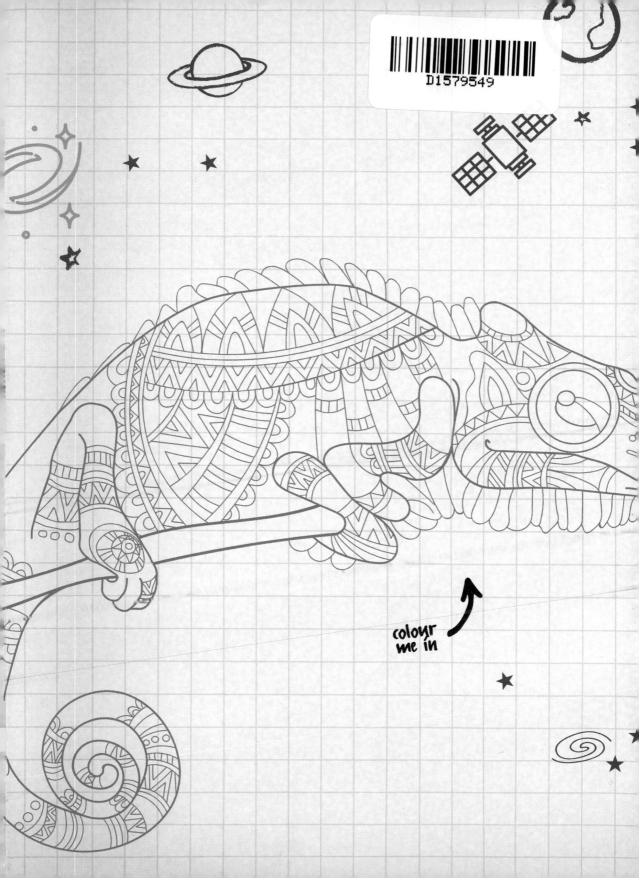

D1579549

colour me in

PICTURE 3:

DATA SOMEHOW HASN'T JUST HAPPENED: WE TAKE ACTIVE CONTROL. IT IS WHERE WE THINK AHEAD, ANTICIPATING HOW THE SYSTEMATIC LOGIC OF STATISTICS WILL WORK FOR OUR OWN SPECIFIC INTEREST. WE DESIGN RESEARCH THAT WILL WORK WELL.

PICTURE 4:

THE REAL BIG PICTURE IS THE POINT WHERE YOU HAVE GAINED ENOUGH KNOWLEDGE AND ABILITY TO ENGAGE WITH THE REAL RICHNESS OF PSYCHOLOGY: WHERE MORE POWERFUL STATISTICS ALLOWS PSYCHOLOGY TO TAKE PRECEDENCE OVER NUMBERS.

THE 4 BIG PICTURES

OUR BOOK  **PAINTS THE BIG PICTURE OF PSYCHOLOGICAL RESEARCH:**

STATISTICS FOR PSYCHOLOGY
A GUIDE FOR BEGINNERS
AND EVERYONE ELSE!
ROGER WATT AND ELIZABETH COLLINS

100

IF YOU CAN UNDERSTAND THE BIG PICTURE, THEN THE DETAILS BECOME A LITTLE BIT CLEARER.

REALLY, THE BIG PICTURE COMES FROM 4 NESTED PICTURES TOGETHER:

100

> "WE WROTE THIS BOOK BECAUSE STATISTICS IS SO MUCH MORE THAN THE RITUAL OF AGONISING OVER WHICH STATISTICAL TEST AND FOCUSING IN ON TINY DETAIL AND TEDIOUS PROCEDURES.
>
> WE ZOOM OUT TO GRASP THE BIG PICTURE AND IT BECOMES APPARENT THAT UNDERSTANDING STATISTICS TRANSFORMS OUR EXPERIENCE OF THE WHOLE RESEARCH CYCLE.
>
> THIS BOOK EXPLAINS EVERYTHING YOU NEVER REALISED YOU WEREN'T TOLD ABOUT THE HOW, THE WHAT, AND MOST IMPORTANTLY, THE WHY OF STATISTICS."

– ROGER WATT AND
ELIZABETH COLLINS

PICTURE 1:

THE SHEER WONDER OF HUMAN VARIABILITY, NOT TO MENTION OTHER ANIMALS. THAT SITS RIGHT AT THE HEART OF THIS – IT IS AFTER ALL WHY WE ARE HERE. RESEARCH, THE PROCESS OF SYSTEMATICALLY INVESTIGATING SOMETHING TO ESTABLISH KNOWLEDGE, INTENDS TO FIND KNOWLEDGE WHICH CAN HELP US TO UNDERSTAND VARIABILITY.

PICTURE 2:

A LOGICALLY STRAIGHTFORWARD SYSTEM OF STATISTICAL ANALYSIS TO PROTECT US FROM MERE WISHFUL THINKING ABOUT PSYCHOLOGY. STATISTICAL ANALYSIS IS SIMPLY THE PROCESSING OF DATA. WE CAN ENVELOP ALL THE FASCINATING VARIABILITY OF OUR SUBJECT IN A SYSTEM OF LOGICAL THINKING ABOUT HOW PEOPLE AND SITUATIONS VARY AND, CRITICALLY, HOW WE CAN USE STATISTICS TO TURN INFORMATION FROM SMALL GROUPS OF INDIVIDUALS INTO UNCERTAIN IDEAS ABOUT BIGGER GROUPS.

YOUR BIG PICTURE

STATISTICS FOR
PSYCHOLOGY

Sara Miller McCune founded SAGE Publishing in 1965 to support
the dissemination of usable knowledge and educate a global
community. SAGE publishes more than 1000 journals and over
800 new books each year, spanning a wide range of subject areas.
Our growing selection of library products includes archives, data,
case studies and video. SAGE remains majority owned by our
founder and after her lifetime will become owned by a charitable
trust that secures the company's continued independence.

Los Angeles | London | New Delhi | Singapore | Washington DC | Melbourne

STATISTICS FOR PSYCHOLOGY
A GUIDE FOR BEGINNERS

AND EVERYONE ELSE!

ROGER WATT AND
ELIZABETH COLLINS

Los Angeles | London | New Delhi
Singapore | Washington DC | Melbourne

Los Angeles | London | New Delhi
Singapore | Washington DC | Melbourne

SAGE Publications Ltd
1 Oliver's Yard
55 City Road
London EC1Y 1SP

SAGE Publications Inc.
2455 Teller Road
Thousand Oaks, California 91320

SAGE Publications India Pvt Ltd
B 1/I 1 Mohan Cooperative Industrial Area
Mathura Road
New Delhi 110 044

SAGE Publications Asia-Pacific Pte Ltd
3 Church Street
#10-04 Samsung Hub
Singapore 049483

Editor: Becky Taylor
Assistant editor: Katie Rabot
Production editor: Imogen Roome
Proofreader: Leigh C. Smithson
Marketing manager: Lucia Sweet
Cover design: Wendy Scott
Typeset by: C&M Digitals (P) Ltd, Chennai, India
Printed in the UK

© Elizabeth Collins and Roger Watt 2019

First published 2019

Apart from any fair dealing for the purposes of research or
private study, or criticism or review, as permitted under the
Copyright, Designs and Patents Act, 1988, this publication
may be reproduced, stored or transmitted in any form, or by
any means, only with the prior permission in writing of the
publishers, or in the case of reprographic reproduction, in
accordance with the terms of licences issued by the Copyright
Licensing Agency. Enquiries concerning reproduction outside
those terms should be sent to the publishers.

Library of Congress Control Number: 2019933332

British Library Cataloguing in Publication data

A catalogue record for this book is available from
the British Library

ISBN 978-1-5264-4125-6
ISBN 978-1-5264-4126-3 (pbk)

At SAGE we take sustainability seriously. Most of our products are printed in the UK using responsibly sourced
papers and boards. When we print overseas we ensure sustainable papers are used as measured by the PREPS
grading system. We undertake an annual audit to monitor our sustainability.

DEDICATION

RW: for Helen and for my grandchildren in case they ever have to learn statistics.

EC: for Tristan Metcalfe, and all past, present and future psychology students.

CONTENTS (BRIEF)

CONTENTS (FULL)

CONTENTS

CONTENTS

LIST OF FIGURES

LIST OF TABLES

ABOUT THE AUTHORS

Roger Watt is a stubborn and persistent Professor of Psychology who has spent many years rejecting 'the system'. He most enjoys his trumpet, his watercolours, and the lettuce tree he's managed to grow in his garden allotment. This book is the culmination of several years of pushing for change in how statistics should be approached by psychologists and students.

Elizabeth Collins is a PhD research student looking into the learning of statistics. A keen world traveller, photographer and bookworm, she fell into statistics accidentally after becoming a peer tutor during her undergraduate studies. She has spent several years contributing heavily to undergraduate statistics teaching, and finding joy in every student success. This book is the culmination of many years spent translating the frequently indecipherable and anxiety-inducing jargon that often appears in statistics to her peers and to her students.

They have collaborated since 2015 on teaching strategies which attracted the first BPS Award for Innovation in Psychology Programmes, and have amassed several teaching nominations and awards from their students.

ACKNOWLEDGEMENTS

The material in this book has evolved as successive generations of students engage with it. Thank you to the countless students who have come to our classes and provided us with helpful insights into what students want and what works with statistics learning. Thank you for the teaching awards and nominations that we have received over the past few years, which have encouraged us further and further.

Thank you also to our department at the University of Stirling, which has allowed us the freedom to transform statistics teaching, including our wonderful statistics lab filled with sofas to complement our different approach to learning environments.

Thank you to those people who have read and supplied comments on earlier drafts, including two of our own students, Janica Niva and Bryan Quinn.

Finally, we must thank our SAGE team, Katie Rabot and Becky Taylor, for making this writing experience a fantastic one. Thank you for not giving up on us when we spent longer working on potential book covers than on the content inside the pages.

HOW TO USE THIS BOOK

Statistics for Pyschology is intended to provide you with a strong statistical foundation for your studies and your research. We will lead you, step by step, into an understanding that develops in a natural sequence where each chapter builds on one that has come before.

This book also contains three Intermezzi chapters which fit between the main chapters to introduce other useful concepts. They each cover something useful for you to learn about.

In this book you will find that our quest to understand statistics leads us to two types of work: sometimes we are building understanding and sometimes we are using that understanding. Building understanding is where we are integrating new theoretical concepts into our picture. Using understanding is where we work through the practical consequences of those concepts.

The book doesn't always follow the chronological process that research typically takes. The table here is a map of how our content connects to the chronological research process.

Identify variables to measure	*Chapter 3*
Specify the logic of relationships between variables	*Chapter 4*
Determine variable types	*Chapter 9*
Determine design for use of participants (with Categorical variables)	*Chapter 10*
Estimate expected effect size and suitable sample size, sampling method	*Chapters 8–10*
Collect and clean data	*Chapter 8 and 10*
Estimate effect sizes	*Chapter 4*
Estimate uncertainty: se or confidence limits	*Chapter 5*
Perform null hypothesis test(s), and/or other advanced analyses	*Chapter 6 and 7, Chapter 11 onwards*
Report results	*Chapter 7, Chapter 13 onwards*
Consider issues of Type I and II errors	*Chapter 6*
Share your results with an audience	*'Finishing with A Bigger Picture'*

KEY WORDS are highlighted in **bold** and can be found in our online glossary, as well as being explained in the text.

A KEY OF ICONS:
In the margin, you will find a variety of icons indicating the purpose of each section, and connections to various online resources.

CHAPTER GRAPHS:
This indicates how much knowledge you are building or using in each chapter.

THE BIG PICTURE:
Each chapter concludes with the '*Big Picture*', which summarises the key information that we consider most important for you to take away. There are also short videos that explore these ideas online.

YOUR TURN:
We have provided a '*Your Turn*' section which has various questions for you to check your knowledge. We have provided the answers online.

FURTHER READING:
We have collated a range of articles and books for you to read if you wish to explore this area further.

WEB ICON:
There is more content online on the website that goes with this book.

ANIMATIONS:
This book is accompanied by 11 animation videos to further explain concepts.

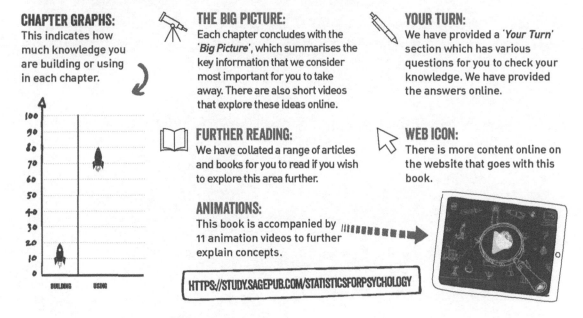

HTTPS://STUDY.SAGEPUB.COM/STATISTICSFORPSYCHOLOGY

Some chapters include mathematical formulae, used to explain concepts. We do not want to assume that you are familiar with formulae, so we have provided a table here that explains the most frequently used elements. Some formulae also have short explanations underneath them in the text, clearly explaining each element.

Symbol	Meaning
$+$	Add, or positive value
$-$	Subtract, or negative value
$/$	Divide
$\times$	Multiply - not to be confused with the letter x
$\pm$ or $+/-$	Plus or minus
a^b	"To the power of b"
sqrt or $\sqrt{}$	Square root
sd	Standard deviation
$<$	(value on left is) less than (value on right)
$>$	(value on left is) greater than (value on right)
Σ	Sum

COMBINING PARTS OF A FORMULA:
Arithmetic By convention, you do arithmetic operations in a specific sequence, not just left to right:

1. powers get done first
2. multiplication and division next
3. addition and subtraction last

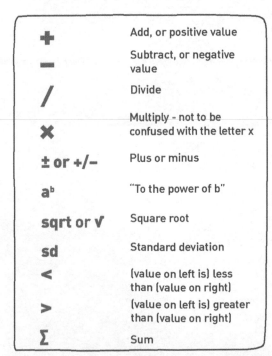

An example:

$$7 - 2 \times 3 + 4^2$$
$$7 - 6 + 16$$
$$17$$

( ) in a complicated mathematical expression, you work inside the brackets first, so:

$$2 \times (3+4) \text{ is } 2 \times 7, \text{ which is } 14$$

Fractions Any formula that has sums above and below a straight line indicates division: divide the top row by the bottom row.

An example: →

$$\frac{7^2}{(1.5 \times sd)}$$

First, square 7 (7x7=49). Then divide this by 1.5 multiplied by the standard deviation.

STARTING WITH FOUR BIG PICTURES

What we have tried to create here is not an ordinary book about statistics. Instead, it is a demonstration of how statistics and research co-exist, fully supplemented with all of the 'whys' that accompany the 'how to' instructions that will allow you to conduct psychological research of your own. Years of experience tells us that knowing *why* is so much more powerful than simply knowing *how*. Our book intends to paint the big picture of psychological research: if you can understand the big picture – the why – then you will realise that the details – the hows – are just a case of looking a little bit closer into the things that you need. Really, the big picture comes from four nested pictures together: imagine a Russian doll, if you will.

A NEST OF BIG PICTURES

The first big picture is the sheer wonder of human variability, not to mention other animals. That sits right at the heart of this – it is, after all, why we are here. Research, the process of systematically investigating something to establish knowledge, is done to find knowledge that can help us to understand as much of that variability as we can.

The second, slightly bigger, picture encapsulates the first. The second big picture is a logically straightforward system of statistical analysis to protect us from mere wishful thinking about psychology. Statistical analysis is simply the processing of data: in the case of this book, we will focus entirely on numeric data, called **quantitative statistics**. We can envelop all the fascinating variability of our subject in a system of logical thinking about how people and situations vary and, critically, how we can use statistics to turn information from small groups of individuals into uncertain ideas about bigger groups.

Once we grasp the second big picture – an understanding of variability and the place of statistics – then we are ready to expand outwards. The third big picture is where data somehow hasn't just happened: we take active control. It is where we think ahead, anticipating how the systematic logic of statistics will work for our own specific interest. We design research that will work well.

The final big picture is where we look right back to the original big picture of the richness and complexity of psychology, recognising how little we gain when we reduce that complexity too far by picking out the bits and pieces of variability that we want to investigate, and relying on rather strict traditional statistics. The real big picture is the point where we have gained enough knowledge and ability to engage with the real richness of psychology: where more powerful statistics allows psychology to take precedence over numbers.

WHERE TO BEGIN

We need to start this book at the innermost picture: human variability. We are going to use one research question throughout this book to illustrate the principles that we discuss. And we found it by looking at ourselves. The innermost picture is one where we see (and celebrate) all the variability between people. The differences between us, the two authors, are, as you would expect, a rich source of research inspiration. We found two or three differences that appealed because they felt like fresh ground to examine.

Our chosen difference for this book is how we approach risk. Maybe we both think of ourselves as risk-takers, but one of us happily steps out of planes and off high bridges, and the other has no intention of stepping off or out of anything higher than a dining chair. He does play the trumpet and wishes that could count instead. There is also a difference in our academic record: the riskier one of us has high exam grades and top-grade qualifications, and the other only studies psychology because his grades weren't good enough to do the things he wanted to (fortunately it has grown into a successful passion…!).

So, our chosen research question is this:

Do risk-takers do better or worse in exams than non-risk-takers?

When we talk about this in the text, we're going to write it out as, 'RiskTaker?', and 'ExamGrade', so that the terms can easily be seen on the page. We use a '?' at the end of RiskTaker to say to the reader that the options are 'yes' – being a risk-taker – or 'no' – not being a risk-taker. We'll use this format again for other examples, so when you see a '?' at the end of a capitalised word, it simply means that there are only two options, called values, which we'll explain in Chapter 3 – yes or no.

Throughout this book we will use diagrams to show research questions. This example, in its simplest form, is shown in Figure PR.1.

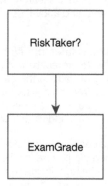

Figure PR.1   Typical hypothesis diagram that we will use to show research questions.

We have chosen this example because, to the best of our knowledge, no-one knows the answer. It is simply something that interests us: any outcome is possible. At the end of this book we won't have told you whether risk-takers really do have an advantage or a disadvantage in exams, but we will have told you how to go out and find out yourself.

THERE ARE MORE ACTIVITIES AND A SHORT
SUMMARY VIDEO FOR THIS CHAPTER AVAILABLE AT:
HTTPS://STUDY.SAGEPUB.COM/STATISTICSFORPSYCHOLOGY

CHAPTER 01

WHY DO WE NEED STATISTICS?

↳ BEING A RISK-TAKER MIGHT MAKE YOU MORE INTELLIGENT

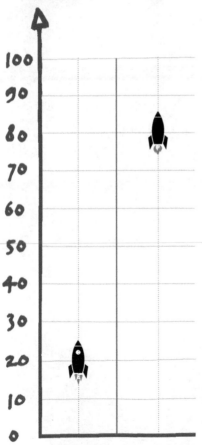

BUILDING   USING

In the previous few pages we have talked about an idea that we are interested in: *do risk-takers do better or worse in exams than non-risk-takers?* In this chapter, we will use this question to illustrate *why* it is that we need statistics, so that you can understand from the start why it is important to learn what will be covered in this book. Although there are plenty of details in statistics, they all fit inside a clear and simple big picture. Fundamentally, statistics is useful to psychological research because it answers two important questions that arise in all research: what does our information appear to tell us and how certain can we be about our findings?

This chapter is a sketch of the whole process to provide the perspective to see the importance of those two research questions. Everything that we discuss here will be explained fully in the subsequent chapters of this book.

1.1 COLLECTING SOME DATA

Before we can do anything statistical, we need **data**: evidence that we collect systematically to provide information about our research question. For our specific piece of research, imagine that we have gone away and found 42 students at a university, classified each of them as low or high risk-taking using a set of questions, and then obtained their exam grades from the last semester. The result is in Figure 1.1.

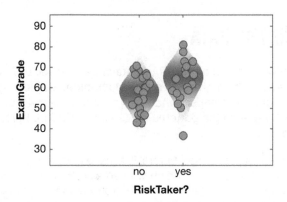

Figure 1.1   Sample graph, comparing a sample of risk-takers and non-risk-takers.

This graph shows the data that we obtained from our sample of 42 participants. Each dot is one participant. The vertical location of the dot in the graph shows the exam grade for each participant. They are split into two groups along the horizontal axis – one for each risk-taking category. This format of graph, with one variable spread across the horizontal axis and the other across the vertical axis, gives us a very simple way of seeing any patterns in the data. In this case, the data suggest that the risk-takers may have higher exam grades.

At a quick glance, it looks like it may be true that being a risk-taker relates to higher grades: the group on the right-hand side of the graph shows some students with higher grades than those in the group on the left-hand side. However, we need to recognise a limitation: this is only *our* impression. How we interpret these results may be very different from the impression formed by someone else; for example, a different observer might look at the right-hand group of risk-takers and focus on the student in that group who has the lowest exam grade of all 42 students together. What we need is a rigorous way of describing what this set of data shows so that all audiences can understand.

We also need to recognise the limitation that we have only found something out about this group of 42 people – our **sample** – and there are millions more students out there who we haven't considered. A different sample of participants would lead to a different set of data, and perhaps a different outcome. We can't be certain about how similar our sample is to other people who we haven't measured.

These two limitations become two questions we must ask of our data, which can be answered with statistics. Statistics exists:

(i)   As a rigorous way of describing evidence: 'what does our data appear to tell us?'

(ii) To calculate the accuracy of our conclusions: 'how certain can we be?'

1.2 DESCRIBING THE DATA

Let's start with question one: 'what does our data appear to tell us?' We can start with the data shown in Figure 1.1 which gives us a nice illustration. But let's go a bit further, using simple statistics. We can summarise what we know from our 42 participants into just a few numbers that will preserve the patterns we are interested in: here, this is the difference between the two groups.

You may have heard the word **'average'** before: it is just a commonly used way of summarising a group of values with a single value, which we can also think of as being the typical value of a group. For our example, we can take each group of participants (non-risk-takers and risk-takers) and say that the people in each group have an overall typical exam grade (one number that summarises the group), and their grades are spread either side of that typical value (spread is also summarised with a number). We will go into this in detail in Chapter 3. But for now, what you need to know is that the first step in looking at data sets is to describe them with a few numbers.

These numbers are examples of **descriptive statistics** and we use them to describe the data set that we have collected, to identify patterns and provide the typical values that we have just mentioned. Figure 1.2 shows what some common descriptive statistics look like: the graph shows the average exam grade for each group as a dot, and the spread of grades as the vertical lines.

The descriptive statistics for each group – a typical value and the spread around that typical value – allow us to examine our original question by comparing typical values. The original question was 'Do risk-takers have higher exam grades?'. That question now becomes 'Is the *typical exam grade* for risk-takers higher than for the non-risk-takers?'. We can go further and use the spread of grades to give a sense of how big the difference is. In Figure 1.2 we can compare the difference in typical exam grades between the two groups with the spread and see that, actually, the difference in typical exam grades is rather small compared with the range of exam grades that were recorded. That gives us a visual suggestion that the effect of risk-taking is small.

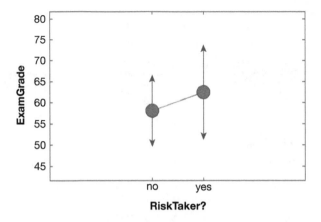

Figure 1.2   Descriptive statistics graph showing means and standard deviations.

This graph shows two types of descriptive statistic, the typical grade and the spread of grades for each group of risk-takers. It summarises the patterns found in the data from Figure 1.1 with a single typical value for each group – shown as a dot – and vertical lines to indicate how spread out the values are within each group. These vertical lines show the magnitude of 1 standard deviation in each direction. The arrow ends to the lines are used to indicate that these are standard deviations. Elsewhere in the book, lines with flat ends will be used to show something different. In Chapter 3 we will see that in this particular situation, the typical value is called a mean and the spread shown in this graph is called the standard deviation.

1.3 UNCERTAINTY IN THE DATA

The second question we have about our data (or any data) is 'how certain can we be?'. The answer to this is to understand the difference between a **sample** and a **population**. Our 42 participants are a sample; the millions of students studying around the world are the population that we are interested in. When we say 'how certain can we be?', we mean 'how certain can we be that our *sample* tells us something reliable *about the population*?'. We'll look at samples and populations in much more detail in Chapter 5, but one important thing to note here is that a population is the whole group we are interested in: it can be everyone in the world, or it can be more specific (e.g. all university students).

We can be certain about our sample quite easily just by examining it, but that is usually not very satisfying – especially if we want to build knowledge about the whole population of interest. Our fundamental problem is that no two samples will ever be the same, as you can see in Figure 1.3, and they will all differ somewhat from the population, just because of the random nature of how we selected our participants and their individual differences. This randomness is called **sampling error**. We can't avoid sampling and so we must live with sampling error. Let's think about why we should care about our sample being different from a population.

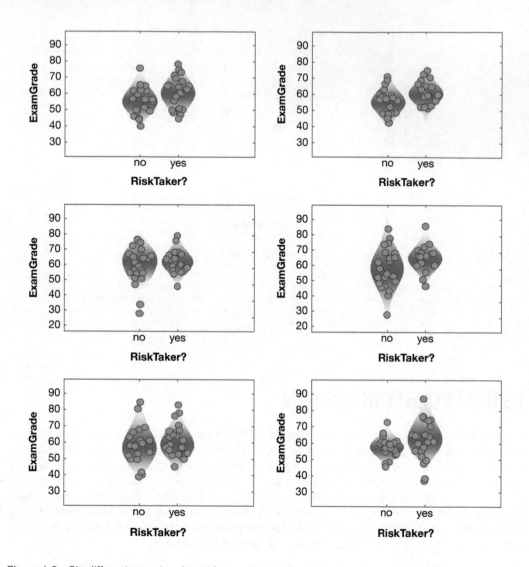

Figure 1.3   Six different samples drawn from a single population to indicate sampling error.

This figure shows what we might find if we collected six different samples of 42 students. These graphs all differ from each other and show quite a lot of random variability (as explained in Section 1.4) due to the samples they contain. This variability between samples illustrates sampling error.

It really boils down to one very important question: if the sample is always different from the population, then how can we find out things about the population? This is where statistics come in: we can calculate the uncertainty in our data so that we can make an inference about the population using the information from a sample. An **inference** is a conclusion that we recognise is always uncertain, and statistics enables us to measure how much uncertainty there is in our findings. Just by looking at Figure 1.3 we can see that six different samples from one population provide different glimpses of what might be happening within that population. This means that one sample on its own is a fairly uncertain source of knowledge.

Using **inferential statistics**, as they are called, in this manner is really about assessing the amount of uncertainty to remind us of the limits of what we can infer from one sample alone.

1.4 VARIABILITY

Central to everything we will learn is the idea of **variability**, which is most simply defined as how spread out the values in a data set are; or the extent of the differences between participants. It is often said that statistics focuses on the typical person, particularly because the typical values we mentioned above in Section 1.2 are frequently used to summarise data sets. When we only provide the typical value when describing a set of values then we are indeed treating everyone as if they were the same and ignoring all the interesting differences between people: the variability.

Failing to include the differences between individuals is to fail to recognise the variability between people and that would be wrong, because the differences between people are so much more interesting than just knowing about the typical person.

In our original example here, we took 42 people who varied considerably in their exam grades. Our analysis of risk-taking is an attempt to understand some of this variability in exam grades: can some of the variability be attributed to the effects of being a risk-taker? The results suggest that some of it can, because we can see a clear difference between our two groups in Figure 1.1 and in Figure 1.2. Our data can be described with a brief formula:

Total variability in grade attainment = variability explained by risk-taking + unexplained variability due to other factors

By thinking about research in this way we can immediately be reminded of two important things. The first is that our research is an attempt to explore, and hopefully understand and explain, the variability in exam grades, and the second is that we are aware that there is variability that we haven't explored or explained yet: for example, student hunger at the start of an exam, the number of hours they have spent studying, or which high school qualifications they have. The amount of unknown variability is just as important as the variability that we do measure when we make inferences from our findings.

THE BIG PICTURE

This chapter is simply an explanation of why we need statistics in research. Each concept we have covered here will be explained further ahead in the book. Table 1.1 summarises the two main roles of statistics.

Table 1.1   The two purposes of statistics:descriptive and inferential statistics.

This is a summary table with the most important two things that you need to know about why we use statistics in research.

Role	Overview	Name
Description	Statistics gives us an objective way to describe patterns in data sets, in order to make sense of data and explain it to audiences	Descriptive Statistics
Uncertainty	Statistics allows us to calculate precisely how much uncertainty there is in the information we have collected, so that we are aware of how much knowledge we have gained about a population	Inferential Statistics

 # YOUR TURN

ANSWER THESE QUESTIONS IN THE SPACE PROVIDED.

1. What is data?

2. What is a population?

3. What is a sample?

4. What is variability?

FILL IN THE GAPS TO COMPLETE THESE SENTENCES.

1. Descriptive statistics are used to describe _____ in data sets.

2. We can calculate uncertainty using _____ statistics.

 THE ANSWERS ARE AVAILABLE ONLINE

YOUR SPACE

REFERENCES AND FURTHER READING

Hand, D.J. (2008) *Statistics: A Very Short Introduction*. Oxford: Oxford University Press.

Gentle introduction.

IIIIIII■■■■■■■■→

THERE ARE MORE ACTIVITIES AND A SHORT
SUMMARY VIDEO FOR THIS CHAPTER AVAILABLE AT:
HTTPS://STUDY.SAGEPUB.COM/STATISTICSFORPSYCHOLOGY

CHAPTER

02

THE RESEARCH CYCLE

↳ THE BIG PICTURE IN A (FAIRLY) SMALL CHAPTER

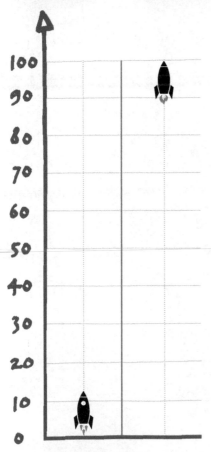

100
90
80
70
60
50
40
30
20
10
0

BUILDING   USING

Let's start with a reminder: all research begins with an **idea**. We established our idea right at the beginning of this book and we are going to continue using it in this chapter: do risk-takers do better or worse in exams than non-risk-takers?

In Chapter 1, we used our idea to illustrate why we use statistics, focusing on what happens when you have some **data**. Now that we have established the place of statistics in research, we are going to take a step back and look at the whole research cycle, broken down into three phases. Various different statistical concepts emerge during each phase, which will become clear as you read each chapter of this book. Our intention here is to introduce you to research as a complete picture, before we examine each element in detail. We're going to avoid using too much technical language here as this is only an introduction.

2.1 THE RESEARCH PROCESS

Once an idea has been established, the process of doing the research can be separated into three distinct phases, illustrated in Figure 2.1. Phase one consists of turning the idea into a testable **hypothesis** and picking an appropriate design to collect evidence in the form of data. This is the decision phase, where most of the important choices about what to do and how to do it are made.

Phase two consists of **data analysis** to produce results. While most people associate data analysis with lots of difficult decisions, analysis is usually already fixed by the decisions you made in phase one. Moreover, although we can't deny that there are lots of different tests that are used to analyse data, we will be showing you how they all ultimately do the same thing – and usually by the same method.

The third phase is the process of presenting results and using them to persuade others that we have found new knowledge. This phase – not strictly the final phase, as research is really more of an ongoing cycle than a single process – will then inspire new hypotheses, and the whole research cycle will begin again.

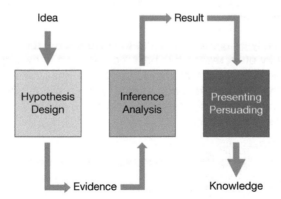

Figure 2.1   The research cycle, split into three phases.

This figure demonstrates the research process, where the three phases are indicated left to right with the three boxes – Phase 1: hypothesis and design. Phase 2: inference and analysis. Phase 3: presenting and persuading. The process begins with an idea and ends with knowledge, and should then begin again with updated ideas, hypotheses and design.

2.2 PHASE 1: IDEAS, HYPOTHESES AND DESIGN

All research begins with an idea, and phase one of research concentrates on turning that idea into something that can lead to a real piece of research. By developing an idea into an explicit statement about what we are interested in investigating, the idea becomes a testable hypothesis. We can then make a series of decisions about what and who to measure, and how to go about gathering them and their data: the design.

2.2.1 IDEAS

We have an idea here which we might develop into a testable hypothesis: risk-takers do better in exams than non-risk-takers. It may be that I have known someone who I think of as a risk-taker and that person usually does really well in exams. This is my idea: what I see in that person may be more widely true of people in general. This is quite a bold claim, and we can come up with many reasons as to why it might be true, and many as to why it might be false – or maybe even why the opposite is true. If you, the reader, are a risk-taker, then you will have a feeling about this hypothesis. If, on the other hand, you are not, then you will have a different feeling. We, the authors, also have feelings about this idea (secretly we hope it's true). These feelings are just wishful thinking. We need to find out what the real situation is.

There is a very important principle here. When we just said that we need to find out what the real situation is, we are also saying clearly that we don't know what the situation is. Research tries to answer the question: is my idea right or wrong? Does risk-taking affect exam grades? We want to find out the answer.

Ideas can come from many different places and they are the most difficult part of the whole process to tie down. Very often research is based on existing knowledge and is devised to clarify or challenge something about that knowledge. Sometimes, research is based on some new observation that the researchers made and it has no obvious direct source in existing knowledge. We give some examples in Table 2.1, and at the end of this chapter we will invite you to make a few ideas of your own.

Table 2.1   Observations, ideas and hypotheses.

Observations turned into ideas and then hypotheses. Note that the hypotheses are clearly testable: for example, it is evident that hypothesis 3 requires two tests of reaction time with a 5-minute gap and a glass of orange juice in the middle.

Source	Observation	Idea	Possible hypothesis
A theory	Dyslexia shares symptoms with stress	Mindfulness might have an impact on issues that dyslexic learners face	Reading speed is increased by mindfulness (compared to control) in people with dyslexia, but not in people without dyslexia
A journal article	Short words have a stronger affective effect	Is this really an effect of word frequency (short words are usually common words)?	Affective effect of words is stronger for common words than rare words.
Newspaper	'10 ways to avoid dementia'	Does orange juice really have some kind of impact on the brain?	Reaction times on a computer simulation are faster than normal 5 minutes after drinking a glass of orange juice.

Source	Observation	Idea	Possible hypothesis
Social Media	People are only friends with people who share their political views	How similar are people to their friends on social media?	Facebook users will have significantly more friends who share the same political affiliation as them than friends who differ

Of course, there are unlimited questions that we could research, but the real skill in research is to be able to find questions that will make for good research. Broadly, research falls into two categories: **exploratory** and **confirmatory**. Exploratory research is where we may not have strong grounds for knowing what to expect: it explores new ideas without any strong expectations of what might be true. Conversely, confirmatory research is where the researcher has some knowledge of what effects are thought to exist and tests these to see whether further evidence is supportive. Referring back to our idea that risk-takers get higher grades, this is exploratory because we are not aware of any evidence or theory to lead us. If we did have strong reasons for thinking they might, such as a theory, we would be conducting confirmatory research to try to find evidence that supports our theory.

But where did our idea come from? And what makes a good idea? There are four rules:

1. Good ideas are *precise*.

2. Good ideas have many different *plausible* outcomes that are *interesting*.

3. Good ideas *connect* with what we already know.

4. Good ideas *matter*.

GOOD IDEAS ARE PRECISE

If you have a precise idea, it is much easier to come up with sensible testable hypotheses to match it. And so 'risk-takers are more intelligent' is more difficult to test than 'risk-takers get higher exam grades' because intelligence can be measured in many ways – and people disagree on how it should best be done. Table 2.2 illustrates different levels of preciseness.

Table 2.2   Ideas ranked from vague to precise.

This table ranks some ideas by their precision. Ideas at the top are rather vague and unsuitable; ideas at the bottom are very precise. It is clear to see that precise ideas will make it much easier to design hypotheses.

Vague	Being a peer-mentor is good for you.
	Peer-mentors have higher self-efficacy
	Peer-mentoring statistics will increase your own confidence in statistics
Precise	Teaching your peers how to do a t-test will enhance your heart rate variability

GOOD IDEAS HAVE MANY PLAUSIBLE AND INTERESTING ANSWERS

If a piece of research realistically can only produce one outcome, then we won't learn much by doing it; if there are lots of possible outcomes, then finding out which one happens would mean we have learned a lot. Think first about this idea: (i) *getting a low exam grade makes you unhappy*. It is hard to see that it could be wrong – it is the only realistic outcome of a study that looked at happiness as a function of passing or failing an exam. Then think about this similar idea: (ii) *getting a low exam grade makes people temporarily more likely to take risks*. It is easy to see that this idea could equally well be right or wrong. That makes it a better idea for research.

Table 2.3   Table indicating plausible outcomes.

In this table we have graded some ideas by the number of plausible answers they have. At the top, although in theory there are several answers, only one outcome seems plausible. At the bottom, a number of different outcomes seem almost equally likely.

Only one plausible outcome	Risk-takers frequently take risks
	Risk-takers are happier when they are taking risks
	Risk-takers have low perfectionism scores
All outcomes equally plausible	Risk-takers do well in exams

GOOD IDEAS CONNECT WITH EXISTING KNOWLEDGE

When people read about a piece of research, they automatically integrate it with what they already know and that works best if there is a connection. Ideas can result in several different changes to knowledge: they can add new knowledge; they can replace existing knowledge; and they can remove existing knowledge (illustrated in Table 2.4).

Table 2.4   Connecting ideas to existing knowledge.

Here are some examples of how good ideas connect to existing knowledge. Please note: none of these is a real research result.

Add new knowledge	Risk-takers do better in exams
Replace existing knowledge	Writing essays in short bursts works better than in long sessions
Remove existing knowledge	Caffeine doesn't help concentration
Fails to connect to existing knowledge	Saying the number '7' repeatedly makes you smile

GOOD IDEAS MATTER

Psychology is a powerful subject: it reflects aspects of the world around us that really matter to us: how we feel, how we and others behave, and so on. Although no single piece of research can change something fundamental, research that has the potential to lead to a positive change in the world around us is of particular value.

We have used for our examples throughout this book various ideas that concern the exam grades that students achieve. If any of the ideas we have here were to produce strong clear results, then those results would matter because keeping exams fair matters.

2.2.2 HYPOTHESES

Let's move on to the key step in any piece of research: hypotheses. We have our idea which involves two separate ways in which people differ: how much of a risk-taker they are, and what their individual exam grades are. Ways in which people (or other types of participant) differ are called **variables**. The term 'variable' captures the fundamental purpose of psychology: to investigate and understand how and why we all vary (differ from each other). If we look at our idea, our variables are exam grades and risk-taking, which we'll label 'ExamGrades' and 'RiskTaker?' to make them easy to spot in the text of this book. Variables are covered in full detail in Chapter 3.

The **variability** of people is fundamental to psychology: if psychology treated us all as the same, research would be dull and usually incorrect. A variable is one specific way that variability can be seen. We all vary in how tall we are and how much of a perfectionist we are – there is a lot of variability among us in these regards. We formulate that variability into two variables: height and perfectionism.

Our hypothesis concerns the relationship between the two variables from our idea. A hypothesis is a formal way of saying that we believe/hope/expect/fear that one of those two variables influences the other: being a risk-taker leads (somehow) to better exam grades. We can use a simple diagram to state this hypothesis. Figure 2.2 uses short labels to name the variables and an arrow to show the way we think the influence flows.

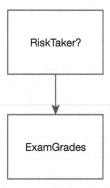

Figure 2.2   Typical hypothesis diagram.

Our idea is turned into a hypothesis that explicitly predicts that one variable will affect the other (indicated by the arrow). We will consider this diagram and others like it in more detail in Chapter 3. In that chapter we will see that it is an important part of most hypotheses to identify which variable we think is affecting which. RiskTaker? and ExamGrades are our two variables that we shall continue to use in this book.

An important part of any hypothesis is a statement of how the individual values of the variables will be represented. In this case, exam grades are easy: they are numbers that already exist, potentially on a **scale** from 0–100. Risk-taking is slightly different as it does not have an obvious way of being measured, and so in our research we have decided to use **categories** derived from a simple test.

To measure risk-taking, each of our participants will be given a plate of chilies, spicy red and mild green, and asked to eat one. Only risk-takers will choose red ones and so we can categorise everyone as a risk-taker or not. The important point here is that we are using a continuous scale (0–100) to describe the ways exam grades vary and a pair of discrete categories (yes=red/no=green) to describe the ways that people's risk-taking varies. We'll look at scales and categories again in Chapter 3.

Finally, to complete our hypothesis we should decide how strong is the effect we are looking for (a relationship between risk-taker and exam grades). In this case, we think that the relationship is not very strong because there are probably lots of other personal and environmental variables that might also affect exam grade, so we give it a score of 0.2 (out of a maximum of 1.0, where 0 is no effect at all). Chapter 4 will explain relationships between variables and the values that we use to describe their strength.

So now we have a complete hypothesis, which is illustrated in Figure 2.3.

> 'Higher risk-taking, as measured by individual chilli-eating decisions, will have a small effect on exam grades.'

We have made some important decisions in building our hypothesis. We will soon see whether the hypothesis is supported by some real evidence. That evidence is going to be a set of data: a record of risk-taking and exam grades for a set of participants.

2.2.3 DESIGN

We can't just jump straight in and start collecting data from anyone we can get our hands on; we must come up with a research **design**. The design is a recipe for how we are going to obtain the data. There are three main considerations: how many participants we need, how we are going to recruit participants, and what we will ask them to do.

There are many ways to recruit participants into a study as a **sample** of the **population**. We have decided to recruit 42 participants – this is our sample size, commonly denoted using the label 'n', so $n=42$ *for our research*. Later on, in Chapter 10, we'll go through the formal way to decide on a sample size, but we've picked 42 here simply because it's one of our favourite numbers.

Next, we must choose a method for recruiting our 42 participants. The ideal way is to use a wholly random process so that each member of the population has the same chance of

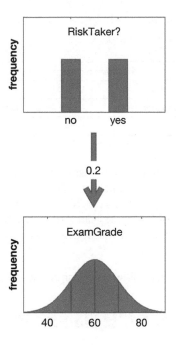

Figure 2.3   Typical hypothesis diagram including more information about the variables and a predicted effect size.

The complete hypothesis, including our small predicted effect of 0.2. We will explore effect sizes fully in Chapter 4.

being recruited – this called **random sampling**. A simple way to do this would be to randomly select student email addresses from a database and send out a request to participants. Doing this randomly means that we are trying to be as fair as possible, with every student equally likely to be picked. There are many ways to recruit participants, which will be explored in Chapters 8 and 10.

When we have our 42 participants, we decide how to use them. Each one will only be assigned to one risk-taker category (yes or no), because a person cannot be both. This means that we are going to compare the exam grades between two different groups of participants. If we were interested in the effects of doing, or not doing, a risky action, we could have used each participant twice: once in each group, as they could participate in both behaviours over different academic semesters. This would mean that we were comparing results from two different situations, both experienced by the same set of participants. However, our original RiskTaker? affecting ExamGrades idea will always use *two separate groups of participants* (risk-takers and non-risk-takers) unless we say otherwise.

Table 2.5   Summary of our chosen research design.

Research design will be covered in Chapters 8–10 in detail.

Research design	
Sample size (total number of participants)	42
Sampling type (how we choose participants)	Advert for sampling
How we will use participants	Belong in one group or the other

These are our main decisions finished. Our design has three basic elements: sample size, sampling type, and the way we will use participants, which are summarised in Table 2.5. These design decisions, along with our hypothesis decisions, will all affect our data, its analysis and our results. Since the influence of these decisions has very considerable influence over the quality and usefulness of the results we will get, we have three chapters devoted to them later on (Chapters 8–10).

What follows is straightforward: we follow our design and collect our data.

2.3 PHASE 2: EVIDENCE, ANALYSIS AND INFERENCE

2.3.1 ANALYSIS

This phase will look very familiar to you: we are using the same data that we had in Chapter 1, which you can see in Figure 2.4. The raw data is on the left – it shows each participant, placed according to their value for each of the variables. The graph on the right shows a summary of the raw data: the typical grade for each group (in this case we use the **mean**, which we'll explain in more detail in Chapter 3). The **axes** on the two graphs are different: the vertical scale in the graph on the right is zoomed in and covers a smaller range compared to the graph on the left.

The first thing to do is just look at the raw data to see what we have and see whether or not it is encouraging. We can see that the lowest grades are in the non-risk-taker group and the top few grades are within the risk-taker group. This suggests that we might have found some evidence to support our hypothesis.

We then can compare the typical exam grades for the two groups and see whether there is a noticeable difference. In Figure 2.4 we show the typical exam grade for each group as the average grade for that group. We briefly touched on this in Chapter 1 and will explore this in much more detail in Chapter 3. The average grade for risk-takers (63.0) is definitely higher than the average grade for non-risk-takers (57.5), as seen on the right-hand graph. However, the left graph also shows that the grades for each group are quite spread out, and there is considerable overlap between the two.

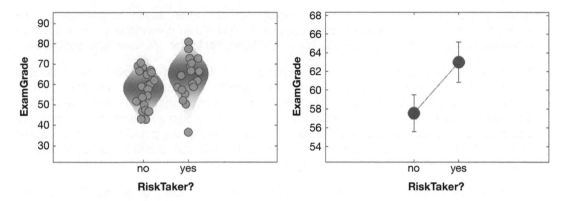

Figure 2.4   Sample graph and descriptive statistics graph side by side.

The left graph shows each participant as a small dot. The right graph shows the typical values (descriptive statistics) for the yes and no RiskTaker? groups. In the right graph, the data in each group are replaced by the typical, or average, exam grade for that group. The vertical lines, which show the spread of the data set, are called error bars and show how uncertain we are about our average: if the error bars are very long, then the average score is not a very reliable summary of our data set. The horizontal bottom of the graph with 'yes' and 'no' plotted is one axis (x-axis), and the vertical left-side of the graph with ExamGrade values plotted is the other axis (y-axis). Notice how important it is to check the scales on the vertical axes: they differ here.

The difference in average grades between our two groups sounds quite large: 5.4 points. But when we put it alongside the natural scatter in grades across the sample, which range from less than 40 to greater than 80, then a difference of just 5.4 is maybe less compelling. So, is the difference between risk-takers and non-risk-takers small or large? There is a calculation we can do that helps with this question.

We can calculate a quantity known as the **sample effect size**. Much of Chapter 4 is devoted to this, and for now all we will say is that the sample effect size is a number that goes from 0 to 1 and measures the strength of relationship between any two variables. The sample effect size gives us more information than just the typical values because it takes into account both the difference in mean grades, and the spread of grades. A big difference in means and a small spread of grades in each group would lead to a larger effect size. This particular sample has a small difference in means compared to the spread of grades in each group, and we would calculate that it has a small effect size.

2.3.2 INFERENCE

In simple, numerical terms, we have found the effect we hypothesised – remind yourself of our hypothesis in Figure 2.3. But…

To be clear, what we have found is a set of 42 people, for whom collectively our hypothesis is correct. That is undeniable, and we can say it with complete confidence. But no-one else is going to be interested in a conclusion that applies exclusively to our 42 participants: we need to use our sample as a guide to the population. This is the *inferential step* that we looked at briefly in Chapter 1: going from the known (our sample) to the unknown (the population).

So, before celebrating a new discovery, we need to ask the question 'How uncertain should we be in our inference?'. Before we jump to the conclusion that there is an effect of risk-taking on exam grades, we must ask whether our result could just be the result of chance. Our sample of participants is a random one, so how often would a random sample produce this result or an even stronger one if there was no real effect in the population? This process is conventionally known as statistical testing and is formally called **null hypothesis testing**. Null hypothesis testing is covered in Chapter 6.

Null hypothesis testing on our sample tells us that the probability of our result, or a more extreme one, happening purely by chance is 0.13 (or 13% of the time). This is not a small enough probability for us to be confident that our finding rules out the possibility that it happened by chance. So, our sample does not allow us to safely infer that risk-taking leads to better exam grades in the population. We should be very uncertain about inferring anything about our hypothesis in this case.

2.4 PHASE 3: RESULTS, PRESENTING AND PERSUADING

Phase three is the presentation phase of research. There are several standard practices for presenting the results of statistical tests in a formal way: there isn't really a right or wrong way. If you are a student in a university, your department may give you specific guidelines; researchers have to use the format specified by the journal they are sending their results to. The most common format used by psychologists is 'APA', developed by the American Psychological Association (hence the name), which looks like this:

'A small difference in exam grades was found between non-risk-takers and risk-takers. A t-test found that the result was not **statistically significant** t(40)=1.54, p=0.132.'

This brief statement has a description of the result ('a small difference') and finishes with a series of numbers including the test-statistic (the 't' value, in this case) and the p-value. Typically, descriptive statistics are also included, which we will discuss in Chapter 3 and later on in Chapter 7. Test-statistics and p-values will be covered in detail in the coming chapters too. For now, it is enough to know that there are various standard ways to present results. Using these values in this layout makes it easy for a reader to find and understand your results quickly.

2.4.1 PERSUADING OTHERS

In this case there is little to persuade others of, as we did not find a significant outcome and our effect size is not very big. However, had our result turned out to be statistically significant, we would have tried to persuade others that much of grade attainment can be explained by the risk-taking element of someone's personality. By getting caught up in the excitement of getting a significant result, we might have been tempted to overlook other factors that contribute to exam grade (such as how much work a student has done!).

By overlooking other factors, we are forgetting how much variability there is in a sample. As we mentioned in Chapter 1, variability means the differences between individuals. Finding one significant outcome does not explain all of the differences between people, because so many individual differences exist. What other factors may contribute to grade attainment? We will look at how to measure more than one variable working together in Chapter 11.

THE BIG PICTURE

The whole research cycle is as simple as this:

1. Start with an idea, turn it into a hypothesis (or multiple hypotheses), and make decisions about the what/who/how of your research.

2. Collect data, analyse it using descriptive and inferential statistics.

3. Present information using common formats such as APA, illustrate your work with graphs, and use your statistical evidence to persuade.

 # YOUR TURN

Below, we have suggested two ideas. Use the space to turn them into a specific, testable hypothesis.

IDEA 1: SCOTTISH SMOKED SALMON INCREASES THINKING POWER.

_____

_____

Does this idea meet the four rules?

☐ precise

☐ plausible & interesting outcomes

☐ connect with existing knowledge

☐ matter?

IDEA 2: BEING A RUNNER MAKES YOU FEEL BETTER.

_____

_____

Does this idea meet the four rules?

☐ precise

☐ plausible & interesting outcomes

☐ connect with existing knowledge

☐ matter?

THE ANSWERS ARE AVAILABLE ONLINE

Use the open space underneath to write out two testable hypotheses of your own, based on the abstracts of two journal articles. You can find journal articles through Google Scholar, by asking for recommendations from your lecturers if you are a student, by looking at class reading lists, or through our online resources where we have provided a few to get you started. Highlight, underline, capitalise, coat in glitter or somehow otherwise indicate your variables within the hypothesis.

📖 REFERENCES AND FURTHER READING

Popper, Karl R. (1959, 2005 revised edition) *The Logic of Scientific Discovery*. New York: Routledge.

A philosophically technical read.

THERE ARE MORE ACTIVITIES AND A SHORT
SUMMARY VIDEO FOR THIS CHAPTER AVAILABLE AT:
HTTPS://STUDY.SAGEPUB.COM/STATISTICSFORPSYCHOLOGY

CHAPTER

03

VARIABLES

↳ YOU MIGHT WANT TO BLEND
IN BUT BEING DIFFERENT IS
MORE INTERESTING

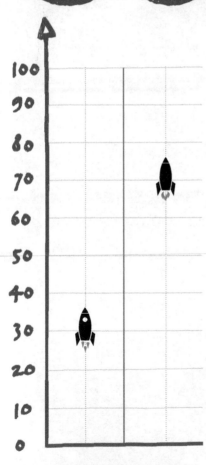

A central notion in psychology is that interesting things like a person's behaviour, thoughts and feelings have their roots in a complex combination of that person's psychological make-up and their situation. Their psychological make-up comes from long-term traits such as their personality and brief states such as their emotions, while their situation is made up of other people, experiences and meaningful objects that shape and constrain their behaviour. The first task in doing research is to break down all of this complexity into something that is simple enough to study and ultimately to understand. We do that by focusing on ways in which people and situations differ, and we call these ways they differ by the term **variables**.

Normally we encounter a person and all of their various qualities as one whole, but as a researcher we have to reduce that whole to a few distinct concepts or moments. These distinct entities become variables in research. For example, we might be interested in how happy a person becomes when they receive an unexpected compliment. Their happiness is a feeling or thought that they are experiencing, and the compliment is an element of their situation. We are taking the whole person and reducing them to these two parts – the compliment and their happiness, leaving everything else about them and their situation unexplored.

It is important to recognise that we are examining a very selective part of the person and their situation but the bits we aren't exploring (most of the person and situation) might still be very important.

3.1 WHAT ARE VARIABLES?

Let's begin by specifically defining the term 'variables'. Variables are key to everything that follows in psychological research, and they come from two important sources. Variables are ways in which:

1. People or objects vary (differ from each other).

2. Situations or occasions vary (differ).

When we choose variables, we must always remember that we are engaging in a creative process: we are splitting the whole down and selecting parts of our own creating. There is nothing really in statistics that can tell us whether a variable is a good choice or not. That is not to say that decisions made about variables don't impact statistics, because they do, as you will learn over the course of this book. Instead, it is important to realise that this is the first of many instances where we must learn that thinking like a psychologist is much more important than thinking like a statistician.

3.1.1 VALUES

A variable is a way in which people or situations can differ. A **value**, on the other hand, is a specific description of a variable for one person or situation. The values that we use try to capture as much of the variability, the differences between individuals, as possible. For our RiskTaker? variable, 'yes' and 'no' are possible values, as are specific numeric scores, such as the number of skydives done. For ExamGrade, the values could be a number between 0 and 100. For the variable 'trial phase', the values will depend on how many phases the research has been divided into but might be 'before' and 'after' treatment.

There are two important properties of values:

1. For any given variable, each person has a value. No-one is left out without a value. For the variable Smoker?, for example, we will all have a value that is either 'yes' or 'no'. We might add a third value of 'occasionally', if that is more useful to know.

2. For any given variable, each person has just one value for it (*at any one time* or in any one situation). For the variable Smoker?, no-one is both 'yes' and 'no' at the same time.

Some values are relatively fixed for each participant, such as their eye colour. So the values for the variable eye colour are likely to be 'green', 'grey', 'brown' and 'blue', with an 'other' category to assign to people who don't fit into the common colours. It is straightforward to assign people to these categories just by looking at them.

Some values, however, change from time to time or in different circumstances. A person's value for the variable 'hungry' will depend on how long it has been since they have eaten. Some different variables and potential values are listed in Table 3.1.

Table 3.1   Variables and possible values.

Note that the last two are variables where the variable is a situation or occasion and the values of the variable correspond to different groups. In these cases, we can choose either to have separate sets of participants for each group or to use the same participant for both situations.

Variable	Potential values
Height	Any value, usually measured in cm or inches
Perfectionism	High to low, measured on a scale determined by researchers
Age	Any value, usually measured in years or months
Birth order	First born, middle child, youngest, only child
Smoker?	Yes or no
Caffeine	Before and after drinking a caffeinated drink
RiskTaker?	Yes or no
TreatmentType	Placebo **or/and** active
Intervention	Before **or/and** after an intervention

3.1.2 SITUATIONS AS VARIABLES

We are using the same concept of a variable to describe both different types of person and different situations. This is unusual but, as we will see in Chapter 4, it makes talking about relationships between variables a very simple general concept.

A variable situation might be whether you are in an active treatment group or a **placebo** control group (the term 'placebo' is used to describe a treatment or situation that has no intended value, to act as a comparison to an active group). We could call the variable TreatmentType, with the values 'active' and 'placebo'. We've included this in Table 3.1. We have two ways of proceeding:

1. We can easily think of an experiment designed so that each participant is allocated to one group *or* the other and we compare between the two groups of participants. This is easy: each person has a single value for TreatmentType and also for Outcome. When we ask, in Chapter 4, whether there is a relationship between TreatmentType and Outcome, we are asking whether the active treatment works.

2. It is easy also to think of an experiment where each participant is placed first in the placebo group *and then in the other group* and we measure their outcome separately in each situation. The logic is the same as before. All that has changed, logically speaking, is that each person in our study now appears twice. Note that each person still has only one value for each variable in any one situation. On their first appearance, they have specific values for each of the two variables, TreatmentType and Outcome, and on their second appearance they have different specific values for those two variables, because the situation has changed.

Table 3.2   Values: one per participant or situation.

In the top example, each participant appears once (provides one data point) and has only one value for each variable. In the bottom example, each participant appears twice (provides two data points) and has just one value for each variable on each occasion.

	RiskTaker?	ExamGrade
Participant 1	yes	69
Participant 2	yes	65
Participant 3	no	67
etc.		

	TestPhase	ExamAnxiety
Participant 1	before	62
Participant 1	after	45
Participant 2	before	55
Participant 2	after	35
etc.		

There are more formal names for these different ways of allocating participants to groups: when each participant exists only in one group, the arrangement is called a **between-participants design**. When the same participants experience more than one situation and therefore have more than one value for a variable (e.g. being in both the 'before' and 'after' groups), it is called a **within-participants design**. We will explain in detail the properties of this in Chapter 10. An example is given in Table 3.2.

3.1.3 EXPERIMENTS: CREATING VARIABLES

Variables may just exist: people have personality variables and find themselves naturally in different situations. However, a key insight in psychological research is that we can also create variables. The commonest example is where we make specific novel situations and place people in them to see what happens. The creation process is described as an experiment. We can distinguish experimental variables from observational ones.

Observational variables describe characteristics and situations that already exist and we merely measure them as they already are. For example, if we ask someone to fill in a questionnaire about their stress level, then we have not made the variable: they were already stressed or not. We are observing their pre-existing stress level. Our RiskTaker? example would be observational if we took a score of how risky each participant naturally is.

Experimental variables are ones we cause to happen, such as when we put participants into an experimental group or a control group. For example, the variable TreatmentType, with values 'experimental' and 'control', is a variable that we have caused. Our Risk variable would be experimental if we divided our participants into groups doing high- and low-risk activities.

This distinction is important because it underlies one of the clearest ways in which we can establish **causation** in a psychological study. When we create an experimental variable, we can explain exactly how each participant's value for this variable happened – by assigning them to a group. This is true, even if we used a random process to choose: nothing else has caused their value. We will return to this topic in Chapter 9.

3.2 VARIABILITY AND VARIABLES

Variability in our variables is where our information comes from. If all our participants have the same value for a variable, then that variable is telling us nothing. If we only have non-risk-takers in a sample, then we won't find out anything about how differences in risk-taking affect anything else, and our research is not a good use of time. So, when we make decisions about our measurement, we are guided by the desire to capture as much variability in our participants as possible with our variables. Let's see how more variability usually means more information.

3.2.1 VARIABILITY AND INFORMATION

In thinking about variables, it is important to understand that we make them to capture and reason about specific types of difference among participants. The function of variables is to represent those differences between participants. The more differences between participants that a variable captures, the more information it provides for us.

Let's use a familiar example: using an exam to find out how much statistics students have learned. We can suppose that each student has learned a different amount and we really want an exam that will capture this.

To start with, imagine we have used an exam with a single question, but because of how it was designed everyone got the same grade (because it was too easy). This exam would be of little or no value: it doesn't distinguish between students. It provides no information about any possible differences between the students.

Now think about a question designed to be more informative. It is designed so that those who have studied will get it right and those who haven't won't. This question splits the class into two groups, which is an improvement. With more questions of varying difficulty, we can split the class with ever finer distinctions between students.

Eventually we have an exam where everyone has a chance to show the extent of their own individual knowledge. We would then say that the exam distinguishes successfully between students who have different levels of learning, and that it has captured that variability. Such an exam gives us much more information about the students than ones less carefully constructed, such as we began with. This is demonstrated visually in Figure 3.1.

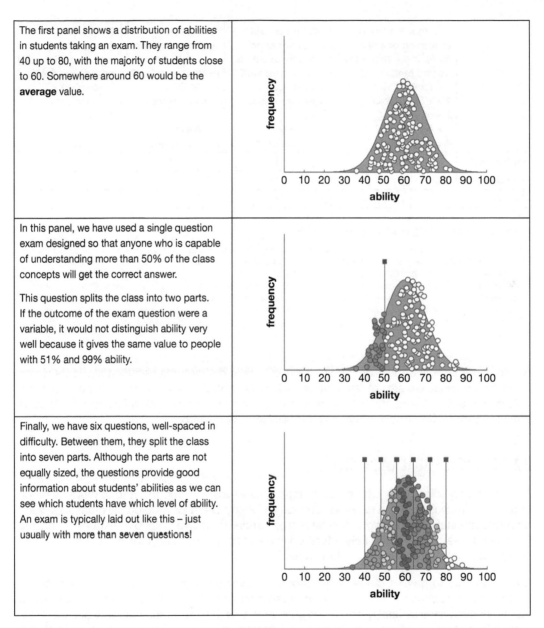

The first panel shows a distribution of abilities in students taking an exam. They range from 40 up to 80, with the majority of students close to 60. Somewhere around 60 would be the **average** value.

In this panel, we have used a single question exam designed so that anyone who is capable of understanding more than 50% of the class concepts will get the correct answer.

This question splits the class into two parts. If the outcome of the exam question were a variable, it would not distinguish ability very well because it gives the same value to people with 51% and 99% ability.

Finally, we have six questions, well-spaced in difficulty. Between them, they split the class into seven parts. Although the parts are not equally sized, the questions provide good information about students' abilities as we can see which students have which level of ability. An exam is typically laid out like this – just usually with more than seven questions!

Figure 3.1   Graph showing variability and information.

When we create a variable, we must decide how it will be measured. It is important that we make choices that will capture as much information about the variable as possible.

	Q1. Imagine standing at the top of a tall steep mountain. How do you feel? 0 = terrified 1 = a bit restless 2 = ok 3 = happy 4 = exhilarated	Q2. You are sitting on a park bench in warm sunshine. How do you feel? 4 = terrified 3 = a bit restless 2 = ok 1 = happy 0 = exhilarated	Q3. Imagine waiting to go into a statistics exam. How do you feel? 0 = terrified 1 = a bit restless 2 = ok 3 = happy 4 = exhilarated	Q4. Imagine driving home through a blizzard. How do you feel? 0 = terrified 1 = a bit restless 2 = ok 3 = happy 4 = exhilarated
Participant 1	0	0	3	1
Participant 2	3	1	2	1
Participant 3	4	3	1	3

Figure 3.2   Risk-taking questionnaire example.

We have invented an example risk-taking questionnaire. The purpose of this example is to show how asking various different but related questions can help to produce a good measure. Notice first that Q2 has an opposite sense to the others and so its numbers are flipped around. Then we can see that the responses our participants give to questions 1, 2, 4 are all quite closely related, but not identical. The responses to Q3, on the other hand, are quite different. We would probably decide to remove Q3 from the analysis. By allowing five different responses for each question, we have ensured that we get useful variability from our participants. By asking about four (or three after the removal of one) topics, we have ensured that we avoid spurious variability – for example, if we hadn't asked Q1, then participant 2 would look much more like participant 1 than they should.

At the same time, we must be careful we don't make distinctions between students which don't matter. Since we are not really interested in which particular facts students have learned, only how many of them, any difference because our exam focuses on a few specific facts is a meaningless difference: and we call this **spurious variability**.

3.2.2 PSYCHOLOGICAL VARIABILITY

The same principles apply with a psychological measure: it is important to capture as much information as possible and to avoid spurious variability. Many psychological measures, such as a questionnaire, are designed to have many more than two possible responses: having from five to seven is more likely. More possible responses mean that the question splits participants into more groups to start with.

It is also usual to have a range of questions to cover different but equivalent experiences so that each question should split participants slightly differently. For this reason, most questionnaires have several questions to gather more of the important variability and therefore more information about the variable we are interested in. Figure 3.2 shows an example of this.

We must set considerable importance on and effort into capturing as much of the natural variability as we can. Choosing measurements that give us a detailed picture of what we are interested in – as much variability as we can – is important to really understand the answer to our research question.

When a set of questions has been created, then it is reassuring to know how well they work and, in particular, whether they make a coherent measure of a single variable: are they internally consistent? A simple way of doing this involves a quantity called **Cronbach's alpha**, which is calculated from the responses to the questions, usually with statistical software. Alpha is a number between 0 and 1, with higher values indicating stronger internal consistency; statistically speaking, the calculation looks for a relationship between the questions. Typically, a value of 0.8 or higher is considered desirable, although it should always be taken with a pinch of salt because more questions (and so more information being fed in) often lead to a higher value regardless of how coherent they actually are.

3.3 MEASURING VARIABLES

Before we can obtain the value of a particular variable for a person/situation, we need to determine how that variable will be measured. There are often many ways in which we can measure a particular variable, and it is important we choose the way that will collect as much useful information as possible. Of course, sometimes it is as easy as writing a list of all the possible eye colours and assigning participants a label that puts them in one group or another, but often the researcher has to think a lot harder.

Something that is very important to consider when we plan our measurements is this: when we talk of variables, we often mean some internal state that we only have indirect access to, which we cannot directly observe. A person's willingness to take risks lies inside their mind and beyond our reach. The thing we measure, on the other hand, of course has to be observable – usually the result of some behaviour or activity of our participants, even if it is only them ticking a box on a form.

If we wish to examine risk-taking, which is an internal and not directly observable quality of the person, we must either use observable behaviour like eating chillies or a history of skydiving, or rely on the person's self-assessment of their general risk-taking by having them answer a questionnaire. Watching someone take a risk or avoid it provides us with a more direct insight into the internal state, at least at that moment. Using someone's answers to a questionnaire is of course much less direct and is heavily influenced by what they wish were the case or what they want us to believe is the case.

An unobservable variable, such as an internal state, that we infer from things we can measure is a type of **latent** variable. A latent variable is any variable that we didn't directly measure but that we extract from our data. In the example we just looked at, we can't directly measure someone's willingness for risk-taking – it is a latent variable. We measure things that we think it will influence so we can infer it.

When we use self-reporting measures to collect data, we ask lots of similar questions of participants and hope that the answers are largely influenced by the internal state that we are intending to examine. This is illustrated in Figure 3.3. The answers our participants make are also influenced by other unseen latent variables (that we aren't interested in) and we hope that these other influences are small. We have to make careful decisions about the questions we use to keep our measurement close to the internal state we are wishing to measure. We will examine this in more detail when we come to research design in Chapters 8 and 9.

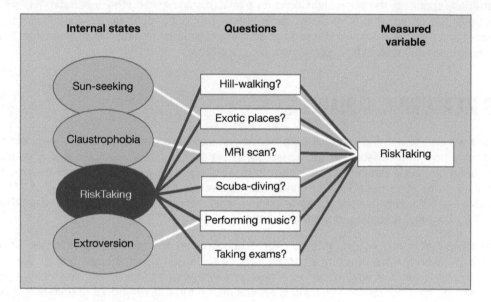

Figure 3.3   Latent variables diagram.

Imagine RiskTaking as a numeric score version of our yes/no RiskTaker? variable. This score might come from combining questions that identify different things that relate to a risky personality. The process of measuring an internal unobservable state with a set of six observable behaviours (using responses to six questions in this example). Since the observable behaviours are all influenced to some extent by other factors, each of them is a combination of the internal state (these are a type of latent variable) of interest and these other factors. If the other factors affect some of the responses differently, then the effects of the other factors are cancelled out to some extent when the responses are combined. Any remaining consequence of the irrelevant internal states will create a measurement error.

3.3.1 MEASUREMENT ERROR

There is always some meaningless variability in between the internal state we are interested in and the measurement we make of it. Any particular internal state can generate lots of external behaviours and responses, and we must try to choose the most appropriate ones for our research. However, each of these behaviours or responses that we measure is also influenced by other internal states that we are not interested in, and so our measure will be contaminated to some extent. This is the basic concept of **measurement error**: the difference between the value we obtain and the real value of the internal state. We can't quantify the size of this error; instead we must make the best decisions we can when measuring our variables to keep it low. Figure 3.3 illustrates this measurement error between what we are interested in and what we choose to measure.

An important way we can improve how we measure an intended internal variable is by using multiple measurements. For example, there are many different ways of measuring risk-taking. A common ploy in psychology is to ask people to imagine a scenario and then to report how they think they would feel or to recollect an occasion when something happened and recall how they felt. If we do this, then we must be careful to include enough different scenarios to be fairly sure we give everyone a chance. Scuba-diving on its own won't suffice; we need to add quite different examples of risk-taking. We could add in playing lead trumpet, inventing a new theory, and so on. By combining more pieces of information, we are more accurately measuring our variable of interest, and hopefully reducing measurement error.

3.4 TYPES OF MEASUREMENT VALUE

Now that we have decided what variables we are interested in and how we are going to measure them, we can look at how those measurements give us different types of value. Recall that values are how we label the differences between participants within a variable: we have chosen our values for the variable RiskTaker? to simply be yes and no, while our values for the variable ExamGrades are all the possible grades that a student could get.

First, we need two distinctions. Values can be ordered or not; they are ordered if they have a natural sequence that can be represented by a number. Values can be **discrete** or **continuous**; they are discrete if there is a fixed, usually small set of values with no half-values in between. RiskTaker? has discrete values with no order – we can't say that 'yes' is more or less than 'no', while ExamGrade has ordered continuous values.

There are three main ways the value from a measurement can be represented: using categories (e.g. playing trumpet, fiddle, guitar, other, none); using continuous numbers (e.g. IQ of 102); or using ordered discrete values (e.g. coming first or second in a race). The most important thing to learn here is that most of the time, the types of value we use for a variable are not predetermined: they are the result of the decisions of the researcher.

3.4.1 CATEGORICAL VARIABLES

Categorical variables are the most straightforward type of measurement value: the values of a Categorical variable are categories (or groups). For example, when we divide our RiskTaker? variable into a 'yes' (risk-taker) group and a 'no' (non-risk-taker) group, we are making two values (the two categories) for the variable RiskTaker?, which makes it a **Categorical variable**.

Sometimes you'll see Categorical variables referred to as **nominal variables**. This is just a different word for the same thing.

There are some variables where the concept itself requires categories and no other variable type would be suitable. Think about a variable, Which RiskType, that captures the different types of risk-taking behaviour that people undertake. There will be lots of different categories, such as bungee jumping, sky diving, no risky activities, etc. The only way we can describe different types is by giving them different labels. Categorical variables have values that are labels. Because they are not amounts, we cannot place them in any logical order or use numbers for values.

3.4.2 ORDINAL VARIABLES

Now think about another example where we give people their exam results using six labels: 'outstanding', 'very good', 'good', 'pass', 'fail' or 'catastrophe'. These are still labels and categories, but now we can put the categories into a natural and clear order: it is better to be 'very good' than 'pass' and 'pass' is better than 'catastrophe'. This ordering means that we are using another type of variable: an **Ordinal variable**. We can also use numbers for the different categories, such as asking someone to rate themselves on a scale from 1 to 5, and so long as the numbers are really just a set of ordered labels, then it is still an Ordinal variable.

3.4.3 INTERVAL VARIABLES

However, when we look at exam grades in a multiple-choice exam, there is usually a simple relationship between the grade and the number of correct answers. Someone who gets 70/100 has 10 more points than their friend who got 60/100, who has 20 more points than someone else with a score of 40/100. The difference between two values is a meaningful measure of the difference between two people because a difference of 10 means the same number of additional right answers at any point on the scale. This technical property that the differences between values are meaningful in mathematical terms means that we are using an **Interval variable**. As a counter-example, when we ask someone to rate themselves on a scale from 1 to 5, the result is probably not an Interval measure. Despite it using numbers, there is not necessarily a fixed difference between adjacent values.

This use of differences between values for an Interval variable has a very important consequence: it allows us to use addition and subtraction with the values. So, these mathematical processes are available to us when we use values from an Interval measurement. This is very useful, as we shall see, because we can compare two numbers by subtracting one from the other to look at the difference between them.

Another very useful consequence of using numbers in this way is that the values can then be treated as being continuous. Ordinal values (labels or numbers as labels) are discrete: everyone has to belong to one of the available values. This means that there are jumps along the scale from one category to the next. Interval values are continuous: there are no jumps from one value to the next.

These two properties, (i) allowing addition and subtraction and (ii) being continuous, tend to go hand in hand. If a numerical scale is continuous, then the values can usually be treated as Interval values. Technically, a variable is continuous if there is always a possible third value in between any two that we have. If we have the values 2 and 3 and are happy that there is also a possible value of 2.5 (between them), then the values are continuous. Real numbers (which include fractions) are continuous. Whole numbers (which don't include fractions) are discrete.

3.4.4 SUMMARY

It is quite simple to determine the type of data we have or are choosing to collect using these two properties:

(i)   Whether the possible values are ordered or not: can we determine whether one value is more or less than another?

(ii) If so, whether the possible values are continuous or limited to discrete steps. If not, then it is normal for the variable to have the property of meaningful addition and subtraction.

Table 3.3 shows how these two properties can be used to determine variable type.

Table 3.3   The properties of values and how they relate to variable types.

Note that you can't have values that are continuous but not ordered, because being in order is required for a set of numbers to be continuous.

	Discrete	**Continuous**
Ordered	Ordinal	Interval
Not ordered	Categorical	

It is important to realise that variable type is rarely outside our control: we can usually measure a variable using several different types. Table 3.4 provides examples.

Table 3.4   Measuring variables using different types of measurement.

Notice that some variables (the top ones) can be represented by all the types of variable. Others, such as car-make, cannot because there is no plausible or useful continuum that links them.

Variable	**Possible continuous numbers**	**Possible discrete values**	**Possible categories**
Weight	Kg or pounds	Clothes size (S, M, L, XL)	Underweight, healthy, overweight
Exam result	0–100	Outstanding/very good/good/pass/fail	Pass/fail

(Continued)

Table 3.4 (Continued)

Variable	Possible continuous numbers	Possible discrete values	Possible categories
RiskTaking	0–10	Professional/amateur/ hobby/none	High/low
Perfectionism	Score calculated from a questionnaire	How much of a perfectionist are you on a scale from 1 to 7?	High or low perfectionist
Degree class	Final GPA score	1st, 2:1, 2:2, 3rd	Pass or fail
Make of car			Toyota, Audi, BMW, Volvo, other

3.4.5 RATIO VARIABLES

While we examine different types of measures, we should briefly address a fourth variable type: Ratio variables. A Ratio variable is an Interval variable with the added property that the value zero corresponds to an absence of the thing being measured. A bank balance is a Ratio variable: zero means it is empty. Note that Ratio variables, just like bank balances, can be negative as well as positive, although negative values mean something different from positive ones. For the deeply curious, Ratio variables allow us to use multiplication and its close cousin, division. This type of variable allows a comparison of two numbers by looking at their Ratio: dividing one by the other. However, from a statistical analysis perspective, we treat Ratio variables in exactly the same way as Interval variables.

3.5 DISTRIBUTIONS OF VALUES

Now that we have established how to measure variables, we can move on to understand what we learn about our data from these measurements. Different types of variables give us different amounts and types of useful information.

Regardless of the type of the variable, the set of values that we obtain can be combined into a **distribution**: a pattern that can be depicted on a graph showing how frequent the different values are. This distribution of values contains a lot of useful information about the variable and also has the virtue of being easy to describe or summarise. So when we treat our set of values as being a distribution, we can move from seeing them just as a list of numbers or labels, and instead describe the distribution that they collectively form.

We will use a very specific word to describe the relationship between the characteristics of a sample and the population. We use characteristics of the sample to **estimate** the corresponding characteristics of the population. Note that the word 'estimate' tells us that the process involves some uncertainty about how accurate we are – which we cover in Chapter 5.

There are two important types of information we can get from the distributions of values.

3.5.1 CENTRAL TENDENCY

The first step is to describe the single most typical value from all the values we have for a particular variable. We have described this typical value so far as an 'average', but in more statistical terms it is called the **central tendency**. The most familiar type of typical value is called the mean. The central tendency is a **descriptive statistic**.

3.5.2 DISPERSION

The second step is to describe the spread of the values. This is called the measure of **dispersion** and is used to capture how widely the values in the data set differ from the central tendency or typical value. Dispersion is another descriptive statistic.

3.6 INTERVAL VARIABLES

Interval variables have values that are numerical, ordered and continuous with meaningful differences between values. A graph showing the distribution of values for an Interval variable is shown in Figure 3.4. This graph shows the relative frequency of each possible value. Because the variable is ordered, we can see that the values plotted horizontally along the bottom (called the **x-axis**) are numerical, and because the variable has continuous values, the distribution is also smooth and continuous.

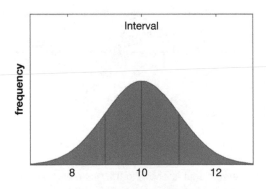

Figure 3.4   The distribution of values for a typical Interval variable.

The graph shows how frequent or common each possible value is. In this case, the value of 10 is the most common and values above 12 or beneath 8 are much less frequent.

In 'How To Use This Book', we included a table of all the common elements of mathematical formulae, so if anything you see from here onwards looks a bit confusing, it would be sensible to go back to the table and have a look.

3.6.1 CENTRAL TENDENCY: MEAN

We use the **mean** as a measure of central tendency for Interval variables. The mean can be calculated for a set of values by adding the values together, and then dividing by the number of values present. In mathematical terms, if x_i stands for each member of a set of values (i goes from 1 to n so that x_3 is the 3rd data point in the set), then:

$$xmean = \frac{sum(x_i)}{n}$$

This formula is just a way of writing down the instructions: sum (add together) all the values (x_i) and then divide by the sample size, denoted as n.

There are two important reasons why we use the mean. Imagine we have a sample of participants and for each we have their exam grade. Figure 3.5 shows this set of data points and its mean. The figure also shows a thin vertical line drawn from each point to the mean value. These vertical lines are the differences between the individual data points and the mean itself – which we will call deviations from the mean. In later chapters we will also call these **residuals**.

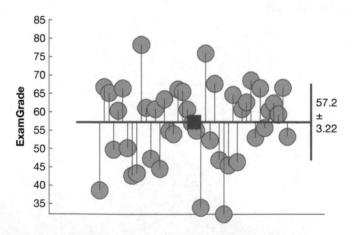

Figure 3.5   Sample from an Interval variable showing the mean and deviations from the mean.

This figure shows a set of data points (dots). The mean for the set is drawn as a horizontal line through the data points. None of the data points actually lie exactly at the mean and for each there is some numerical difference between the data point value and the mean. The size of this deviation of a data point from the mean is called a residual.

Then the mean we obtain has these two properties:

1. The sum of deviations from the mean is zero.

$$sum(x_i - xmean) = 0$$

A deviation is the difference between each person's own grade and the mean and can be calculated by subtracting one from the other. The sum of these deviations for the whole sample is zero. In Figure 3.5, the mean is the thick horizontal line. The difference between each individual value and the mean value is indicated with a thin vertical line. The total length of all the vertical lines above the mean is equal to the total length of the vertical lines below the mean.

2. The sum of squared deviations from the mean is minimum.

$$sum((x_i - xmean)^2) = minimum$$

Because deviations can be positive or negative, when we square each person's deviation (squaring is when you multiply a number by itself) we make a positive number – a negative number squared is like two negatives and they cancel out. The larger this squared deviation is, the less useful the mean is as a guide to that individual's particular grade. We can add up these squared deviations from everyone in the sample to produce the sum of squared deviations. The mean is then the value that, overall, produces the smallest possible total sum of squared deviations.

These are the mathematical ways of showing the two reasons why the mean is a good value to use as a central tendency. It isn't biased up or down: there is as much deviation above as beneath. It is the number that comes closest to matching each data point in the set; any other value would lead to a higher sum of squared deviations.

Those steps aren't strictly necessary to do, but they are a good way to understand why we do this. Doing this also means that we can follow through very easily to learn about measuring dispersion in Interval data.

3.6.2 DISPERSION: STANDARD DEVIATION

For an Interval variable, we use the **standard deviation** as a measure of dispersion. The standard deviation only requires a little bit more work:

$$sd(x) = sqrt\left(\frac{sum\left((x_i - xmean)^2\right)}{n} \right)$$

1. We divide the sum of squared deviations by the number of participants that we have. This gives us a value called the **variance**, which will come in useful later on.

2. We then take the square root of the variance and call the result the standard deviation. We use the square root because it gives us a sensible value which is in the same units as the original data. In the previous figure (Figure 3.5) the standard deviation is shown as the thick vertical line at the right side of the diagram. It shows 1 standard deviation away from the mean in each direction.

The standard deviation is a measure of dispersion, because it tells us how much our values typically differ from our measure of central tendency (the mean). A small standard deviation means that the values do not differ much and are therefore not very spread out, and a large standard deviation means the opposite.

3.6.3 ESTIMATES

We are usually interested in a sample because of what it tells us about the population we took it from. So our sample mean and standard deviation can be used to estimate what the population mean and standard deviation might be.

- Population central tendency: the sample mean is the best estimate of the population mean.
- Population dispersion: the sample standard deviation is always a little bit smaller than the population standard deviation, more so the smaller our sample size (n) is. We can correct for this by replacing n in the calculation of standard deviation by (n–1).

This is explained in further detail online

3.6.4 DISTRIBUTION OF VALUES: THE NORMAL DISTRIBUTION

We can also look at the shape of the distribution of values. When we have Interval data, these values often appear in a very specific shape: the **normal distribution**, which forms a symmetrical bell curve, shown in Figure 3.6. Any variable that is affected by a lot of separate causes usually has a normal distribution. A person's exam grade can be influenced by many causes: their hours of sleep, how much they have studied, their diet, their optimism, and so on. Taken together, this results in a distribution of grades that will follow this normal pattern. Since nearly everything of interest in psychology has lots of causes, normal distributions are very common. From looking at the normal distribution, it is clear to see that most people have a grade somewhere in the middle of the range of values, while much fewer people have grades in the top and bottom tails.

Why is this important to know? Well, because we can say a lot about our data with just a very small set of numbers. The normal distribution itself can be completely described and pictured by using just its mean and standard deviation: no other information is needed. This is a fortunate outcome of mathematics, the first of several we will encounter.

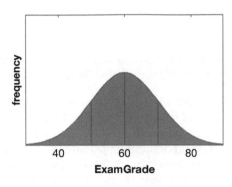
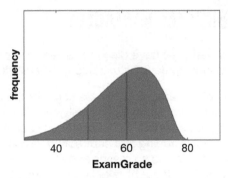

Figure 3.6   Normal and skewed distributions.

Left: The bell-shaped distribution of values in this example is called a normal distribution. A normal distribution is useful because it depends on only two numbers: its mean and its standard deviation. The narrowest part of the graph at each end of a distribution is called a tail. A normal distribution as pictured here has two equal tails. Right: a skewed distribution. This distribution has a negative skew – it has a longer tail towards low values.

However, data do not always fall in this nice neat pattern. For example, the distribution of exam grades may be quite different: the exam may be set up so that too many questions are very difficult and most people will not get them right. The result of this will be a distribution that is skewed: one 'tail' is longer than the other (as shown in Figure 3.6). Skew often arises because the measurements we use are biased, due to how difficult it can be to devise a very good measure that collects the intended information we are looking for. Both the normal distribution and skew are explored in a little more detail in our online resources, if you are interested in learning more.

This is explained in further detail online

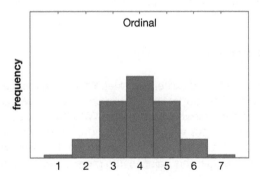

Figure 3.7   The distribution of values for a typical Ordinal variable.

This figure shows the distribution of values for a typical Ordinal variable. There are seven discrete values and the central values are more common than the extremes.

3.7 ORDINAL VARIABLES

Ordinal variables have discrete values, with order but with no meaningful distance between each value. Figure 3.7 illustrates the distribution of values for a typical Ordinal variable.

With Ordinal variables, we lose some of the mathematical opportunities that we just used with Interval variables; specifically, we should not add or subtract values. If we calculated a mean and standard deviation for an Ordinal variable (where the values are numbers), this would involve adding and subtracting the values. Adding or subtracting Ordinal values is not a safe process and so means and standard deviations calculated in this circumstance might be misleading. It might take little to nudge a 3-level risk-taker up to level 4 while taking an enormous amount to nudge a level 4 to a 5. This means that the difference between a value of 3 and a value of 4 may not be the same as the difference between a value of 4 and a value of 5, and so treating those two differences as the same is misleading.

3.7.1 MEDIAN

Consequently, we use the **median** as the measure of central tendency for Ordinal variables, which is illustrated in Figure 3.8. The median is simply the middle value of the data set, when all of the values are put in order: to do this, we don't have to add them up as we do for the mean. The median may end up being a full value or being a value halfway between the two in the middle, depending on whether we have an even- or odd-sized set of data.

The median has the nice property that as many values lie below it as above it, which means that any individual value is equally likely to be larger than or smaller than the median. This is weaker than the equivalent for the mean where the summed deviations are equal either side of the mean.

3.7.2 INTER-QUARTILE RANGE

Measuring dispersion in an Ordinal data set is trickier. We can say that a particular Ordinal value is higher or lower than the median, but not by how much. However, we can state that a particular value is so many places above or below the median. With this, we can divide the data set into quarters. The difference between the value at the boundary of the first and second quarters and the value at the boundary of the third and fourth quarters is the **inter-quartile range**, which is illustrated in Figure 3.8. The bigger this value is, the more spread out the values are.

3.7.3 ESTIMATES

Both the sample median and the inter-quartile range can be used as estimates of the population without correction.

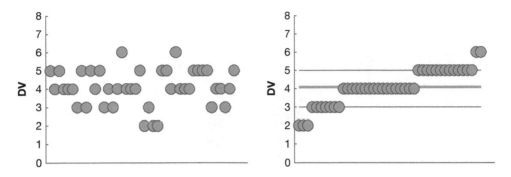

Figure 3.8   Sample from an Ordinal variable showing the median and inter-quartile range.

The same data, presented twice. On the left the data is unsorted. On the right, the same data is shown, but sorted by value. The central thicker line shows the median and the two thinner lines show the inter-quartile range.

3.7.4 DISTRIBUTION OF VALUES: LIKERT SCALE

The use of Ordinal measures in psychology is very common, although largely for an uninteresting historical reason. The often-used Likert scale is a simple device: you ask a question and provide an ordered set of possible answers and the participant is asked to choose one. In the days of paper and pencil, it was the most convenient way of doing this (it isn't any longer but old habits …). There would typically be five to seven possible answers, resulting in an Ordinal variable.

Years of experience have shown that there is a typical distribution of values that this produces – it isn't as mathematically tidy as the normal distribution, but superficially looks similar. Responses to the Likert scale tend to cluster around the middle and are fewer out in the extremes.

3.8 CATEGORICAL VARIABLES

Categorical variables have values that are categories (groups). No additional detail is provided; all that is known is whether a participant belongs to a group or not. Figure 3.9 illustrates the distribution for a simple Categorical variable.

3.8.1 MODE

With a Categorical variable, the only measure of central tendency that may be useful is the **mode** – the value that appears the most times. This is simply the value that has the highest

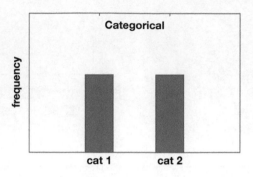

Figure 3.9   A Categorical variable with two groups.

There is no limit to the number of groups a Categorical variable can have: learn more about how to choose sensible groups in Chapter 9. In this case, there are two groups, and both have the same number of participants.

count and is the most common. Sometimes when we have a Categorical variable, such as trial phase or experimental condition, the mode will not tell us anything useful because we have deliberately set the group sizes to be equal.

In the most straightforward terms, looking at the count for each category also tells us about the dispersion of the data: are the categories roughly equally sized, in which case there is a lot of dispersion, or is the distribution focused into a small number of the available categories, in which case the dispersion is small? There is no spread within the categories, as each person within the category has the same label.

Categorical data gives us the least amount of information about our sample.

THE BIG PICTURE

The concept of variables is the most fundamental building brick for the whole of statistics. When we choose which variables are of interest, we are choosing the components of a person or situation that will matter for the research. We are responsible for our variable choices.

VARIABLES

1. Variables are distinct ways that people or situations vary.

2. Variables have values which can be numerical or labels.

3. Normally, each participant has one value for each variable.

   a. In a between-participants design, participants only belong in one group of a Categorical variable: they only have one value for this variable.

   b. In a within-participants design, participants are allocated to every group of a Categorical variable: they will have multiple values for this variable.

VARIABLE TYPES

4. We can choose how to measure our variables. The different types are Categorical, Ordinal, or Interval. While some variables only suit one type, most can be made to work with any of the different variable types.

5. Different variable types provide different information about the thing they are measuring. Ordinal and Interval provide ordering information. Interval also provides information about differences in values.

DISTRIBUTIONS OF VALUES

6. Across a population, the values of a variable form a distribution. It is useful to be able to describe these distributions of values by their typical value (central tendency) and their spread (dispersion).

7. The different variable types each have different measures of central tendency and dispersion.

   a. The three types of central tendency measure are the mean median and mode.

   b. Dispersion can be measured using the standard deviation, inter-quartile range or comparing frequencies.

IMPORTANT ISSUE TO THINK ABOUT

8. Variability plays a big role in choosing what variables to use and how to measure them. We want to capture as much variability as possible, without letting unwanted spurious or unwanted variability creep in.

 # YOUR TURN

DEFINE THESE KEY TERMS IN THE SPACE PROVIDED:

1. Latent variable

2. Mean

3. Standard deviation

FILL IN THE GAPS IN THESE SENTENCES:

1. The median is the ------------- value in an ordinal data set

2. The inter-quartile range can be used to measure dispersion in an ------ variable.

3. The measure of central tendency for a Categorical variable is the ------

Identify the variable type for each of the variables in the following table:

Variable	Method	Type of Measurement? Interval/Categorical/Ordinal
Happiness	Self-rated report using a Likert scale	
Dog	Organised by breed	
Height	Scale in centimetres	
Weather	Mm of rainfall	
Caffeine status	Measurements taken before and after drinking coffee	
Social Media	Hours spent on social media	
Pain	Self-rated using a low–high set of options	
Top Level of Education	Categorising from primary school through to postgraduate	

THERE ARE MORE ACTIVITIES AND ANSWERS ONLINE

YOUR SPACE

 ## REFERENCES AND FURTHER READING

Rosnow, R.L. & Rosenthal, R. (1997) *People Studying People: Artefacts and Ethics in Behavioural Research*. New York: Freeman and Co.

Classic text.

THERE ARE MORE ACTIVITIES AND A SHORT
SUMMARY VIDEO FOR THIS CHAPTER AVAILABLE AT:
HTTPS://STUDY.SAGEPUB.COM/STATISTICSFORPSYCHOLOGY

CHAPTER

04

RELATIONSHIPS BETWEEN VARIABLES

RELATIONSHIPS: BECAUSE VARIABLES ARE STRONGER TOGETHER

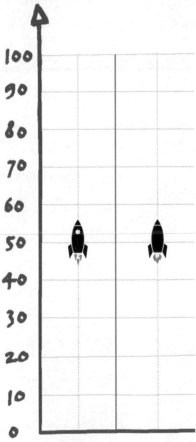

Recall that we began this book by establishing an **idea** that risk-takers do better in exams than non-risk-takers, which involves two **variables**: risk-taking (which we have labelled RiskTaker?) and exam performance (labelled ExamGrade). In the last chapter we saw how we can get values for our variables from a **sample** of participants capturing as much as we can of the relevant differences between those participants. Each participant will have one **value** for each variable, so in this case, that is two values because there are two variables.

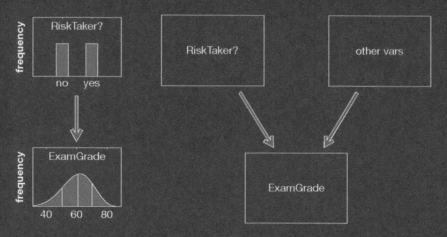

Figure 4.1   Our basic hypothesis diagram.

Our basic hypothesis: there is a relationship between RiskTaker? and ExamGrade. On the left we show our normal diagram for this. On the right, we see the full situation: we are studying RiskTaker? as one among many other influences on ExamGrade that we aren't considering. We have used 'other vars' to stand in for all the influences that we are ignoring.

The sets of values that we have for each of our two variables do not on their own tell us anything much. The **mean** exam grade for each group on its own may or may not be interesting, but it doesn't help with our question. We are really interested in looking at both sets of values together, to see whether there is a relationship: the analysis phase of research begins.

Our idea about the relationship between risk-taking and exam grades is schematically illustrated in Figure 4.1 as a **hypothesis**: risk-taking scores affect exam grades. Of course, we must recognise right from the start that many other variables could also be involved – this is certainly not an exclusive relationship. We aren't saying that exam grades depend solely on risk-taking. In a bigger picture, we should imagine that the influence of risk-taking on exam grades works alongside the influence of many other variables also shown in Figure 4.1.

In this chapter we will focus on situations where there are just two variables, as this will allow us to cover all the fundamental principles that we need to know for now. This is not a real-world limit: it is perfectly normal to have more variables (we shall discuss this in Chapter 11). A relationship between two variables is enough to see a number of important characteristics that we are going to learn about in this chapter.

4.1 WHAT IS A RELATIONSHIP BETWEEN VARIABLES?

All psychological research methods are designed to explore relationships between variables, whether those variables are characteristics or situations. A good starting point is to think about relationships as being **associations** between the values of two different variables. Getting slightly higher exam grades could be associated with being a high risk-taker; or the association could go the other way – getting slightly lower exam grades is associated with high risk-taking. Being 'associated with' just means 'tends to occur with'. Association is a good neutral word for a relationship.

When we say that we think risk-takers have higher exam grades, we don't actually mean that every risk-taker has a higher grade than every non-risk-taker. We mean that, everything else being equal, we think it is more likely than not that a risk-taker will have higher exam grades than a non-risk-taker. There is a tendency to describe results as 'Risk-takers do better in exams', when what is meant is 'Risk-takers have some amount of advantage in exams'.

A person's exam grade is the result of myriad different factors all coming together at that moment. These factors, aspects of the person and their situation, are all potential variables. If the exam had been a day later, then some of those factors would be different and the exam grade would be different. In among all of those factors, there will be (tiny) effects of almost everything that is happening in the person's life. Any pair (or more) of variables could have a relationship, and one could argue that every pair of psychologically interesting variables are related in some sort of way.

4.1.1 TWO QUESTIONS ABOUT RELATIONSHIPS

There are two questions we can ask about a relationship:

1. Does the relationship exist?
2. How strong or weak is the relationship?

The first question is common in psychology but is the less useful and interesting of the two. The possible answers for the first question are 'yes', 'not sure' and 'no'. The possible answers to the second question are much more interesting because they could give us a lot more information. As we shall see in Chapter 6, the question of 'does a relationship exist?' is always answered by saying how strong the relationship must be for us to accept that we are not just seeing some kind of pattern by chance.

4.2 THE LOGIC OF RELATIONSHIPS

A relationship between two variables can mean many different things: 'A is related to B', 'A affects B', or 'A depends on B'. It might also mean that 'A and B are both dependent on C', something we shall come to in Chapter 11. All of these different meanings involve some manner of statistical relationship between the variables.

Although we would usually prefer to think of relationships as having a direction – such as 'A causes B' – usually the statistical processes we use to examine the relationship do not distinguish a direction, which could be 'A causes B' but could just as easily be 'B causes A'.

Instead, the psychology and the general logic of the situation may let us identify one of the variables as affecting the other. Even if we are uncertain about our choice, it is often reasonable to work as if we are going to use the value of one variable for predicting the value of the other variable. This introduces a logical difference between the roles of the two variables. The two variables are no longer interchangeable because one is predicting the other and we can think of this difference as introducing an asymmetry: the relationship is not balanced; one variable is being influenced by the other.

Asymmetry in the logic of a hypothesis is important, and there is some common terminology used. The variable that affects or predicts is called the **Independent Variable** (IV); the variable that is affected or predicted is called the **Dependent Variable** (DV). Figure 4.2 demonstrates this logic where 'RiskTaker?' is the IV, affecting 'ExamGrade', which is the DV. A hypothesis or research project can have multiple IVs and/or multiple DVs.

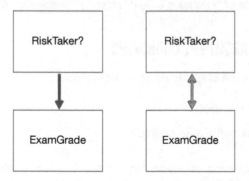

Figure 4.2   Psychological thinking determines the asymmetry of a relationship.

The basic logic of the relationship between two variables. On the left, the Independent Variable (IV) predicts or affects the Dependent Variable (DV). The figure is drawn to show the asymmetry of role. It is important to understand, right from the start, that data and statistics cannot be used to determine that asymmetry: it is a matter of psychological thinking. Strictly speaking, the data and the statistics cannot be used to determine which direction the influence flows and the diagram on the right is more appropriate.

The IV is called independent because, so far as our study is concerned, it is independent of everything we are interested in: we are not measuring any of its causes or predictors in our work. Of course it does have causes, but we are not interested in them. In our example, although the variable RiskTaker? will have lots of interesting causes, our study is not considering them.

The DV, on the other hand, is thought to be dependent on the IV (hence the name). Our hypothesis is that the value any one person has for the DV depends to a degree on the value they have for the IV. In our example, we are asking whether risk-taking might be a source of some of the differences in exam grades.

The statistics will say that there is a relationship between IV and DV, but never that we are justified in treating one as IV and one as DV: this logic is a psychological decision.

Sometimes, situations exist where the variables are treated as equal in status and the association between them is assessed without identifying any psychological asymmetry. This is a practice that leads to dead ends: there is very little valuable knowledge to be gained. Usually, not identifying asymmetry is used as a starting point for planning and experimenting with research before it moves onto further, more interesting analysis.

4.2.1 GRAPHS TO SHOW RELATIONSHIPS

Perhaps the easiest way to see and understand a relationship between two variables is to illustrate it with a graph. The purpose of the graph will determine the form it takes, as you will see in Figure 4.3, but there are a few simple, fundamental rules behind every graph:

1. The values of the IV are plotted horizontally along the bottom of the graph, called the **x-axis**; the values of the DV are plotted vertically along the side of the graph, called the **y-axis**. This will always be the case in this book. This is in important convention because it means we will not have to say which is which.

2. The values for a variable are arranged along the corresponding axis. If the variable has numerical values, then the convention is that values increase rightwards and upwards.

3. Typically, a graph only has content where there would be corresponding data. If you think of making a graph in terms of applying ink to paper, then there will only be ink where there might be data.

We will encounter three main uses for graphs. In order to make these graphs easy to distinguish as well as easy to read, in this book we give each type a specific form throughout. The types are illustrated in Figure 4.3.

Think of graphs as a language that has evolved to be highly effective for presenting patterns in data. There are few, if any, concepts in this book that aren't easily demonstrated with a graph. It is important to become adept at reading a graph and also at producing clear graphs: often they are the most vivid and immediate way of conveying a pattern to an audience.

Populations Graphs showing the distribution of values for a variable, or the joint distribution of values for two variables in a population. These are always plotted as filled areas. Each person in the population is placed somewhere in that filled area. Since the population is usually extremely large, it is not possible to show each person individually.	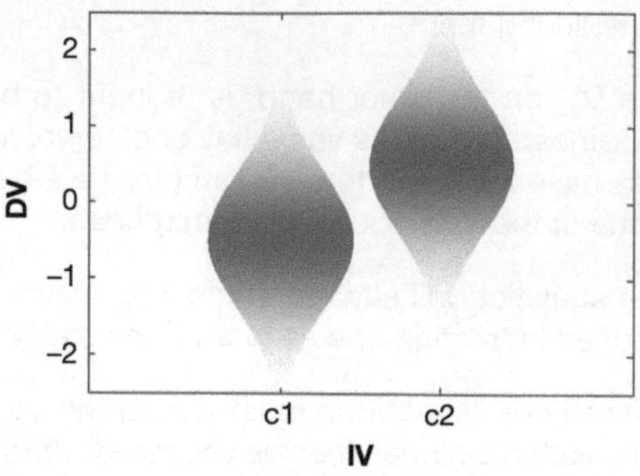
Samples Graphs showing the distribution of all the values for a variable, or the joint distribution of values for two variables in a sample. The value for each participant is usually plotted separately using a marker of some type, such as a small symbol (circle, square, cross, etc.). The example here shows a graph that would suit our RiskTaker? hypothesis, with a Categorical IV. Each participant is plotted as a circular dot	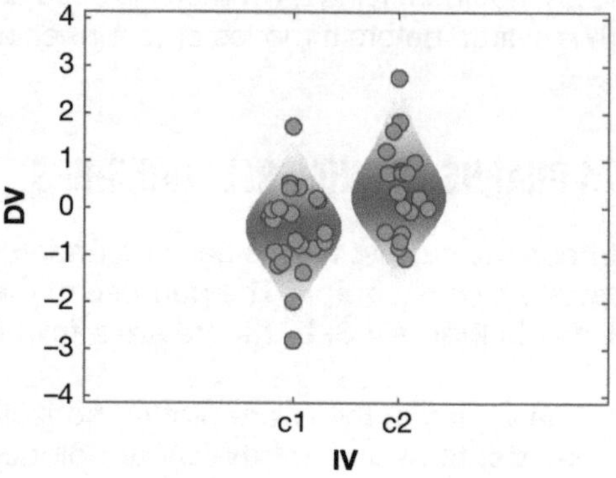
Descriptive statistics Graphs showing how the measure of central tendency of a DV varies with the values of an IV. These will take two forms, depending on the variable type of the DV. If the DV is Interval (or Ordinal), then the central tendency is mean (or median) and a circular dot (or similar icon) will be placed at that value. If the DV is Categorical, then the central tendency is a count or frequency and a **bar chart** will be used to show this.	

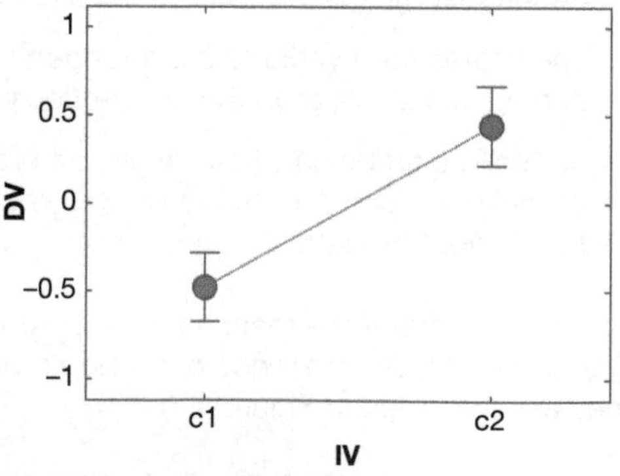

Figure 4.3   Examples for population, sample and descriptive statistics graphs.

In this book, there are three basic purposes for a graph: to show a population, a sample, or descriptive statistics. This figure provides an example for each graph type. More examples for these three basic purposes will be shown later as they become useful.

4.3 TYPES OF RELATIONSHIP

Each variable can be illustrated using a graph that shows the separate distribution for its own set of values. However, this tells us nothing about the relationship between the variables. Figure 4.4 shows both the separate distributions for two individual variables (on the top and left of each panel) and their joint distribution. For this figure we have used two Interval variables as this makes the effect particularly easy to see.

As Figure 4.4 shows, the differences between no relationship (middle), a negative relationship (left) or a positive relationship (right) are only visible in the joint distribution of both variables – where both variables are plotted together on a graph. The distributions of the variables on their own separate graphs (these are called **marginal distributions**) are the same regardless of whether there is a relationship between them or not. The joint distributions in this figure show the relationship.

In the central panel there is no relationship and the joint distribution is not oriented in any obvious direction. The panel on the right shows something different: it shows that for those individuals whose value on the IV is high (to the right) also have higher values for the DV, and vice versa for the panel on the left. These patterns indicate that a relationship exists.

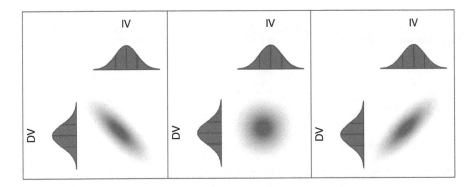

Figure 4.4   Distributions of two variables plotted together.

In this figure we can see the appearance of three different relationships. The joint distribution is shown in the centre of each panel with the distributions for the individual variables on the edges. For each of them, the two individual variables (IV and DV) on their own show normal distributions. Looking at these single distributions doesn't show the relationship. It is only when they are put together that the relationship emerges. In the middle panel the value that DV has is unaffected by the value for IV. On the left and right, the value that DV takes is related, in part, to the value of IV.

We can say that a relationship can be expressed as a pattern where the values of the DV depend, to some extent, on the value of the IV. If the values of the DV depend strongly on the values of the IV, the relationship between them is stronger. Look at the population graph in the right panel of Figure 4.4, where there is a positive relationship. Each person is somewhere in this distribution. For just those people who have a high value for the IV (on the right side of the distribution), their set of DV values is slightly higher than average. Conversely, for those people with low values for the IV, their set of DV values is slightly lower than average.

4.3.1 RELATIONSHIPS IN POPULATIONS

The way a relationship shows itself across the whole distribution in a population depends on the variable types that are being used. For this first step, we just need the fundamental distinction between discrete (Categorical) and continuous (Interval) variables. Ordinal variables are, as always, a nuisance here. Depending on whether they are really discrete or not, they will behave like either discrete or continuous variables.

If you look at the four different combinations of continuous and discrete variables in Figure 4.5, you will see that the basic pattern is the same: in each case there are more participants in the lower left and upper right corners. It is important to realise that these four different cases reflect a single fundamental idea: the distribution (of people, in this case) in the population. All of the four populations illustrated have the same pattern: more people in the top right and lower left. The exact forms of the graphs reflect the difference due to variable type.

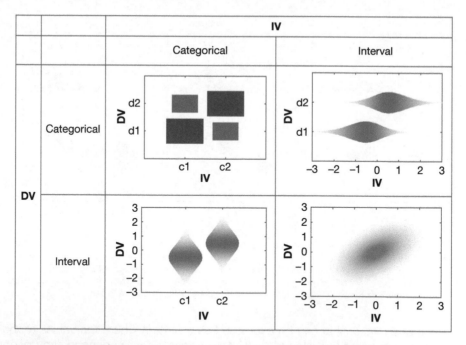

Figure 4.5   Relationships between two variables as they appear in populations.

Each variable can be discrete or continuous, and the four combinations of these two types gives the populations shown.

4.3.2 RELATIONSHIPS IN DESCRIPTIVE STATISTICS

The next step is then to describe that relationship. We can apply our knowledge of **central tendencies** from Chapter 3 here, thinking now in terms of the central tendency of parts of the population that share similar common values for their IV. A relationship between two variables will usually manifest itself as a way in which the central tendency of the DV depends, to some extent, on the specific value of the IV. Note the main point here: if we change the specific value of the IV we see corresponding changes in the central tendency of the DV.

A relationship concerns changes in the central tendency of the DV. You may recall from Chapter 3 that we described three different possible measures of central tendency.

- For Interval DVs, the **mean** is suitable and we can use that same concept in this new context of a relationship: when the DV is Interval, a relationship will show up as different means depending on the specific values of the IV.
- For Ordinal DVs, the **median** is used as a measure of central tendency and so we can think of relationships where the DV is Ordinal as being cases where there are different medians depending on specific values of the IV.
- For Categorical DVs we need a bit more. The measure of central tendency of a Categorical variable is the **mode** (commonest value). In this context of a relationship, we will use the relative frequency of the different categories rather than the mode: when the DV is Categorical, a relationship will show up as different relative frequencies of the categories depending on the specific values of the IV. Switching from mode to relative frequencies is done because the relative frequencies will change much more than the mode might.

A relationship concerns the specific values of the IV. In practice, what matters about the IV is whether it is ordered and continuous or not. Here the distinction between Ordinal and Interval doesn't matter: both are ordered and we can safely treat both as if they were continuous.

- An Interval or Ordinal IV has values that are continuous (or can be treated as such, for the purposes of looking for a relationship) and so the values for the changes in DV that we look for are also continuous.
- A Categorical IV has values that are discrete and so the changes in the DV will also be discrete.

Table 4.1 illustrates the different combinations of variable type and the change in central tendency that they cause. You will see that we have considered all three types of variable for the DV but only two for the IV. We are going to suppose that any Ordinal IVs are treated as Interval.

Table 4.1   Variable combinations and relationships, part 1.

The various different variable combinations and what they mean for the way a relationship between the variables will appear. Ordinal IVs can be treated as Interval.

		Changes in the value of the IV are associated with	
		Categorical	**Interval**
	Categorical	discrete changes in frequency	continuous changes in frequency
DV	**Ordinal**	discrete changes in median	continuous changes in median
	Interval	discrete changes in mean	continuous changes in mean

4.3.3 RELATIONSHIPS WHEN DV IS INTERVAL

When the DV is Interval, the measure of central tendency, as we have just mentioned, is the mean. A relationship would manifest as the value of the IV having an influence on the corresponding mean of the DV.

This is easy to apply when the IV is Categorical: the mean of the DV depends on the value of the IV. The values of the IV are a set of categories, and the relationship shows itself as different means for the DV in the different categories of the IV.

A graph that shows the effect directly is therefore a **line graph** with points showing the mean DV value for each category of the IV (as seen in Figure 4.6). If the line joining those points is not horizontal, then the mean DV varies from category to category and we can say that there is a relationship between the IV and the DV in our sample.

With a little bit of imagination, we can use this approach when the IV is also Interval. We can't treat the IV as groups each with its own mean, but we can do something similar. To start with, imagine that we split the IV into three sections: low, mid and high, which can be seen in

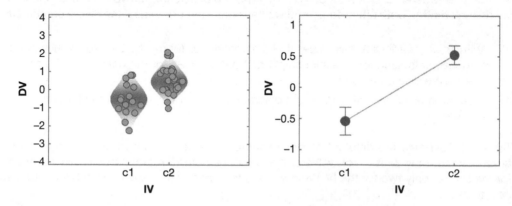

Figure 4.6   The distribution of participants and a line graph showing the effect of a Categorical IV on an Interval DV.

Figure 4.7. For each of these sections there is a corresponding mean value for the DV for that section. Let's call this a **local mean** – localised to one specific section of the IV – to distinguish it from the global or overall mean. This is more conceptual than anything else – you wouldn't really split your sample up to calculate many local means, but it helps to understand where the maths has come from. Now we think of a line that joins these local means together: this is shown in the figure and is called the **regression line**. You may also come across the regression line labelled as the line of best fit – which is quite a self-explanatory name, as ideally it is the line that best fits all of these imaginary local means.

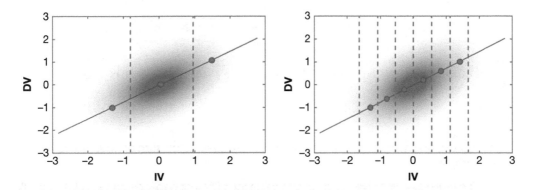

Figure 4.7   Illustration of the concept of a regression line.

Although the IV is continuous, we can think of it as having lots of small sections. For each of the small sections (three are shown on the left, many more on the right), we can imagine calculating a local mean of the corresponding DV values. These local means are shown as dots in the figure. The regression line then joins up the local means.

Now imagine splitting the IV into a larger number of infinitesimally small sections (instead of just three) and finding the local mean of the DV for all the data points in each tiny portion. Again, we are interested in the question of whether there is an overall trend. Once again, we link our local means using a regression line.

In practice with a realistic sample size, we can never have enough data points to actually do that process of infinitesimal groups and draw a regression line. However, there is a realistic way of achieving this same outcome that just builds very slightly on the work we did in understanding the idea of the mean in the previous chapter.

- The mean is the single (best-fitting) value that minimises the sum of squared deviations in a sample.
  - The mean of a DV gives us an overall expected value for a DV.
  - The actual value of the DV for each individual data point has a deviation from this best-fitting value.
  - The mean is the value that makes the sum of squared deviations minimum.

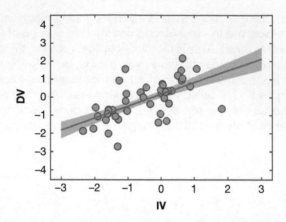

Figure 4.8   Scatter plot with the regression line showing the effect of an Interval IV on an Interval DV.

- The regression line is the (best-fitting) line that minimises the sum of squared deviations in a sample.

    o   The regression line gives us an overall value for a DV that depends on the value of the IV

    o   The actual value of the DV for each individual data point has a deviation from this line.

    o   The regression line is the line that makes the sum of squared deviations minimum.

This is illustrated in Figure 4.9.

The regression line gives us an overall best-fitting line: a best-fitting value for the DV for each possible IV.

Normally, psychology research restricts its interest to cases where that line is straight. If the line is horizontal, then there is no relationship (the DV mean does not change as the IV changes). If it is sloping one way or the other, then there is a relationship.

There are two simple principles in this section:

1.   If the DV is Interval, then the relationship is seen as changes in the mean of the DV with changes in the value of the IV.

2a.   If the IV is Categorical, then the relationship is differences in a set of group means: one for each category.

2b.   If the IV is Interval, then the relationship is a continuous regression line showing how DV mean value varies with the IV.

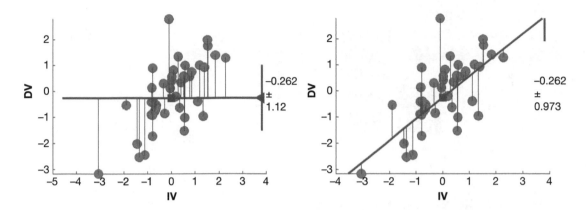

Figure 4.9   Illustration showing how the regression line reduces the sum of squared deviations.

This figure shows how the regression line reduces the sum of squared deviations. On the left is the pattern we have already seen in the previous chapter for the mean. The mean is the single value that minimises the sum of squared deviations. On the right, the line centred on the mean is now rotated to show that the deviations between the data points and the line are reduced further. The best fitting regression line is the one that achieves a minimum for the sum of squared deviations from the line.

4.3.4 RELATIONSHIPS WHEN DV IS CATEGORICAL

When the DV is Categorical, the central tendency is captured by looking at a **count** or **frequency**: how many (counts) or what proportion (frequencies) of the whole sample/ population belong in each category. Relationships with a Categorical DV therefore use frequencies: how often or how likely the DV is in one category, depending on the value of the IV. Frequencies are proportions and so are limited to lie between 0 (none) and 1 (all).

When the IV is also Categorical, then the relationship appears as a change in the relative frequencies of the DV categories when the IV category changes. If we measured both our variables as Categorical, then a relationship between them would be that the relative frequencies of high grades versus low grades was different for risk-takers than for non-risk-takers, which is illustrated in Figure 4.10. A convenient graph for showing relative frequencies is a bar chart where the height of the bars corresponds to the frequency.

When the IV is Interval, then we do the same thing as before: we think of splitting the IV into a large number of infinitesimal parts and finding the local relative frequency of the different DV categories for each part. This becomes another regression line – but this time it is a regression of frequencies. In this case, research in psychology is usually interested in an S-shaped line called the logistic regression line, which can be seen in Figure 4.11. The line is S-shaped so that it remains within the frequency limits of 0 and 1 – because less than 0 would suggest a category occurring less often than never, and above 1 would mean a category occurring more often than always. We have some more information about logistic regression in our online resources.

This is explained in further detail online

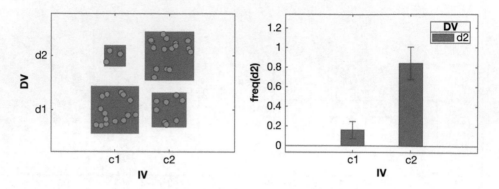

Figure 4.10   Bar chart showing the effect of a Categorical IV on a Categorical DV.

This bar chart illustrates with simple counts on the left and relative frequencies on the right. The right-hand graph shows, for each category of the IV, the frequency (proportion) of participants in the d2 category of the DV.

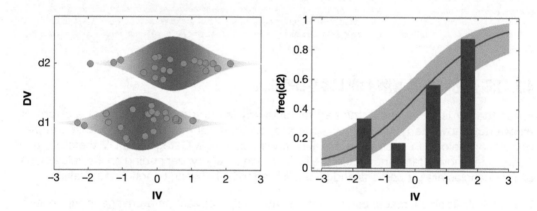

Figure 4.11   Bar chart showing the effect of an Interval IV on a Categorical DV, with a logistic regression line.

The smooth S-shaped curve is the logistic regression line.

There are two simple principles in this section:

1.   If the DV is Categorical, then the relationship is expressed as a variation in the frequency of the different values of the DV.

2a.   If the IV is Categorical, then the relationship is shown as a set of differences in group frequencies.

2b.   If the IV is Interval, then the relationship is shown as a continuous regression line showing how DV frequency varies with the IV.

4.3.5 RELATIONSHIPS WHEN THE DV IS ORDINAL

It is almost possible to provide this section in one short sentence: 'The same as when the DV is Interval.' Very often that is quite reasonable, provided we present our results with careful consideration of how much less information an Ordinal variable has provided us with. But…

A statistical purist would wish to see relationships as difference in medians, when the DV is Ordinal. This is easy to do for a Categorical IV: we are looking at differences in median in the different groups – exactly analogous to the differences in mean for Interval DVs. Medians have to be either one of the values or a midpoint between two of the values. This means that differences will have discrete values.

An Interval or Ordinal IV poses a more serious problem for the real purist. In these cases, for an Interval DV we talked about continuous changes in the mean of the DV. For an Ordinal DV we cannot, as purists, talk about continuous changes in the median – medians don't change continuously. So, we use a variety of logistic regression called ordinal logistic regression. In essence, this uses the same ideas as we just saw for Categorical variable – amended a little to allow for the fact that the multiple categories of the DV (the discrete Ordinal values) are ordered.

4.3.6 RELATIONSHIPS SUMMARY

Table 4.2 summarises these four typical ways that relationships appear, depending on how we have chosen to measure the variables:

Table 4.2   Variable combinations and relationships, part 2.

The basic types of relationship between variables and how they depend on the type of the variables. If the DV is Ordinal, then the effect can appear as either a change in means (or medians) or as a change in frequencies, depending on whether we are treating the DV as discrete or continuous.

		IV	
		Categorical	**Interval**
DV	**Categorical**	Difference in frequencies	Regression of frequencies
	Interval	Difference in means	Regression of means

The overall pattern can be seen: the DV determines whether we are looking at frequencies or means; the IV determines whether we are using differences (discrete changes) or regression (continuous changes).

There is a lot of detail here, but it is really important to keep the bigger picture: the overall pattern is always the same. A relationship between two variables changes their joint distribution but not their individual distributions. How we will see that relationship depends (in the detail) on how the variables are measured.

4.4 THE STRENGTH OF A RELATIONSHIP: EFFECT SIZES

Now that we have understood how different relationships appear between basic variables, we can move on to the most important step. All relationships, regardless of the variables, have two important elements: a strength and a sign (positive or negative). For example, the relationship between RiskTaker? and ExamGrade probably has a weak strength, meaning that whether you are a risk-taker or not would only have a small effect on your grade. The relationship between RiskTaker? and ExamGrade might have a positive sign, meaning that an increase in the value of RiskTaker? goes with an increase in ExamGrade. If participants with a value of 'yes' for RiskTaker? tended to get poorer grades, then the effect sign would be negative.

An **effect size** is a numerical description of the strength of the relationship, with a sign (+ or −) to show the sign of the relationship. Effect strength is at the heart of how psychological and statistical results are presented, although sometimes you will notice that it is neglected in published journal articles. Effect sizes are illustrated in Figure 4.12 and Figure 4.13.

When we talk about a relationship and its effect size, this is a property of the whole sample or the whole population and not specific people in the sample or population. Since each person only has one value for IV and one for the DV, we can't see those variations in any one person and so we can't see the relationship.

A quick look at any of the graphs of effects shown above demonstrates that even in the presence of a positive effect, there are plenty of individuals who are not risk-takers but get high exam grades (this is seen best in Figure 4.12). They don't seem to fit our hypothesis. This is a key principle: understanding that our chosen IV is only a part of the variation in the DV, which we illustrated back in Figure 4.1. In our example, there are lots of other reasons why exam grades might vary between people. The effect size is a measure of how much of the variability in the DV can be attributed to the IV. When we put it like this, we maybe shouldn't often expect strong effects in psychological research.

Now that we have examined what different strengths of effect size look like, whether they are positive or negative or non-existent, we can move on to another important detail: the effect size form. Effect sizes can be represented in many different forms. So far, you have seen us use a decimal number to describe our effect size predictions in Chapter 2, where we predicted a small effect of 0.2 (as seen in Figure 2.3). This is just one numerical form that effect sizes can be expressed in, and there are plenty of others. They are all interchangeable with various mathematical transformations. We will describe the three most common forms here, plus one that was introduced quite recently but is useful. To do this, we will use an example set of data, shown in Figure 4.14.

Effect size & sign	Categorical → Interval	Interval → Interval
Large negative		
Small negative	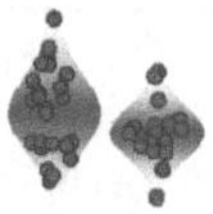	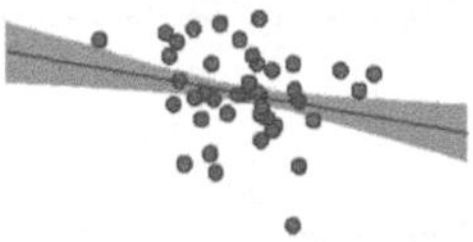
Zero/close to zero	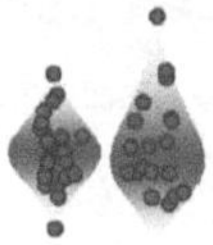	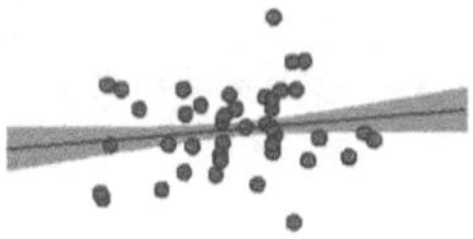
Small positive	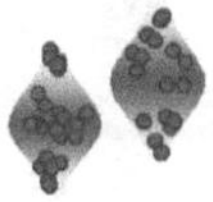	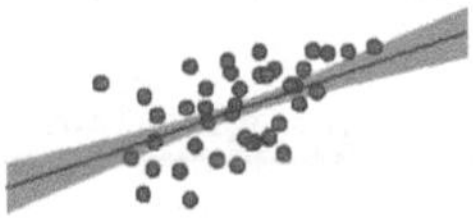
Large positive		

Figure 4.12   Effect sizes when the DV is Interval.

The graphs on the right-hand side are formally called **scatter plots**.

- *The sign of the relationship is given by whether the sample points rise from left to right (+ve) or fall (–ve).*
- *The size of the effect is given by how much vertical scatter of data points there is over and above that caused by the IV.*
- *Ordinal data will typically look the same as Interval data when plotted unless it is being treated as a set of discrete categories.*

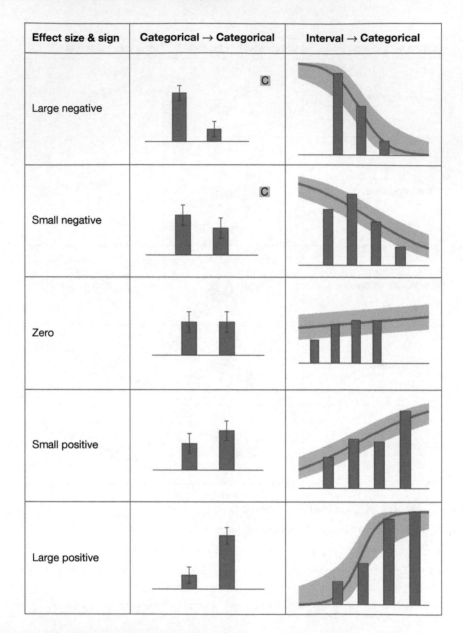

Figure 4.13   Effect sizes when the DV is Categorical.

These graphs show the frequency of the second of two categories for the DV.

- *The sign of the relationship is given by whether the frequency rises from left to right (+ve) or fall (–ve) – which side of the graph has the tallest column.*

- *The size of the effect is given by how steep the rise is, indicated most clearly on the Interval–Categorical diagrams with the curved lines.*

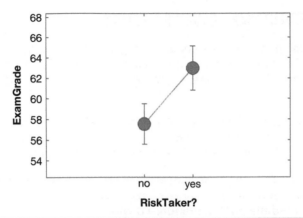

Group	Group size	Mean	Standard deviation
no	22	56.2	8.45
yes	20	60.9	7.29
Whole sample	42	58.5	8.18

Figure 4.14   Descriptive statistics for a sample.

This example data will be used to illustrate the different types of effect size. We have data from risk-takers and non-risk-takers.

4.4.1 NATURAL EFFECT SIZES

Often it can be useful to provide a **natural effect size**: a measure of the strength of the effect in the units of the variables themselves. Using our basic example with its Categorical IV, it is straightforward to grasp an effect size that is a difference of 4.7 exam grade points in favour of risk-takers. This would be a particularly sensible way to describe an effect if your audience isn't used to statistics but does regularly sit exams. The use of grade points to express the effect of risk-taking on exam grades allows any audience that understands exams to get a sense of how meaningful this effect is, because 4.7 is on a scale that they will be familiar with. They will be able to understand whether a difference of 4.7 exam grades points is important or not.

When the IV is Interval, there is an equivalent natural effect size. We could say that for every increase of 1.0 in risk-taking score, the typical exam grade goes up by 2 grade points. The natural effect size would be the increase in exam grade points for a change in a risk-taking scale of 1 unit. This is still partly understandable, although an audience will need to know how the risk-taking scale is constructed to find out whether 1 unit is a lot (because the risk-taking scale only goes from –2 to +2) or is tiny (because the risk-taking scale goes from –100 to +100).

Generally, however, natural effect sizes are of limited usefulness because the variables involved in psychology tend to have arbitrary or not widely-known scales.

4.4.2 STANDARDISED EFFECT SIZES: COHEN'S D-FAMILY

Imagine that several different researchers are all looking into the question of risk-taking and exam grades. This is a good idea, because the relationship may differ a bit from university to university. The problem is that the different universities have different grading scales such as: 0–100, 0–25, 0–42.

This will make it very difficult to compare results with natural effect sizes. For this reason, **standardised effect sizes** were devised. These provide a way to represent effect sizes on a common scale regardless of what system of measurement is used for the DV.

A standardised effect size is one where the natural effect size is adjusted to remove the effect of the scale of the DV. This adjustment is achieved by dividing the difference in means by a quantity that is usually called the **pooled standard deviation**:

$$d = \frac{m2 - m1}{pooledSD}$$

This is explained in further detail online

The pooled standard deviation is a misleading name, and before saying what it is let us say what it isn't: it *isn't* the standard deviation of the whole sample. The pooled standard deviation is the typical standard deviation within the groups. Actually, we have learned enough already to be able to use a better name for it: it is the standard deviation of the residuals (a residual is the difference between one participant's score and their group mean score). We have included some mathematical information about the standard deviation of the residuals in our online resources, if you are interested in some more details.

In the example of Figure 4.14, the two groups have standard deviations of 8.45 and 7.29 but the first group has 22 participants and the second has 20. So the pooled standard deviation is not just the simple average of the two groups: we need to give a bit more weight to the first (larger) group:

$$pooledSD = \sqrt{\frac{n1 \times sd1^2 + n2 \times sd2^2}{n1 + n2}}$$

$$pooledSD = \sqrt{\frac{22 \times 8.45^2 + 20 \times 7.29^2}{22 + 20}}$$

Applying this formula to the data in Figure 4.14 gives us a pooled standard deviation of 7.9.

Since the value for the pooled standard deviation depends quite directly on the scale for the DV, dividing the difference in means by it removes the effect of the measurement scale. The standard deviation we are using for this division is not the standard deviation of the whole sample, just the standard deviation within the categories.

If we then put these numbers into the formula for the standardised effect size, we can calculate that the standardised effect size is 4.7/7.9 = 0.59:

$$d = \frac{60.9 - 56.2}{7.9} \qquad d = \frac{4.7}{7.9} \qquad d = 0.59$$

We have already said that the pooled standard deviation, the bottom part of the formula for d, is the standard deviation of the residuals. We can add one more point here: the difference in group means, the top of the formula for d, is the same as two times the standard deviation of the group means. Our group means are 56.2 and 60.9. The standard deviation of those two numbers is 2.35, and twice that is 4.7, which is the pooled standard deviation we calculated before. So there is another way of calculating the standardised effect size, which uses this formula:

$$d = \frac{2 \times sd\,(group\,means)}{sd\,(residuals)}$$

$$sd\,(residuals) = pooled\,SD$$

The standardised effect size is twice the ratio of the standard deviation of the group means to the standard deviation of the residuals. The importance of this will become apparent in a minute.

This is explained in further detail online

Standardised effect sizes range from zero outwards to ± infinity. A standardised effect size of +infinity is where the relationship between the variables is perfect. If all risk-takers got a grade of 60 and all non-risk-takers got a grade of 40, then the standardised effect size would be infinity (which is, of course, a very big effect) because the group standard deviation is zero; divide anything by zero and mathematically speaking you get infinity.

In order to understand how the d-family works and why it is sometimes difficult to interpret, think about this. Let's suppose that our RiskTaker? Categorical variable gives us a 5-point difference in exam grades. We are interested in how this compares with other factors, such as whether you are a mature student or not. Mature students have a 10-point advantage in exam grades. This is easy to interpret: 10 points is twice 5 points. If we represent these two results with d-family effect sizes, then that nice feature is lost. The reason is that we standardise the effect size by dividing by the group standard deviation, which is less when the difference in means is more.

This means that these effect sizes can be quite difficult to use: on a scale of 0 to infinity, a value of 100 and a value of 1000 are maybe not as much different as you might think, whereas going from 1.0 to 1.5 is a considerable change in effect size.

4.4.3 NORMALISED EFFECT SIZES: R-FAMILY

Another family of effect sizes is even more useful to researchers. **Normalised effect** sizes are effect sizes that range outwards from 0 to +1 or –1: a value of –1 means a full-strength negative relationship; 0 means no relationship; and +1 means a full-strength positive relationship. The meaning of the word normalised in this context is just that the scale ranges up to 1. This is known as the r-family of effect sizes (the most familiar use of it is the correlation coefficient).

This effect size is easy to use because it is simple to understand a scale that goes between –1 and +1. A reader can quickly understand that 0.2 is a fairly modest effect and 0.8 is a very strong effect. The normalised effect size in the example of Figure 4.14 is calculated using a slightly different formula from the final one we showed for *d*, standardised effect sizes:

$$r = \frac{sd\,(group\,means)}{sd\,(sample)}$$

The standard deviation of the group means is 2.35 and the standard deviation of the whole sample is 8.18 (still using the values found in Figure 4.14), so the normalised effect size is 0.29.

The r-family of effect sizes has all the same benefits that the d-family has, but it also has the added benefit, thinking about our comparison of risk-taking with other factors, that $r = 0.4$ means twice as much benefit as $r = 0.2$. For example, if we found that energy drink consumption has an effect of $r = 0.4$ on ExamGrade, then it would have twice as much influence as our RiskTaker? variable.

4.4.4 BINOMIAL EFFECT SIZE DISPLAY (BESD)

This final measure of effect size is not yet common but is actually very useful. It works by telling us how many members of the sample or population broadly follow the effect. If you look at the scatter plot of ExamGrade as a function of our risk variable measured as an Interval variable – perhaps RiskScore, or NumberofRisks – then you can see that everyone who is in the left-bottom quadrant has lower than average risk-taking *and* lower than average exam grade. Similarly, for the top right quadrant: higher than average risk-taking *and* higher than average grade. We can say that these participants are following the effect. If the relationship is perfect, then everyone would lie in one of those two quadrants. If there is no relationship, then 50% of the sample or population lie in one of those two quadrants.

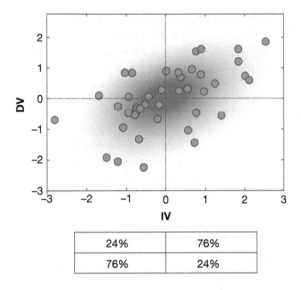

24%	76%
76%	24%

Figure 4.15   Illustration of binomial effect size display (BESD) effect size.

We can see that an effect of the relationship between the IV and the DV here is to cause more of the data points (participants) to lie in two of the quadrants (top right and bottom left). If there was no effect the four quadrants would all have equal numbers, so an interesting and sometimes really useful way of describing the strength of the relationship is to calculate how the participants are split between the quadrants.

Figure 4.15 shows the data split into four quadrants (the split is done at the median values for IV and for DV). The percentage of participants in each quadrant is written in the table beneath. If there was no effect, then we would expect the same number of participants in each quadrant. If we compare the actual split 76:24 with the null effect 50:50, then we can calculate that 26% of participants have been moved to another quadrant by the effect (the difference between 50 and 76 is 26, and the difference between 50 and 24 is 26).

The BESD just gives the percentage of the sample or population in each of the four quadrants – and by convention the % sign is left out. It is very nice because it gives us a good intuitive sense of how strong a relationship is – and is something we can readily compare with our expectations. Conveniently, it is very easy to convert the r-family effect size to a BESD:

Table 4.3   The calculation of BESD from normalised effect sizes.

50 – r×50	50 + r×50
50 + r×50	50 – r×50

If a dandruff cure has a normalised effect size of 0.26, then it has a BESD of (50 – 0.26×50): (50 + 0.26×50) which = 37:63. This means the treatment only has a positive effect on 13% of participants, because the difference between the observed count of 63 and a zero-effect count of 50 is 13.

4.4.5 EFFECT SIZES AS COMPARISONS

There is another way of thinking about these effect sizes that will prove very useful soon. Both the d-family and the r-family involved dividing one quantity by another. Division of this sort is a basic mathematical way of comparing two quantities, and in that way they are both comparisons.

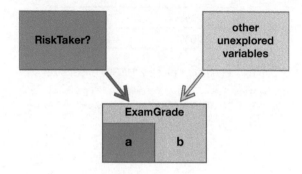

Figure 4.16   Variability diagram.

Now we can see that the variability of ExamGrade attributed to RiskTaker? and shown by area (a) can be compared to either the total variability in ExamGrade (a+b) or just the variability in ExamGrade unaccounted for (b). Note that as (a) increases, (b) decreases. Standardised effect sizes are related to a/b; normalised effect sizes are related to a/(a+b).

We can think of the effect as accounting for some of the variability in the DV. Some of the variability between people in exam grades comes from the variability between people in risk-taking. And, of course, the rest of the variability in exam grades doesn't come from the variability in risk-taking. Figure 4.16 shows this. The variability in ExamGrade caused by RiskTaker? is *a*. The left-over variability in ExamGrade, *b*, is therefore caused by other variables that we have not considered.

- In the case of the d-family, we are comparing the variability in the DV that is due to the IV with the variability in the DV that is not due to the IV. We are comparing *a* with *b*:

$$d = \frac{a}{b}$$

- In the case of the r-family, we are comparing the variability in the DV that is due to the IV with all of the variability in the DV. We are comparing *a* with *(a+b)*:

$$r = \frac{a}{a+b}$$

4.4.6 EFFECT SIZE: SUMMARY

The way an effect size is described is critical for two different types of understanding: (i) how important is the effect, and (ii) how does the effect compare with other effects? For the first question, natural effect sizes are sometimes useful and the BESD is always useful. For the second question, either *d* or *r* are good ways of comparing the effect sizes for different situations.

Table 4.4   An effect size interpretation table.

There's some more helpful information about effect sizes online. We use 'Cat2' as the shorthand for a Categorical variable with two groups, such as our RiskTaker? variable. The variable before the arrow (Cat2 here) is the IV and the variable after the arrow (Int here) is always the DV.

Effect size type	Examples	When?	Possible values	Interpretation
Natural	Difference in means Regression line slopes	When scale of DV (and IV) are commonly understood	Any values that match the scale of the variable	Use the variable measure as a guide to interpretation, e.g. *if DV is IQ, natural effect size of IV may be 7 IQ points*
Standardised	Cohen's *d* Cohen's *f* Hedge's *g*	Cohen's *d* is typically used for the result of a Cat2 → Int hypothesis	–infinity to +infinity	–inf is perfect negative effect 0 is no effect +inf is perfect positive effect
Normalised	*r*	Any time	–1 through to +1	–1 is perfect negative effect 0 is no effect +1 is perfect positive effect

4.5 EFFECT SIZES IN PSYCHOLOGY

So far, this discussion has left one important question unanswered: What sort of effect sizes do we usually see in psychology? The answer is that we tend to see small to medium-sized effects.

4.6 RELATIONSHIPS, STATISTICS AND VARIABILITY

Let's remind ourselves of how these actions relate to our exploration of the variability in our sample. A relationship between the IV and the DV means that the IV accounts for some of the overall variability in the DV. We have established ways of expressing the strength of a relationship, and the stronger the relationship – or as we have put it, the larger the effect size – the more of the variability in the DV is explained by the IV. In our examples, there remains plenty of unexplored/unexplained variability and we should not lose sight of this.

Suppose that our task is to estimate the value of a DV variable for a person. At the start, our best estimate of their value is that it is the population mean. That value minimises the sum of squared deviations and means that it is the best guess.

$$\text{best estimate of DV} = \text{mean of DV}$$

Now suppose that we know their value on some IV and moreover that we know the effect size for that IV. This means that we can make a small improvement in predicting what their DV value will be.

$$\text{best estimate of DV} = \text{mean of DV} + \text{effect of IV on DV}$$

THE BIG PICTURE

All of the variability that distinguishes people is the basic material for statistics. We capture the variability by choosing variables and look to explain the patterns of variability by considering the existence of relationships between variables. The first purpose of statistics is to objectively describe patterns of variability as relationships between variables.

THE LOGIC OF RELATIONSHIPS BETWEEN VARIABLES

1. Relationships between variables are the heart of psychological research methods.

2. In a statistical relationship, we identify one variable as the Dependent variable and one as the Independent variable.

   a. Dependent variable (DV): is assumed to be the one that is affected by the other variables. We are often seeking to understand the DV.

   b. Independent variable (IV): is assumed to affect the DV. It is only affected by things we are not interested in (in our study).

3. When you explore some data, always start by asking: what is the Dependent variable (DV)? Think about the logic of the situation.

FORMS THAT RELATIONSHIPS CAN TAKE

4. The form a relationship takes will depend on the choices made about how to measure variables.

   a. Type of the DV: determines whether the relationship will be a pattern of changes in means (Interval DVs) or frequencies (Categorical DVs).

   b. Type of the IV: differences or continuous trends, i.e. what is the type of the IV? Will it use means or frequencies, i.e. what is the type of the DV? These decisions are made for us already.

QUANTIFYING RELATIONSHIPS

5. Relationships can be quantified by their strength (effect size) and the sign of that effect (positive or negative).

   a. On a graph, the strength of a relationship can be seen by inspecting how scattered the data points are. The more scattered, the weaker the relationship.

   b. The sign of the relationship is shown by whether the effect goes up (positive) or down (negative) as you look from left to right.

6. The strength of a relationship can be quantified using different types of effect size.

   a. A natural effect size can help translate an idea to an audience.

   b. Standardised effect sizes are more suitable for comparing across studies and range from 0 to infinity.

   c. Normalised effects are also easier to compare and range between -1 and +1, with 0 indicating no effect.

 YOUR TURN

DEFINE THESE KEY TERMS IN THE SPACE PROVIDED:

1. Independent variable

2. Dependent variable

3. Effect size

FILL IN THE GAPS IN THESE SENTENCES:

1. The horizontal axis of a graph is called the ....

2. The vertical axis of a graph is called the ....

3. A natural effect size is measured using the same scale as the .... variable.

4. The range of possible values for r is ....

THE ANSWERS ARE ONLINE

YOUR SPACE

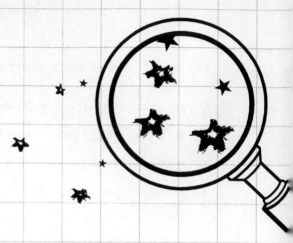

 REFERENCES AND FURTHER READING

Cohen, J. (1988) *Statistical Power Analysis for the Behavioural Sciences*. New York: Psychology Press.

The classic text on standardised effect sizes.

Cumming, G. (2012) *Understanding the New Statistics*. New York: Routledge.

A book intended for a wide audience.

Ellis, P.D. (2010) *The Essential Guide to Effect Sizes: Statistical Power, Meta-Analysis, and the Interpretation of Research Results*. Cambridge: Cambridge University Press.

Quite technical but very useful summaries.

Rosenthal, R. & Rubin, D.B. (1982). A simple general purpose display of magnitude and experimental effect. *Journal of Educational Psychology* 74: 166–169.

The source publication.

> **THERE ARE MORE ACTIVITIES AND A SHORT SUMMARY VIDEO FOR THIS CHAPTER AVAILABLE AT:**
> **HTTPS://STUDY.SAGEPUB.COM/STATISTICSFORPSYCHOLOGY**

INTERMEZZO 1

Correlation

Now that we have begun to explore the relationships that may exist between variables, we are going to pause and focus on one specific type of relationship: **correlations**. Why are we dedicating space to correlations when there are many types of potential relationship between variables? Well, primarily because correlations crop up over and over again in student courses and in research, as the 'easiest' way to measure a relationship between two sets of numbers. Too large to fit into a text box and yet too small (and really not consequential enough) to justify its own chapter, we have instead written this intermezzo: a slight tangent from the timeline of the main book.

IM1.1 CORRELATION: WHAT IS IT?

A correlation is a type of relationship between two variables: if they are correlated, then a **linear** relationship exists between them. Linear in this context means that the relationship is easily visualised as a straight line, shown in the left graph of Figure Im1.1.

The degree of correlation between two variables is calculated as a value that ranges from –1 to 0 to +1, called a **correlation coefficient**. The correlation coefficient is exactly the same as the **normalised effect size** '*r*', which we looked at in Chapter 4. Extreme values for the correlation coefficient are where the two variables are perfectly associated; the central zero is where there is no association, illustrated in the two graphs in Figure Im1.1. It is often accepted that anything from 0.5 to 1 or –0.5 to –1.0 is a large effect, but really there is no conventional agreement on what constitutes small, medium and large.

The term correlation is a general term for a **bivariate** linear relationship: bi means two, and so bivariate means between two variables. There are several specific types of correlation, although the most common one, often just given the blanket label 'correlation', is actually called a Pearson correlation, which will pop up again in Chapter 7 when we examine two-variable hypothesis testing. All the different types of correlation rely on the same mathematical formula, produce the same type of r-family effect size, and measure the same type of relationship between two variables. They differ only in what types of variable are used. These differences are minimal, and we'll touch on them in a moment.

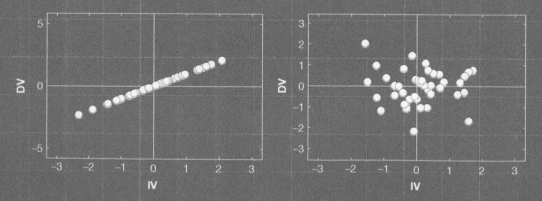

Figure Im1.1   Another way of thinking about correlations between two variables.

The left diagram shows a very strong positive correlation between two variables: all the data points are in the lower-left or upper-right quadrant. The right diagram shows no correlation between the two variables: the data points equally occupy all four quadrants on the graph.

We can calculate correlation coefficients between any two variables that use ordered numbers for their values. The calculation doesn't, of itself, require that the variables are Interval or conform to any particular distribution. We could technically re-label a Categorical variable that has two categories with values of 0 and 1 for each category (or any other pair of numbers), then we can use those numbers in a correlation. When this is done, the process is called point-biserial correlation. If we replace the values of one or both variables by their rank order, then the same process does a Spearman's rank correlation. All of these are just different labels for what is effectively the same process.

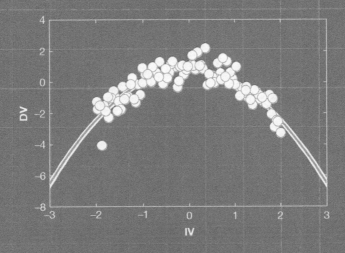

Figure Im1.2   A quadratic effect.

In this figure we show a type of effect known as a quadratic effect, where the relationship between the IV and the DV is not a straight line. Despite the fact that there is obviously a very strong relationship between the IV and the DV, because it is not a straight line, it has a correlation of zero.

IM1.2 SOME FORMULAE FOR CORRELATIONS

There are several formulae involved in the process of calculating a correlation – although, of course, many statistical packages will do this for you. However, let's briefly examine the relevant formulae in order to understand all of the theory that goes into a correlation.

Let's begin by considering one important formula. **Variance** is the square of a standard deviation. It is a measure of the **dispersion** of a distribution, which we learned about in Chapter 3. The formula for a variance is the sum of squared deviations divided by the sample size:

$$var(x) = \frac{\sum_i (x_i - \bar{x})^2}{n} = \frac{\sum_i (x_i - \bar{x})(x_i - \bar{x})}{n}$$

where $\bar{x}$ stands for mean(x)

Here we have given two versions of the formula. The second version (at the right) of this is the same as the first version (in the middle), but we have written the squared out long-hand. Remember that we have included a handy table of formula elements at the beginning of this book, if you need to check what any of the symbols mean.

The next formula we need to calculate a correlation is for a quantity called the **covariance** and is almost the same as the second version of the formula for variance but with one critical difference:

$$cov\left(x,y\right)=\frac{\Sigma_i\left(x_i-\bar{x}\right)\left(y_i-\bar{y}\right)}{n}$$

In this formula one of the appearances of x from the second formula for variance is replaced by a y (if you look at the top line of the formula). Instead of calculating the variance for one variable, we can calculate the covariance, which is the dispersion of the two variables together, so x is our first variable and y is our second variable. Note that $cov(x,y)$ means the covariance of x and y and is the same as $cov(y,x)$. It doesn't matter which way round they are written.

Now we can take this formula for covariance and put it into a formula for a correlation coefficient. This formula has covariance (the bit that says $cov(x,y)$ on the top row) divided by the standard deviation of each variable:

$$corr\left(x,y\right)=\frac{cov\left(x,y\right)}{sd\left(x\right)sd\left(y\right)}$$

The size of a covariance depends on the scales we are using for the quantities x and y, just as variance does (look back at Chapter 3 to go over this again). To produce a quantity that does not depend on the measurement scales, we divide the covariance by quantities that are related to those scales: the two standard deviations.

IM1.3 CORRELATION AND REGRESSION

In Chapter 4 of this book we explained how relationships between two variables can be thought of as situations where the mean value for one variable, the DV, changes as the other variable (the IV) changes. That made it easy to visualise the **regression** line as a straight line that joined up a set of **local means** at different places along the x-axis – a mean that continuously changes across a graph. That is simple because it links the closely related ideas about relationships between variables of different types as all being changes in typical values in some way. And whereas regression sits very well in that idea of a steadily changing local mean, correlation doesn't fit so well.

However, there is a nice straightforward relationship between correlations and regressions. We've included some maths here to explain the relationship, but if you would rather just know the most important information, jump to the last paragraph of this section.

For our more curious readers: if the slope of the regression line is called $b(y,x)$ meaning y is the DV and x is the IV, then the correlation between x and y is given by:

$$corr\left(y,x\right)=\frac{b\left(y,x\right)\times sd\left(x\right)}{sd\left(y\right)}$$

For those readers who like tinkering with mathematics, it is easy from this to produce a version that gives $b(y,x)$ in terms of the covariance of x and y and their individual variances:

$$b(y,x) = \frac{cov(y,x)}{var(x)}$$

What we have shown here, even if the maths was of no interest to you, is that these quantities – regression slope, covariance and variance, and correlation – are all linked concepts. Since they are all actually closely related, we don't need all three. When we get to Chapter 11 and beyond, dealing with relationships between more than two variables, the one we need most is b, the regression slope, which is why we have used it here. And it will be useful to know that b can be found using the $cov(x,y)$ and $var(x)$.

IM1.4 CORRELATION COEFFICIENT AND VARIANCE EXPLAINED

In the main text, we have noted that the squared value of the normalised effect size is the proportion of variance in the DV that the IV explains. Here we will show how that happens, using this to tie the ideas here together and then return us to the main text again. The maths is a little heavier than usual and is only here for any readers who are still curious. Otherwise you will lose nothing by jumping to the final section of this intermezzo.

The formula of a simple regression line:

$$yfit_i = a + b_i$$

tells us how to calculate the fitted value for the DV ($yfit$) for a given value of the IV (x).

The variance in the DV that the IV explains is the variance of $yfit$ in this formula. Notice that we can drop the subscript (i) now since the variance is a property of all the values for $yfit$, not just the one identified by i. So the variance explained is this:

$$var(yfit) = var(a + bx)$$

Since the a part of this is not varying, and since it is added to everything else, it doesn't contribute to the variance of y and we can remove it. At the same time, b doesn't vary either, but since it is multiplying something that does vary we can move it outside the bracket. So we have:

$$var(yfit) = var(a + bx) = var(bx) = b^2 \times var(x)$$

Now, we already have this from earlier:

$$r = corr(y,x) = \frac{b \times sd(x)}{sd(y)}$$

which means when we square each side that we can write r^2 as a simple ratio:

$$r^2 = \frac{b^2 var(x)}{var(y)}$$

We only need one last step now. We notice that the top half of this ratio is the same as *var(yfit)*, and this leads us to this formula:

$$r^2 = \frac{var(yfit)}{var(y)}$$

This says that r^2 is a ratio of the variance of the fitted values of the DV (i.e. the variance in the DV explained by the IV) to the total variance of the DV. So r^2 is the proportion of the variance in the DV that is explained by the IV.

IM1.5 SUMMARY

Correlation is a term that typically has been used to describe the strength of a relationship between two interval variables. Some would see correlation as being central to the use of statistics in psychology and may be puzzled that we haven't said more in the main text about it. The reason for this is that, used in that way, it is too narrow a concept – it leads to a theory of statistics that is made up of lots of specialised quantities and procedures.

To keep everything in a single coherent framework, we have talked of all effects as being recognised as either changes in (local) means for Interval DVs or changes in (local) frequencies for Categorical DVs. The natural way to talk about the effect of an Interval IV in an Interval DV is then linear regression.

In this brief intermezzo, we have shown you how these two concepts – correlation and regression – can be related, via the overarching concept of covariance. In this context, we have also been able to show you how the square of the correlation coefficient is the proportion of the DV that is explained by the IV.

We have used a much wider concept of the correlation coefficient throughout this book: *normalised effect sizes*. We prefer normalised effect sizes: the r-family, with it's easy-to-interpret values from −1 to +1. We like the observation that on top of this – r-family effect sizes can be thought of as a comparison of the variance in a DV explained by a relationship to the whole variance of that DV. That is a nice extra, and it gives the r-family of effect sizes a very clear meaning.

CHAPTER

05

UNCERTAINTY

AFTER ALL THAT WORK, YOU MIGHT BE WRONG ANYWAY

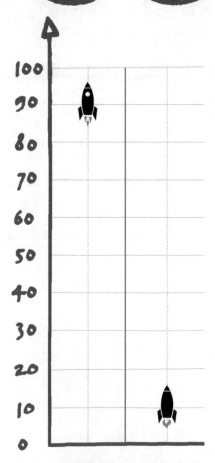

BUILDING   USING

Now that we have looked at the most fundamental elements of research – **variables** and relationships between them – it is time to look at the most fundamental principle: **uncertainty**. We know how to identify and measure variables; we know what kinds of relationships might emerge, and even how to assess the strength of those relationships. Now we need to know one more thing: how certain can we be that relationships we think we have found really exist? How certain can we be that an effect size – calculated from one or more samples of participants – is close to the **effect size** in the full population that we are interested in?

In this chapter, we will explore the idea of the uncertainty that is associated with inferences about **populations** using **samples**. Once obtained, the sample itself is certain: we have it. But we are using our sample to learn about the population: how can we determine our uncertainty in doing so?

Let's begin with a recap here: the population is the whole set of individuals who we are potentially interested in. If we have a **hypothesis**, then that hypothesis will refer to a population. Our hypothesis that risk-taking affects exam grades is a statement about the population of all students – everywhere and always. If it wasn't, our hypothesis would need to be more specific. The population of interest is usually extremely large and well beyond any possibility of studying as a whole, which is why we take a smaller sample from the population. We hope that our sample is representative of the population and we put some effort into our research design to ensure so (more in Chapter 8). Because our sample will never be identical to our population, there will always be some uncertainty about what the sample tells us about the population. In this chapter we shall examine uncertainty in more theoretical detail; later chapters will concentrate on the practical matters used to minimise it.

Because we are building an understanding of uncertainty in this chapter, there are lots of diagrams and graphs that illustrate uncertainty using various formulae. These are not something you would expect to produce for yourself: when we say 'we can plot', it is to illustrate our points. However, if you are interested you will find details online.

5.1 WHY IS UNCERTAINTY IMPORTANT?

Psychology is a dangerous subject. What the discipline claims to know about mind and behaviour can have the potential for great change in the world. It follows that research in psychology is under an ethical obligation to think it might be mistaken, and to be clear about how possible that is when presenting research results to the wider world. In this chapter we see how to do that. The key concept is uncertainty. The uncertainty lies in the word 'could' in this statement: the outcome we reach _could_ be different if we had a different sample.

- A different sample _will_ lead to different statistics, including a different sample effect size, simply because everyone is different and every set of data is different in some way.
- That different effect size _might_ cause us to reach a different inference about the existence or strength of a relationship between our variables.
- We have to be aware of how much the outcome _could_ be different.

This is the crucial role of **inferential statistics**. Without this step of considering carefully what our uncertainty is, research in psychology risks becoming just wishful thinking.

5.2 WHAT IS UNCERTAINTY?

We will repeat this many times during this chapter and in this book: our uncertainty is about what the sample tells us about the population. We are interested in the population, but we usually only have access to a smaller sample. Because different samples vary randomly, their sample effect sizes vary randomly, even though the population has a fixed population effect size. The difference between the sample and the population is illustrated in Figure 5.1, which shows a population and a sample.

We have no uncertainty about the sample effect size – it is a fact: it is what we measured. We can calculate the sample effect size with great precision and certainty. The uncertainty comes in when we use the sample effect size as a guide to the population effect size. The sample effect size is an uncertain estimate of the population effect size: no matter how confident we are with our calculations about the sample, we will not have the same degree of confidence in what we know about the population.

5.3 VARIABILITY: POSSIBLE SAMPLES FROM ONE POPULATION

We'll begin with a scenario that illustrates this uncertainty, demonstrated by the amount of **variability** involved in taking a sample from a population.

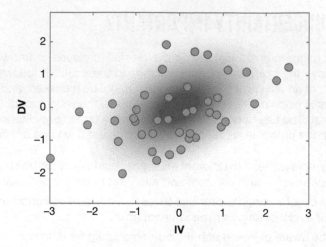

Figure 5.1   Illustration of a population and a sample.

This figure shows the population as the shaded area and the sample as discrete data points (the dots). It shows how this sample and the population differ.

5.3.1 AN EXAMPLE: THE POSSIBLE SAMPLES FROM A POPULATION

This is a *completely hypothetical situation* that could never really exist, which may sound a little unusual, but it's a very helpful perspective to think about. Imagine we have built a population and we are watching various researchers take samples from it. Let's suppose that in our population, the relationship between an Interval version of our main variable, which we'll call RiskTaking here, and ExamGrade is $r = 0.2$ – a fairly typical effect. So we sit back and await the outcomes that the researchers reach.

In Figure 5.2, we show the samples and **regression lines** from the first four researchers who report their results. The respective sample effect sizes (from top left clockwise) are 0.06, 0.24, 0.30 and 0.11. In this realistic – but very much imaginary – situation, we know that the population effect size is 0.2 (we specified that from the beginning) and so none of these sample effect sizes is really close. We might be tempted to think that researcher B, with the sample effect size of 0.24, did their research in the 'best' way, to get a result so close to the true population effect size. However, we also know this: each researcher did exactly the same thing. They each took 42 participants at random from the same population. If you went away and took your own sample from that same population, using the same methods, you would get yet another different sample effect size. Although they don't know it, researcher B was simply the luckiest.

In Figure 5.3 we have an illustration of two different views of the four sample effect sizes. The graph on the left shows what the researchers know: the values of the sample effect sizes. This is

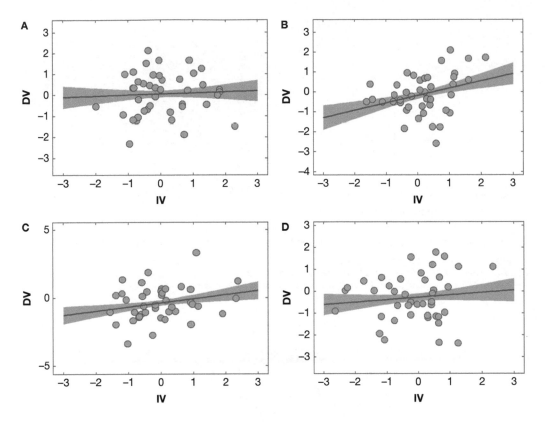

Figure 5.2   Four samples from one population.

These four samples are all taken from the same population in the same way. Each has 42 participants chosen at random. The fact that they differ so markedly demonstrates how much variability there is from one sample to another: the relationship between RiskTaking (the Interval version of our RiskTaker? variable) and ExamGrade is unclear.

the usual situation in research. The graph on the right shows what, from our outside perspective, we also know, which adds in the value of the population effect size they came from.

Each researcher in this example has obtained their own sample effect size. If they each claimed that their sample effect size was the population effect size, they would all be wrong and would all disagree with each other. If, on the other hand, they were each to claim that their sample size was within ±0.15 of the population effect size, then actually they would all be right and they would all agree with each other – which we can see from our outside perspective. That extra bit – the ±0.15 (which for now we have just produced from thin air, but comes from real calculations that we'll get into) – is how we state the uncertainty of an outcome. It defines the limit on how accurate their knowledge is about the population.

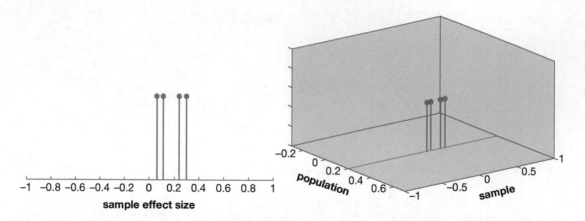

Figure 5.3   Left: four sample effect sizes placed together. Right: shown with the population effect size.

The left panel shows our four sample effect sizes placed at their respective positions within a graph that allows all possible effect sizes. We can see that they are clustered together. The right-hand panel shows the outside perspective, where we can also see what population they have come from (the 0.2 line). The two graphs show the same thing, just from different perspectives.

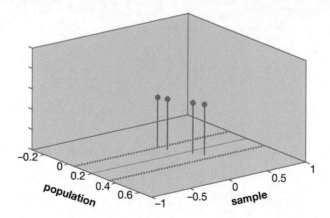

Figure 5.4   Four sample effect sizes plotted with their distance from the population effect size.

In this figure, we have again plotted the sample effect sizes. Each dot is a sample effect size, with the vertical line indicating where they sit in relation to the population effect size (marked with the solid horizontal left to right line at 0.2). With the outsider view, we can see that they are all slightly wrong, but lie within ± 0.15 of the real answer (shown by the dotted lines).

From our outside perspective, we know that researchers A and D have produced results that underestimate the population effect size, and the others have overestimated it. Individually, none of them knows whether they have underestimated or overestimated the effect: they just know that they have each found their own one particular sample size, and that other researchers using different samples will find different effect sizes. That is their own individual uncertainty: none of them can say whether they have overestimated or underestimated the population effect size. There is nothing any of them can do that can fix this.

From our outside perspective, which we've shown in Figure 5.4, we can see that they are all within the range of ±0.15 of the population effect size and that this figure is a good measure of the researchers' uncertainty. If there was a method for each of them to calculate that 0.15 range just by using their knowledge of their own sample, then each researcher would be able to say how uncertain they are. That method does exist and we will cover it in Section 5.4, but we'll start by covering the relevant theory first so that everything makes sense.

5.3.2 SAMPLING ERROR AND SAMPLE VARIABILITY

In our hypothetical, imaginary example, we know the population effect size. This isn't something that we can know in the real world, unless our population is small enough to measure every participant; if it was, we wouldn't need to worry about uncertainty. We know that the sample effect size will differ from one sample to another, despite coming from the same population. This variability means that a sample only provides an **estimate** of the effect size of the relationship between the variables in the population: it is an uncertain guide.

The difference between what we have – the sample effect size, and what we are interested in – the population effect size, is known as **sampling error**. Sampling error is a result of the random nature of sampling. It isn't an error in the colloquial sense of being a mistake; it is simply the unavoidable random difference between sample and population which a researcher should always be aware of. If we can understand sampling error, we can then better understand uncertainty. We've illustrated sampling error in Figure 5.5.

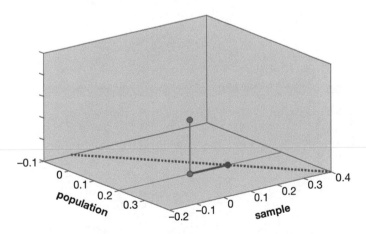

Figure 5.5   Illustration of sampling error.

The population side of this graph indicates the true population effect size for this example: 0.2, marked with a thin line. The sample effect size is seen with the thick vertical line with a small dot at each end to make it visible. If the sample effect size was the same as the population effect size, it would fall on the dotted line. The thick blue line shows the difference between the sample effect size and the population effect size: the sampling error. It will help with later diagrams in this chapter to understand now that sampling error is illustrated as a difference along the sample axis as shown.

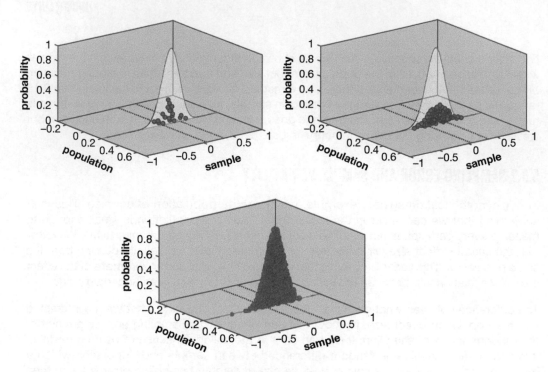

Figure 5.6   Illustration of the distribution of sample effect sizes.

Clockwise from top left: effect sizes from 20 samples, 100 samples, 1000 samples. The samples are all taken with the same sample size from a single population. As the number of samples grows, it becomes clear that they are all coming from a constrained distribution, centred on the population effect size.

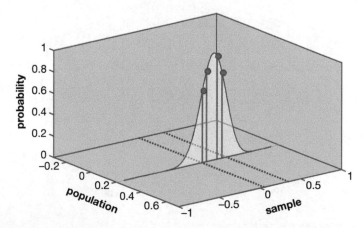

Figure 5.7   Four samples shown on a sampling distribution.

This figure shows the four samples as before on the sampling distribution they came from. They are all placed with the population effect size of 0.2. Each dot (attached to a line to make it clear to see where the value falls on the probability scale) indicates one sample effect size. As they are all quite near the peak of the curve, they are all quite probable. The dotted lines on the floor of the graph indicate the standard error: the standard deviation of the sampling distribution. It can be seen that the standard error is quite narrow, and so big effect sizes, such as 0.5 or higher, are unlikely.

Because we only know our sample effect size, and not the population effect size, we can never really know what our exact sampling error is. All might seem hopeless at this stage. We are saying that when we take a sample, and calculate the sample effect size, we are going to get a number that is wrong: it isn't the same as the population effect size. Not only is our sample effect size probably wrong, we don't know how far wrong our sample effect is, because we can never exactly know the real population effect size – or even whether our sample effect size is more or less than the population effect size. However, there is a way of calculating a range of possible values for our sampling error. Doing this is an important step because it leads naturally and easily to ways that we can use to describe the uncertainty that we have about our sample.

5.3.3 THE THEORY: THE SAMPLING DISTRIBUTION

This is explained in further detail online

To learn how to calculate a range of values for our sampling error, first we should consider the concepts that are involved. Begin by considering the complete set of all possible samples that could come from the population we are interested in using one specific sampling method (e.g. every possible study taking 42 random participants) – what we have just seen with four samples, but on a much bigger scale. This set of potential samples is infinite. In this set, each sample would have its own sample effect size, which means that across all the samples there will be a distribution of these values. Using the single most important piece of maths for statistics – the Central Limit Theorem – we can say that the distribution of sample effect sizes is quite tightly constrained – with more falling close to the population effect size and fewer away from it. This is illustrated in Figure 5.6. We've also included some more detail about it online.

This distribution of all possible sample effect sizes is called the **sampling distribution**. The standard deviation of the sampling distribution (how spread out all of those possible values are) is called the **standard error**. The two terms, sampling distribution and standard error, are illustrated in Figure 5.7.

5.3.4 QUANTIFYING SAMPLE VARIABILITY: THE STANDARD ERROR

This is explained in further detail online

In our first example, we created a population with a known effect size of 0.2 and then watched researchers take samples. That means that we can look at each sample and actually say what the true sampling error was for each, which you can see in Table 5.1.

Table 5.1   Sampling error from the samples taken from our first example.

This is simply the population effect size of 0.2, subtracted from the found sample effect sizes.

Sample effect size	Sampling error
0.06	–0.14
0.24	+0.04
0.3	+0.10
0.11	–0.09

We can think of these sampling error numbers as being samples from a distribution containing all possible sampling error. Once we have that thought, we can easily go one step further and calculate that their standard deviation is 0.1 (just as we learned to do in Chapter 3). This standard deviation of the sampling errors is an indication of the spread of sampling errors we might expect to see.

This has helped us to understand what the sampling error is, but it is artificial. Since sampling error is the difference between population effect size and sample effect size, we can only calculate it when we know both quantities. Normally we don't know what the population effect size is, so we can't calculate the sampling error. Each of our four aforementioned researchers has a sample effect size which is an estimate of the population effect size. None of them knows what the population effect size is and so none can say what the actual sampling error for their study is. Even if they got together and pooled their findings, they still couldn't find out what the sampling error on each study is because they still wouldn't know what the population effect size is.

There is one thing we can notice just now. In this artificial situation where we know the population effect size, we found that the standard deviation of the set of *sampling errors* was 0.1. Actually, if we calculate the standard deviation of the set of *sample effect sizes*, we will get exactly the same result. So the **standard error**, defined as *the standard deviation of all possible sampling errors*, is also the standard deviation of sample effect sizes.

5.3.5 IN PRACTICE: ESTIMATING THE STANDARD ERROR

The standard error is the standard deviation of sample effect sizes from a population – so, a measure of the **dispersion** of all the possible sample effect sizes we can expect to see – and is a way of saying what the variability is for a sample effect size. If we had enough samples we could estimate the standard error from them, but getting enough samples is hard work. So here's the miraculous bit: we can use our one, single, actual sample to get an estimate of the standard error. Doing this will tell us what the spread of other results from the same population should look like.

Calculating the standard error for effect sizes can involve quite complex formulae and we use computers now to do such things. We will illustrate the process with a simple example of the calculation.

Suppose that we just want to estimate the mean for a population from our sample: the mean exam grade, for example. An estimate of the standard error of a sample mean is given by the sample standard deviation divided by the **square root** of sample size:

$$se(mean) = \frac{sd(sample)}{\sqrt{n}}$$

where n = number of participants. Note that this is an estimate of the standard error. It is, however, usually a very good one.

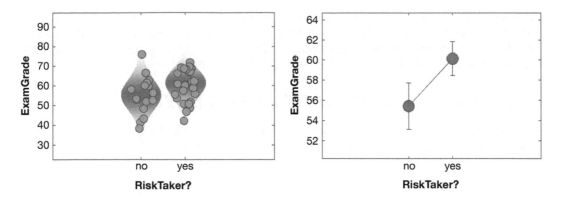

Figure 5.8   A sample set of data used for calculating standard errors.

We show the data points on the left and the graph of group means on the right. The thin vertical lines with a flat end at the top and bottom are known as error bars and are showing the standard error for each mean.

Since many different types of sample effect sizes are built up from combinations of means (such as differences in means of different groups or the travelling mean of a regression line), it is possible to build up formulae from this simple one to calculate the standard error for all the different types of effect size.

For an example, consider the set of data shown in Figure 5.8. It shows some data for the effect of RiskTaker? (this time measured in our typical Categorical type) on ExamGrade. Our two groups are RiskTakers?=Yes and No. The basic statistics for each group are shown in Table 5.2.

Table 5.2   A calculation of the standard errors for group means.

We've included the standard error calculations in the bottom row.

	Yes group	**No group**
Mean(ExamGrade)	60.9	56.2
SD(ExamGrade)	7.29	8.45
Number of participants	20	22
SE(Mean)	7.29/sqrt(20) = **1.63**	8.45/sqrt(22) = **1.80**

5.3.6 ESTIMATED STANDARD ERROR OF NATURAL EFFECT SIZE

The natural effect size is (60.9 – 56.2), which we can now write as (60.9±1.63) – (56.2±1.8), to include the uncertainty that we have calculated as the standard error in Table 5.1. Simple subtraction can be used to combine the two means: 60.9 – 56.2. The answer is 4.7. Combining the standard errors is a bit more complicated:

$$se(m1-m2) = \sqrt{se(m1)^2 + se(m2)^2}$$

where m1 *and* m2 *are the two group means.*

This formula gives a combined standard error of sqrt(1.9×1.9 + 1.8×1.8) – anything squared is just multiplied by itself. The answer is 2.62. So the natural effect size is 4±2.62. Remember that the standard error is the standard deviation of the distribution of all possible sample effect sizes. If it is large, then that would mean our uncertainty was also large.

5.3.7 ESTIMATED STANDARD ERROR FOR STANDARDISED EFFECT SIZE

If we wanted instead to use the standardised effect size, which is d=0.56, we would need to use a different formula to calculate its standard error. The formula is:

$$se(d) = sqrt\left(\left(\frac{n1+n2}{n1\times n2} + \frac{d^2}{2(n1+n2-2)}\right) \times \left(\frac{n1+n2}{n1+n2-2}\right)\right)$$

where d is the effect size and n1, n2 are the numbers of participants in each group.

Using this formula, we discover that the standardised effect size is 0.56±0.32.

5.3.8 ESTIMATED STANDARD ERROR FOR NORMALISED EFFECT SIZE

Another formula is used for the calculation if you are using the **normalised effect size**:

$$se(r) = sqrt\left(\frac{1-r^2}{n-2}\right)$$

where r is the effect size and n is the sample size.

Using this formula, we find that the normalised effect size is 0.278±0.152.

We have included more information about standard errors in our online resources for Chapter 5, where we have more space to go into detail.

5.4 UNCERTAINTY: POSSIBLE POPULATIONS WITH ONE SAMPLE

The previous section has shown how a population with a particular population effect size will produce samples with a range of different sample effect sizes. Now, by reversing the logic, we can realise that any given sample, with a particular sample effect size, could come from a wide range of population effect sizes. We have learned how to understand the uncertainty of our sample compared to other potential samples from the same population. Now let's look at how to understand the uncertainty of our single sample compared to the true population value. First, let's look at the theory behind the practical methods that we can use to describe uncertainty about our possible population.

In the previous section we were starting with a population and asking what possible samples it could produce (in the future); in this section we are starting with a sample and asking what possible populations could have produced it (in the past). In the first case, we talk about the *probability of future events*; in the second case, we talk about the *likelihood of past events*.

5.4.1 AN EXAMPLE: THE POSSIBLE POPULATIONS FOR A SAMPLE

In the first example at the start of this chapter, we had created a population and then watched several researchers taking samples and saw that all the samples were different. Now we want to turn this upside down.

This time we only have one researcher with a sample they have made from the population they are interested in. They have calculated its sample effect size (r=0.12) and now want to know what this tells them about the population. They are aware that the population effect size could, and probably will, be different from this: many different population effect sizes may be viable candidates.

Let's imagine that they have measured RiskTaker? and ExamGrade in a sample of participants. They are being closely watched by two student societies: the Paragliding society and the Cross the Road Safely society. If their sample can be understood to show a benefit for RiskTaker?, then the Paragliders will be happy and the Cross the Road Safely society might feel disadvantaged. If it goes the other way, the two societies will have the opposite reactions.

The sample effect size is slightly positive, at 0.12, which suggests that risk-takers have the advantage. We know that this single sample will have a sampling error, and so we know that we can't just reach a definite conclusion – another sample might tell another story. What our researcher needs here is a way of using what they know about possible sampling error to calculate their uncertainty about the effect size in the population. In the rest of this section we will see how this is done.

5.4.2 THE THEORY: SAMPLING ERROR AND POPULATION LIKELIHOOD

We have a real sample, with an effect size of 0.12, and we have recognised that a lot of different potential population effect sizes could have produced this sample effect size. We are now thinking about these two things:

1. Our actual sample effect size.
2. The full set of possible population effect sizes: where could our sample have come from?

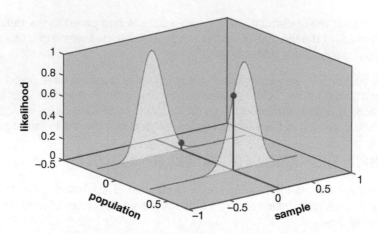

Figure 5.9   Comparing our sample to two different possible populations.

This graph shows the sample effect size for our example sample (0.12) alongside two sampling distributions for populations with an effect size of −0.25 and +0.25. The height of the dot on each sampling distribution gives an indication of the likelihood that our sample came from a population with that population effect size.

In the previous section we saw the idea of the sampling distribution: the set of all the possible sample effect sizes that can come from a single population effect size. This is a way of describing how the single population effect size gives rise to a spread of sample effect sizes. Now, we think of a whole set of possible population effect sizes. The relevant theory is called likelihood theory. Likelihood is a way of measuring how likely it is that a given sample came from a particular population. We will produce a **likelihood function**, which is a graph that shows how likely each potential population effect size is as the source of our sample (which has r=0.12).

Likelihood theory allows us to think about a possible population and ask how likely is it that our sample came from that population. We can then do the same for another possible population, and so on. Eventually we will have worked out, for all the potential populations, how likely each is as the source of our sample.

Let's use a simple example to illustrate likelihood, using two different possible population effect sizes: −0.25, and +0.25. There is no special reason for choosing just two or for choosing these particular values – it's just a place to start. The sampling distributions for each population are plotted in Figure 5.9 – remember, these are graphs that illustrate the distribution of the *potential sample effect sizes* from the two possible population effect sizes we have chosen. The actual sample effect size of 0.12 is indicated on each of those two sampling distributions. We can see straight away that our sample effect size is much more likely to have come from a population with an effect size of +0.25, compared to −0.25 (note the position of the dot right near the tails for the –0.25 distribution, where the frequency of that sample effect size occurring is low).

As you can see from Figure 5.9, the vertical axis now denotes the likelihood of a sample effect size coming from a particular population. This is because we are now looking back from the sample data that we have to see what happened in the population it came from, which is a likelihood. In the previous section, when we were looking at the potential future samples we might collect, we were looking forwards at a **probability**. The words 'likelihood' and 'probability' are sometimes used interchangeably but, as we have just explained, there is a very useful difference.

Our graph in Figure 5.9 shows us the likelihood of two different potential population effect sizes, allowing us to identify which one, from these two, would be more likely given our data. However, we are not limited to two: we simply picked two potential population effect sizes to keep things simple and plotted their sampling distributions. In reality, the relevant mathematics can cover every possible population effect size at once, so that we can see the likelihood of all of them at once. This is illustrated in Figure 5.10. On the left of the figure we have shown 11 different sampling functions and drawn a dot for the value of each at our sample effect size of 0.12. On the right we have replaced the 11 potential population effect sizes with all possible effect sizes – so dense that they make a surface rather than a series of individual sampling functions. The line is still there, following the surface.

Now we can concentrate on just the likelihoods for our sample effect size (shown as the line in Figure 5.10, which is every possible relevant individual likelihood joined up). To make it easier to see, we have extracted it from everything else and shown just this line in Figure 5.11.

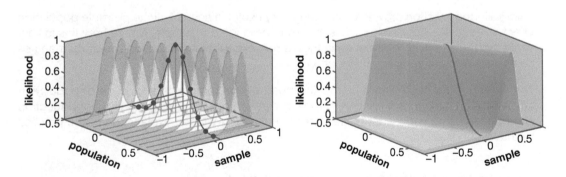

Figure 5.10   Sampling functions for several different possible population effect sizes, forming a likelihood distribution.

This now shows sampling functions for several different possible population effect sizes. The likelihood of our sample for each is shown as a dot, and we can see how that dot varies across the different possible population effect sizes. The dots are joined up with a line. This line is the likelihood distribution.

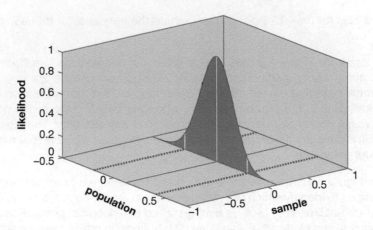

Figure 5.11   The likelihood distribution for a sample with a sample effect size of 0.12.

The graph shows for each possible population effect size how likely it is that our sample, with its sample effect size of 0.12, came from that population effect size. The peak of the distribution is called its maximum. It is placed at the population effect size that has the (highest) maximum likelihood of being the source of our sample. The solid line drawn underneath it shows us what population effect size has the maximum likelihood. The dotted lines show the range of population effect sizes that include between them the population effect sizes that taken together are 95% likely to hold the real population effect size.

We can see that it has the form of another distribution – similar to the sampling distributions themselves, but lined up at right angles to them. This distribution of the likelihood for every possible population effect size is called the **likelihood function**.

The likelihood function provides something very useful: a scan of all the possible population effect sizes to see how likely each is in turn to produce our sample. Notice how this is very similar to the sampling distribution in Figure 5.7, except the distribution lies at right angles compared with the sampling distribution.

The likelihood function shows us the likelihood of our sample as a function of population effect size, obtained from multiple sampling distributions. In reality, the likelihood function is produced using various formulae instead of the long-winded explanation of the process we have just given.

5.4.3 QUANTIFYING UNCERTAINTY WITH LIKELIHOOD

This is explained in further detail online

As the likelihood function depends only on the actual sample we have and not on any specific hypothetical population, it encapsulates our knowledge about the population. We know that the population effect size, whatever it is, is somewhere inside that distribution. We don't know where it is inside that distribution, just that it is there somewhere. There will be one population

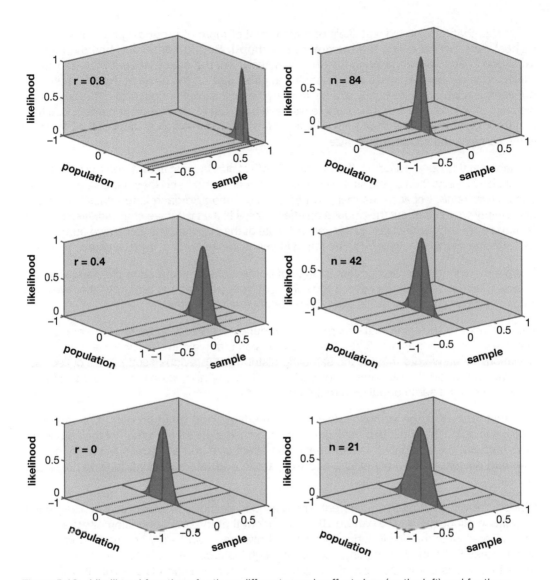

Figure 5.12   Likelihood functions for three different sample *effect sizes* (on the left) and for three different *sample sizes* (on the right).

In each case, it is easy to see how the confidence limits are affected. In the left-hand column, they shrink but also become more asymmetric. In the right-hand column, they also shrink – we have more knowledge about the population as we have more participants, so the spread of likely options gets smaller.

effect size that has the highest likelihood among all of them of producing our sample. This highest likelihood is called the **maximum likelihood**. Saying something has the highest likelihood is equivalent to saying it is the most likely. So, the effect size with the maximum likelihood is our best estimate of the population effect size on the basis of the information in our sample. Happily, it is usually exactly the same as the sample effect size in the situations we are concerned with. For the example we have been using, the population effect size that has the maximum likelihood of being the source of our sample has a value of 0.12 – which is the same as the sample effect size.

Someone at this point asked us: 'So our sample effect size is most likely to be the population effect size? Really, then all the likelihood stuff is unnecessary?' And they deserve an answer. The answer is no, because the real point of the likelihood approach is to tell us how much uncertainty we have about the population effect size, which is what we shall look at next. The fact that our sample effect size is the best estimate of the population is just a nice outcome of all the maths involved – which can be found in our online resources, if you are keen to see it.

Since the likelihood function covers a range of populations, the spread of that range will tell us how much uncertainty we have. If the spread of likely populations is narrow, then we have little uncertainty; if the spread is wide, then our uncertainty is great.

The likelihood distribution that this process produces is spread out across the population effect sizes, shown in Figure 5.12. It has a dispersion that we can describe with a standard deviation. When we did that for the sampling distribution (previous section), we called that standard deviation the standard error and used it to say how widely distributed different samples from the same population might be.

We can't really use the standard deviation of the likelihood function here. We can quite tangibly imagine making lots of real samples and so it makes sense to talk of their standard deviation; but there is only one real population effect size and so it does not really have a standard deviation. It simply exists, and we want to evaluate how confident we are about knowing it.

This is explained in further detail online

Instead, we will do something different. The likelihood distribution shows us how likely each population effect size is. We can be 100% confident that the real population effect size lies somewhere inside the distribution: somewhere between −1 and +1 (when using normalised effect sizes). But that says nothing useful. Although just possible, it is very unlikely that the real effect size is out in the tails of the distribution where likelihoods are very low. So, we could drop them without losing much of that 100% confidence. In practice we drop enough of the two tails so that we are still 95% confident that the real population effect size lies in the range of values which remains. The value of 95% is just an arbitrary choice. The range of population effect sizes that is left is called the 95% **confidence interval**. The extremes of the range are called the **confidence limits**.

5.4.4 CONFIDENCE INTERVALS

Confidence intervals can really be calculated for anything that we estimate about a population from a sample. We will look briefly at two typical cases: estimating the mean of a population and estimating the effect size of a population.

When we are estimating the mean of a population, the likelihood function is a normal distribution. This is convenient because it is known that for all normal distributions, 95% lies within the range of 1.96 times the standard deviation either side of the mean. Since our likelihood function is a normal distribution, this applies to that. Moreover, since the standard error is the standard deviation of the likelihood function, then we can say that the confidence interval for the estimate of a population mean is the sample mean ±1.96 times the standard error.

Calculating a confidence interval for an effect size is more complex and involves a mathematical process called Fisher's z-transformation. This isn't a piece of maths that you would do by hand: it's a function included with typical pieces of statistical software and online calculators. We've included some information in our online resources section, so you can see how it works and calculate your own.

This is explained in further detail online

Look back at the likelihood function in Figure 5.11 and you will see it has the 95% confidence limits drawn on it. As can be seen, the range they cover is quite wide, indicating that we have quite a lot of uncertainty in this result.

Given that the choice of 95% is arbitrary, it is natural to ask what would happen if we changed it. Suppose we decided to quote 90% confidence limits instead of 95%. Two things are changed by doing this: (i) the size of the confidence interval (the range of values that it covers) is reduced, which might be a good thing, but (ii) we are now only 90% confident that that range contains the true population value, which is a bad thing.

When including a confidence interval in a set of results, the two confidence limits (lower and upper) are written in brackets next to the relevant value. For the sample we showed in Figure 5.8, we have found that the sample effect size is 0.278 and the standard error is 0.152. This then means that the population effect size is estimated to be 0.278 and the 95% confidence limits are [–0.015, 0.527].

5.5 PUTTING IT TOGETHER

Just to consolidate this, we finish with Figure 5.13, which shows the two fundamental distributions we have been describing. The sampling distribution, running left right, is what samples may appear in the future from a specific population; the likelihood function, running front to back, is which populations may have been the source of the sample that we have already taken in the past. In the next chapter we will continue using this diagram for one common way of dealing with uncertainty.

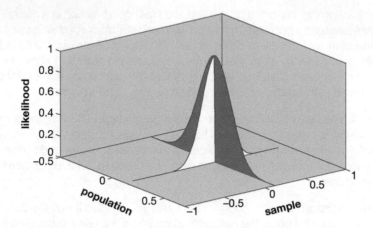

Figure 5.13   Graph combining sampling distribution and likelihood distribution.

The likelihood function is blue and parallel to the population axis; the sampling distribution is white and parallel to the sample axis.

So what do we have to say to the two student societies – Paraglider and Cross the Road Safely? We tell them that we are 95% confident that the effect size lies between –0.015 and +0.527. We can't rule out the possibility that there is no effect, or even a tiny negative effect, but the most likely effect size is reasonably positive.

THE BIG PICTURE

There is always uncertainty in statistical decisions. The second purpose of statistics is to quantify and understand this uncertainty.

UNCERTAINTY IS UNAVOIDABLE

1. Uncertainty occurs when we use a sample to make an inference about a population.

2. Uncertainty is the result of randomness and chance in samples: any sample could contain any set of participants, and each sample from the same population will differ. This difference by chance is called sampling error.

3. We must never forget that uncertainty sets an absolute limit on what we can claim to know.

EXPLORING UNCERTAINTY

1. There are two core procedures for exploring uncertainty, which are summarised in Table 5.3.

    a. The sampling distribution is the distribution of all possible samples that will come from any specific population and research design. It shows us the uncertainty about the samples that a population will produce.

    b. The likelihood function shows us the uncertainty about which population a given sample could have come from.

MEASURING UNCERTAINTY

1. The standard error is defined as the standard deviation of the sampling distribution. It is therefore the spread of all possible sample effect sizes.

    a. The standard error corresponds to the standard deviation of all possible
        sampling errors.

2. Confidence intervals from the likelihood function are a way to quantify the
    uncertainty about a population given a sample.

    a. A confidence interval is the range of values which, given our sample, are likely to
        contain the true population value (such as the population mean or effect size).

    b. Typically, confidence intervals are set to 95% confidence, so it is 95% likely that
        the true value falls inside the two confidence limits.

Table 5.3   Two key concepts from this chapter. It is helpful to think of these as looking in different
directions in time. The sampling distribution tells us what will happen when in the future we make
samples; the likelihood function tells us what population in the past may have produced our sample.

Outcome	uses	to calculate	Tense
sampling distribution	*hypothetical* population effect size	Sample Variability the set of *possible* samples	in the future
likelihood function	*actual* sample	Population Uncertainty the set of *possible* population values	in the past

WORKING WITH UNCERTAINTY

1. If a confidence interval includes zero (e.g. the limits are -0.13 and +0.162), then this
    would mean that the true population effect size could be zero, as well as any other
    effect size within the interval.

2. In the real world, the population effect size should be somewhere in the middle of
    the sample effect sizes that different researchers find when investigating the same
    topic.

    a. If we have access to an unbiased range of studies of a particular effect, then they
        will contain overestimates and underestimates of the population effect.

    b. If we only have access to significant results then we will see a biased selection
        that will tend to contain only overestimates of the population effect.

This all means something very practical. When you do your own piece of research, sampling error, that same chance process, will apply. The sample effect size you get could be large (good luck) or it could be small (bad luck).

YOUR TURN

DEFINE THESE KEY TERMS IN THE SPACE PROVIDED:

1. Sampling error

2. Standard error

3. Likelihood distribution

4. Confidence interval

FILL IN THE GAPS IN THESE SENTENCES:

5. The likelihood function shows the likelihood of different .... effect sizes for a given .... effect size

6. When all possible sample effect sizes are plotted as a distribution, they are called the ....

THE ANSWERS ARE AVAILABLE ONLINE

YOUR SPACE

 # REFERENCES AND FURTHER READING

Barford, N.C. (1985) *Experimental Measurements: Precision, Error and Truth* (2nd edition). Chichester: Wiley.

The best book, now out of print.

Efron, B. & Hastie, T. (2016) *Computer Age Statistical Inference*. Cambridge: Cambridge University Press.

Quite advanced. Chapters 1-4 explain different approaches.

Lambert, B. (2018) *A Student's Guide to Bayesian Statistics*. London: Sage.

Covers a different approach.

Pawitan, Y. (2013) *In All Likelihood*. Oxford: Oxford University Press.

Very advanced. The first two chapters are relevant.

THERE ARE MORE ACTIVITIES AND A SHORT SUMMARY VIDEO FOR THIS CHAPTER AVAILABLE AT:
HTTPS://STUDY.SAGEPUB.COM/STATISTICSFORPSYCHOLOGY

CHAPTER

06

NULL HYPOTHESIS TESTING

↳ BECAUSE UNCERTAINTY MAKES (SOME) PSYCHOLOGISTS UNCOMFORTABLE

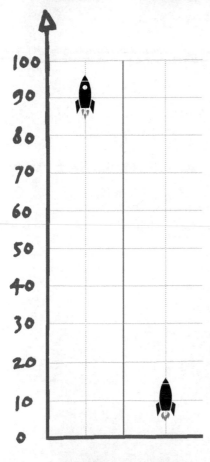

In Chapter 5, we looked at quantifying uncertainty using two fundamental approaches: the **standard error** and **confidence intervals**. In this chapter we're going to turn to a more traditional approach to uncertainty: it is widely used, but frequently problematic, which we will explain later on in this chapter. It is called **null hypothesis testing**. You may have heard of '**p-values**' or '**significance testing**', both of which are part of this same thing.

Null hypothesis testing intends to measure uncertainty, but in reality it is a mixture of quantifying uncertainty and measuring **effect size** strength. For this reason, it is often misunderstood. Let's look at what it is, and why it has problems.

6.1 THE LOGIC OF NULL HYPOTHESIS TESTING

The logic of testing is rather brutal, and we will look at it on its own before going any further. The logic involves a **hypothesis** and some evidence. What we will see is that logic can allow us to confidently reject the hypothesis but can never allow us to accept the hypothesis.

- The starting point is a hypothesis (which is hypothetical) and some evidence (which is real).
- If the two are inconsistent, then one of them must be wrong. The evidence is real and cannot be wrong; the hypothesis is hypothetical and could therefore be wrong. So, if the evidence is inconsistent with the hypothesis, we reject the hypothesis.
- If the two are not inconsistent, then they could both be correct, and we cannot reject the hypothesis.

If the evidence and hypothesis are consistent with each other, this doesn't mean that the hypothesis is correct; it means that it *could* be correct, along with many other hypotheses that are consistent with the evidence.

When we find an inconsistency we can do something decisive, but when we find a consistency we cannot do anything further.

6.1.1 THE NULL HYPOTHESIS

We shall begin with an explanation of the null hypothesis (commonly written as H_0) as this is central to the procedure – hence the name. The null hypothesis states that there is *no effect* of our Independent variable (IV) on our Dependent variable (DV), which means that the population effect size would be zero. So, the null hypothesis is a hypothetical claim that the effect size within the **population** is zero. In this way of doing things, our actual hypothesis is called the **alternative hypothesis**. The sampling distribution for the null hypothesis can be calculated using the concepts of the previous chapter, and is shown in Figure 6.1.

Why would we be considering the null hypothesis that no effect exists, when that's the opposite of what we are interested in? We are usually doing research to pursue some particular hypothesis that there is a relationship between our IV and our DV.

The reason that we need to consider the null hypothesis is because we are going to test it: we are not going to test the alternative hypothesis. This probably sounds quite odd: we hope that our evidence will be inconsistent with the null hypothesis, allowing us to reject it. The intention of null hypothesis testing is to try to find enough evidence to reject the null hypothesis as being false. In the previous chapter, we saw that there will always be some residual uncertainty and so even if we do reject the null hypothesis, we cannot be sure we are

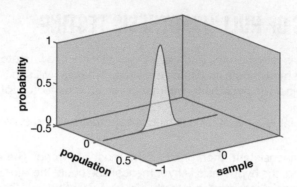

Figure 6.1   Graph showing a sampling distribution for the null hypothesis.

If there is no effect in the population for the variables we are studying, then any sample we get will be somewhere in this distribution (see that the distribution is aligned with 0 on the population effect size scale).

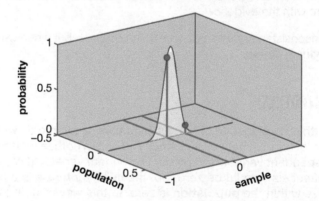

Figure 6.2   Graph showing the sampling distribution for the null hypothesis and two actual samples.

Two sample effect sizes are shown superimposed on the sampling distribution from Figure 6.1 (using lines and dots). This graph shows us that the left sample would be much more consistent with the null hypothesis than the right one, because it is much more probable (using the scale on the y-axis).

right to do so. However, this is just an accepted part of this type of uncertainty testing – and part of the reason it has problems.

Figure 6.2 illustrates this approach. It shows the same sampling distribution from the null hypothesis as before. This time it shows two possible **samples** we might have: one has a sample effect size of –0.05 (the one on the left) and one has a sample effect size of +0.22 (the right hand one). The figure shows us that the first example sample is produced more often by the population with zero effect size and so is potentially more consistent with that population than is the second one.

6.1.2 THE TEST

The basic test is simple. We have two propositions: (i) the null hypothesis that the population effect size is zero; and (ii) an actual sample with a sample effect size that is 0.22 (or whatever we found). Null hypothesis testing asks a simple question: are these two propositions consistent with each other? If they are, then we cannot rule out the null hypothesis: that the population effect size is zero. If they are not consistent with each other, then one of the two propositions must be false. Since our sample must be true because we can see it for ourselves, it has to be the other proposition – the null hypothesis – that is false. So, if our sample effect size is not consistent with a population effect size of zero, we would infer that the population effect size is not zero.

Let's pause for a minute and consider an example. We could be looking at a sample of giraffes and predicting that the more hours of rainfall there are, the more food they will eat. We have two hypotheses:

- Our alternative hypothesis: there is a relationship between hours of rainfall and giraffe food consumption in the population.
- Null hypothesis: there is no relationship between rainfall and giraffe food consumption in the population.

We test the null hypothesis hoping to find that our evidence from a sample of giraffes means that the null hypothesis can be rejected.

The logic of null hypothesis testing isn't quite as firm and safe as we have made it sound. Null hypothesis testing asks the question: are the null hypothesis and our sample inconsistent with each other? Is the behaviour of our sample of giraffes inconsistent with the null hypothesis that no effect really exists in the wider giraffe population? This is a question that is quite difficult to answer because of sampling error and uncertainty. We can never say categorically that the sample is inconsistent with the null hypothesis: there is always some possibility that the two may be consistent.

Because of the uncertainty in our sample, we must use a weaker (and therefore less satisfying) question: what is the *probability* that the null hypothesis would produce a sample with an effect size that is at least as big as the effect size we have found in our sample? Supposing the null hypothesis is actually true, what is the probability of getting a sample with our sample effect size or one that is even more extreme – stronger? This is shown in Figure 6.3 for the two example samples we had in the previous figure. The shaded area in each case contains all the samples that the null hypothesis might produce that have an effect size that is at least as large as our actual one. So, the proportion of the sampling distribution that is shaded is the probability we are interested in.

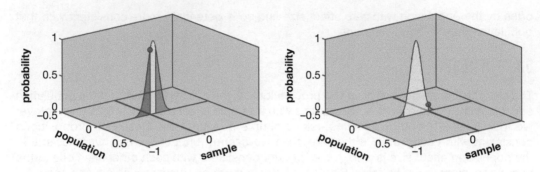

Figure 6.3   Graphs showing how the sampling distribution for the null hypothesis is used to calculate a p-value.

The probability of obtaining a sample effect size at least as large as our actual sample effect size is the proportion of the sampling distribution that is shaded. Each graph shows the distribution for a population where the null hypothesis is true. On the left, where the actual sample effect size is small (–0.05), the probability of it occurring in the null hypothesis population is high. On the right, where the actual sample effect size is larger (0.22), the probability is much smaller.

6.1.3 THE PROCEDURE

We start with our null hypothesis, specifying that the population effect size is zero. We can then use the sampling distribution theory from Chapter 5 to visualise the range of sample effect sizes that could come from a population with an effect size of zero, to see how probable it is that this population could produce our sample effect size or a stronger one. This can be illustrated using the same diagrams as we have seen before, as you can see in Figure 6.3.

The figure shows the sample effect size we have (0.22 in this case) and has shaded the parts of the sampling distribution that are for sample effect sizes, positive and negative, that have a larger magnitude than this. The proportion of the whole distribution that is shaded gives us the probability of getting our sample effect size or stronger from this sampling distribution.

The probability of getting our sample effect size or stronger is so commonly used that it is nearly always shortened to *p*, or **p-value**. The value for *p* is used as an indication of how consistent our sample is with the null hypothesis. The smaller the value for *p*, the less consistent they are (meaning that it is more likely that we have found a true effect).

If the p-value is very small, meaning that a population with zero effect size would rarely produce our sample effect size or an even stronger one, then this is judged to indicate inconsistency between the null hypothesis and our sample. When our sample is inconsistent with the null hypothesis, we can say that we *reject the null hypothesis*.

If the p-value is not very small, meaning that a population with zero effect size would sometimes produce our sample effect size or stronger, then we do something that is very irritating. We cannot judge that there is an inconsistency. That double negative really matters.

When this happens, we say that we have *failed to reject the null hypothesis*. We haven't actually accepted the null hypothesis; we have only reached a point where we cannot reject it, based on the evidence that we have.

The logic of null hypothesis testing is this:

- We start with two propositions:
  (i) the null hypothesis describes our population,
  (ii) our sample came from that population,

and then, third, make a calculation:

  (iii) the probability of the null hypothesis producing a sample with an effect size at least as large as our sample.

- The value of p is treated as a measure of how consistent these two propositions are with each other.
- If p is very low, then we can conclude that the null hypothesis and our sample are not consistent with each other: one must be false. Since our sample is not false (assuming we didn't cheat), the null hypothesis *can be rejected*.
- If p is not very low, then we cannot conclude that the null hypothesis and our sample are not consistent with each other. We say that we have *failed to reject* the null hypothesis. Please be aware that every word in these two sentences matters. The key to understanding this is that 'we cannot conclude …' and that is where we reach – unable to conclude. This indeterminate result is one of the problems with null hypothesis testing.

The decision at the centre of this – about the consistency of the two propositions – is a judgement we reach by comparing the p-value with an arbitrary level, conventionally set to 0.05. That value of 0.05 is called *alpha*. What that really means is that researchers have agreed that a 5% (0.05 = 5%) chance of getting the wrong outcome is acceptable, because we can never really be completely certain. This sounds like a strange thing to accept, but it is entirely arbitrary – it is just a matter of convention. Table 6.1 shows a summary of the decision process.

Table 6.1   Two possible outcomes of null hypothesis testing

The outcomes of a statistical test of the null hypothesis, how we must report them and what they mean.

Outcome	Decision	Meaning	Implication
$p<=0.05$	**reject the null hypothesis** 'result is statistically significant'	there is evidence that the null hypothesis does not reasonably account for our data	the effect probably exists
$p>0.05$	**fail to reject the null hypothesis** 'result is not statistically significant'	there is no evidence that the null hypothesis does not reasonably account for our data	we don't know whether the effect exists

If we reject the null hypothesis, then conventionally we say that the result is **statistically significant**. This sounds like a definite, certain statement; but it is important to realise that it isn't certain at all. The technical term 'statistically significant' must be understood to mean 'uncertainty about the existence of the effect is low'.

If we fail to reject the null hypothesis, then conventionally we say that the result is not statistically significant. This also sounds quite definite, but it isn't; it is in fact why we use the term 'fail to reject'. We don't accept the null hypothesis (say that no effect exists); instead we just don't have enough evidence for anything else yet. There are many other effects that might exist, that we haven't yet investigated. Failing to reject the null hypothesis leaves the idea open for further development. In fact, the technical term 'not statistically significant' must be understood to mean 'we don't know anything new'. This is important: when $p>0.05$, we are saying 'there is no evidence that …' and *lack of evidence for an effect* isn't the same as *evidence for the absence* of an effect.

Figure 6.4 shows the relationship between the actual sample size and the decision to reject or not the null hypothesis. It shows the familiar sampling distribution for the null hypothesis. The shaded areas are drawn to contain exactly 5% of the distribution so that any actual sample with a sample effect size that falls in these areas would be considered statistically significant.

6.1.4 COMMENT

The first thing to notice about null hypothesis testing is that the question that it asks is not the most obvious one to ask and so the result is a little more complicated to interpret. We would expect to ask a question about our actual hypothesis, not a hypothetical null hypothesis. We would also expect to be asking a question about what the sample tells us about the population, not what the null population tells us about the sample.

This is all a slightly odd way of proceeding, and the reason for using it is that it is the best that can be done with pencil and paper. Because of that, it has been a standard approach for nearly a century – since long before we had statistical software to examine our data for us. It leads us to a conclusion: we either reject the null hypothesis or we don't. But we are making that apparently definite statement on the basis of uncertain information. If we reach a conclusion only on the basis of facts supplied, then we are making a deduction. In this case, we are going beyond the facts supplied by involving a null hypothesis, and that means we are making an **inference**.

It is vital to understand that the conclusion we reach is a conclusion about the null hypothesis. It is not a conclusion about the alternative hypothesis – which is what we should really be interested in – because we have only asked a question about the null hypothesis. We are really only reaching a conclusion when we reject the null hypothesis: when we fail to reject it, we are saying nothing at all. We hope this strikes you as weird: we spent the whole of Chapters 1–4 developing and working with our so-called 'alternative' hypothesis, and then we go off and

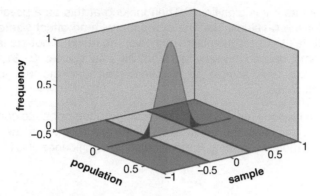

Figure 6.4   The basic rule of null hypothesis testing.

The figure shows the sampling distribution for the null hypothesis. The population effect size is 0 for the null hypothesis. The area of darkest blue regions on the tails of the sampling distribution add up to 5% of the whole area. That means that samples drawn from the null hypothesis have only a 5% probability of falling in one of these regions. The heavy lines, which are drawn to line up with these regions, divide the range of sample effect sizes into three groups: those (paler) in the middle where we would say that the sample effect size is not inconsistent with the null hypothesis; and those (darker) outside where we could say that the sample and the null hypothesis were inconsistent with each other. By chance, 5% of samples from the null hypothesis will fall in the darker area. Note that the actual population we are studying does not appear in this diagram – neither as a real population nor as a hypothetical one. Null hypothesis testing is only a comparison of the sample with the null hypothesis.

test a different hypothesis. If you do find that to be strange, then the rest of this chapter is going to feel surreal. Stick with it.

6.1.5 TWO EXAMPLES

Let's imagine two possible outcomes of a study where we explored the relationship between risk-taking and exam grades. We are going to invite you to think about the outcomes we are about to provide in two ways: (i) as a member of the Paragliding Club or the Cross the Road Safely Club (you choose which suits you best); and (ii) as a psychology researcher.

The outcomes:

*   Our first possible outcome is that we used 42 participants and, to our delight, we found a sample effect size of 0.29 which is quite big.
*   Our second possible outcome is that we used 4200 participants and, to our disappointment, we found a sample effect size of just 0.031, which is fairly tiny.

Looking at this as someone for whom the result might personally matter, the first result seems important and the second seems unimportant. In the usual colloquial sense of the word, the first outcome looks as if it is significant. Then looking at this as a psychology researcher we have to ask for the p-values. The first outcome, with an effect size of 0.29, has found $p>0.05$ and so we fail to reject the null hypothesis: the result is not statistically significant. The second outcome, despite having a much smaller effect size of 0.031, has found $p<0.05$ (because it has a much larger sample size) and so we can reject the null hypothesis: the result is statistically significant.

These two different reasons for looking at the result produce opposite consequences in this (slightly provocative) scenario. For significance as the practical value, then the first outcome is the one that is the more interesting. For the statistical significance, it is the second outcome that matters.

6.2 LIKELIHOOD FUNCTIONS AND NULL HYPOTHESIS TESTING

The sample we have comes from the population that we are studying, but that population hasn't actually featured anywhere in null hypothesis testing. As well as looking at the sampling distribution for the null hypothesis, which is, strictly speaking, all we need for null hypothesis testing, we can look at the sampling distribution for the population our sample might have come from.

Figure 6.5 shows a fairly typical scenario. Once again, we are viewing this from the outside, seeing both the sample that might be visible to a researcher and also the population it came from (which isn't visible to the researcher). The sampling distribution towards the back is the null hypothesis and the regions shaded blue are where a sample has to be to allow us to reject the null hypothesis. The sampling distribution towards the front is the one we are actually sampling from. The shaded area on this is also where the sample has to come from to allow us to reject the null hypothesis. The same single sample is shown, superimposed on both sampling distributions. The sample results in a failure to reject the null hypothesis because it isn't far enough out in the tails of the null hypothesis sampling distribution – although, as we can see, the sample effect size is very close to the population effect size and so the sampling error is actually rather small.

In the light of the work we did in the previous chapter learning about likelihood functions, you should be feeling cheated now. Null hypothesis testing not only doesn't use likelihood, it wilfully ignores it. Either we made you work hard for nothing (no, we didn't), or you can now appreciate that null hypothesis testing involves ignoring a great deal of information in the sample.

The truth is that despite failing to reject the null hypothesis, it is by no means the most likely population in this example. This is a salient example of why failing to reject the null hypothesis cannot be treated as if it means that the null hypothesis is accepted. Here we have failed to reject it, but our evidence is nonetheless less consistent with the null hypothesis than it is with many other population effect sizes.

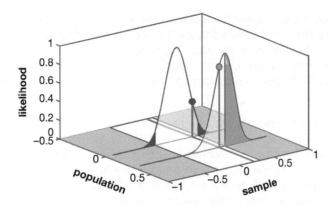

Figure 6.5   Comparing likelihoods of a null hypothesis population and true effect population.

This figure shows a possible situation that a researcher could find themselves in. Unknown to them, they are sampling a population (n=42) with an effect size of r=0.3. Their sample effect size is 0.22. The figure shows the likelihood for the null hypothesis and for the population with an effect size of r=0.3. This tells us that likelihood is twice as high for the population r=0.3 than it is for the null hypothesis. Nonetheless, the sample falls into the middle space where the null hypothesis cannot be rejected. The figure also shows that a significant result can only be obtained in this scenario when the sample effect size is greater than the actual population effect size. In the previous chapter we were quite relieved to find that sampling errors have a mean of zero, meaning no bias. Here, the sampling errors for a statistically significant result are all +ve: there is very considerable bias.

6.3 THE CONSEQUENCES OF NULL HYPOTHESIS TESTING

The outcome of a null hypothesis test is a decision about whether to reject the null hypothesis or not. Because we are making that firm decision about the population on the basis of uncertain information from the sample, the uncertainty becomes converted into a chance that we have made the wrong decision: we have made an error.

6.3.1 IF WE REJECT THE NULL HYPOTHESIS?

If the probability of obtaining our sample or one with a larger effect size from the null hypothesis is less than 0.05, then by convention we reject the null hypothesis. Usefully, the distribution of p-values that we would get for samples from the null hypothesis itself is uniform: each possible p-value between 0 and 1 is equally probable. So, 5% of all samples drawn from the null hypothesis will have $p<0.05$. This means that if the null hypothesis is actually correct, then the probability that we will be rejecting the null hypothesis wrongly is given by alpha, 0.05. We have a probability of wrongly rejecting the null hypothesis of 0.05 and so in the long run we will do so 5% of the time.

When this so-called 'false positive' scenario occurs, we call it a **Type I error**. When we reject the null hypothesis, there is always a chance that we have made a Type I error: we can never know whether or not we have made one. This is why relying on a single piece of research is not a sensible practice. The uncertainty of going from our known sample to an unknown population still exists; it has now become an uncertainty about whether we have made a Type I error or not.

If we want to be mindful of the uncertainty that still exists, then we can say something more. Either we have made a Type I error or we haven't. We can't really talk about the probability that we have made a Type I error because that probability is either 1.0 (we did) or 0.0 (we didn't). Instead we can use the idea of a likelihood: looking back, what is the likelihood that we have made a Type I error? That likelihood that we have made a Type I error normally has just the same value as the p-value we have calculated.

Here is an important distinction. Before we have data (or before we have analysed it) and looking to the future of what that data may be, we have a 5% future **probability** that we will make a Type I error. After we have analysed our data, and looking back to what may have happened in that process, the past **likelihood** that we have made a Type I error is given by the p-value we calculate. See Table 6.2 for a summary of this.

Table 6.2   Prospective and retrospective Type I errors

The two ways of thinking about Type I errors.

	When?	Asking about?	What?	How much?
Prospective Type I errors	Before	forwards to the future	Probability	alpha
Retrospective Type I errors	After	backwards to the past	Likelihood	p-value

6.3.2 IF WE FAIL TO REJECT THE NULL HYPOTHESIS?

If our p-value is greater than 0.05 (alpha), then we fail to reject the null hypothesis and can conclude nothing much at all. That is always unsatisfactory, not least because it might be unfair: the population may have an effect and our sample was just unlucky for us. When we fail to reject the null hypothesis, it may be that there is no effect in the population or it may be that the sampling error (recall, the error caused when the sample doesn't represent the population well) associated with our sample has caused us to reach the wrong outcome. If there is an effect in the population and we have missed it because of sampling error, then we are making a **Type II error**.

A Type II error is a miss (a 'false negative'): we missed the finding that was there to be made. If we have failed to reject the null hypothesis, we can never say whether we have made a Type II error or not.

Unlike Type I errors, when considering Type II errors it is not straightforward to calculate the prospective probability that we will make one, or the retrospective likelihood that we have made one. Type I errors depend on the behaviour of the population of the null hypothesis, which is an invention we can be sure about. Type II errors depend on the behaviour of the actual population we are studying and that we cannot be sure about.

Table 6.3   Prospective and retrospective Type II errors

The two ways of thinking about Type II errors.

	When?	Asking about?	What?	How much?
Prospective Type II errors	Before	forwards to the future	Probability	?
Retrospective Type II errors	After	backwards to the past	Likelihood	?

It is worth saying that the future probability or the past likelihood of Type II errors are not related at all to the p-value we have obtained. In Table 6.3, we have placed question marks in the cells for How Much? In Chapter 8, we will return to this and show how we can sometimes calculate an estimate of the values for these two cells. However, in general, it is accepted that Type II error rates are usually unknown.

6.3.3 INFERENTIAL ERRORS CONSIDERED TOGETHER

You may think that a 5% probability that we will make a Type I error is quite high and then be wondering why we don't set alpha lower. If we set alpha to 0.01 and so use $p<0.01$ for our arbitrary rule, then there would only be 1% of Type I errors. We now consider why. The problem is that if we set the criterion to 0.01, then Type II errors are increased much more than Type I errors are decreased.

Null hypothesis testing has at its heart this unavoidable trade-off between Type I and Type II errors. Recent thinking is beginning to suggest that researchers actively engage with this trade-off rather than simply accept the convention of alpha=0.05. The suggestion is that a specific value for alpha is declared (*before* the data has been collected!) that takes into account what is already known.

Type I errors are very serious: once a result has made its way into our understanding of psychology, it can be hard to eradicate if it turns out to be mistaken. We need to keep those very much under control for the integrity of our science. At this point, it would be good to be able to show you a famous example of a piece of psychology that turned out to be based on data that had a Type I error. We can't. Just as a researcher cannot know whether they have made a Type I error because of the uncertainty in their results, nor can we as readers of their research. The closest we can come to this is to replicate their study a few times, and if each replication fails to reject the null hypothesis, then the likelihood that they made a Type I error increases. Because of this, Type I errors and correct results are difficult to distinguish without a lot of **replication**. Everyone knows that there must be Type I errors in the literature, we just don't know where.

Type II errors are also problematical. When we fail to reject the null hypothesis, we are saying we have learned nothing new. All the effort involved in collecting data from participants is wasted when we get a Type II error and so we appear to have made no progress.

Finally, it is worth pointing this out: before you have data, looking forwards to what outcomes you might expect, you must consider that you may make a Type I error *and* that you may make a Type II error. After you have data, looking back to what may have happened, you can only have made one of those two errors – which you should consider depends on whether p<0.05 or not.

Table 6.4   How data analysis changes how we think about Type I and II errors

The situation before and after data analysis.

		Type I error	Type II error
Looking forwards:	No test yet: p unknown	maybe	maybe
Looking backwards:	Test done: $p <= 0.05$	maybe	no
	Test done: $p > 0.05$	no	maybe

6.4 A CONVERSATION ABOUT TESTING FOR NULL EFFECTS

Two paragraphs back we said something quite shocking: when a Type II error occurs, then time has been wasted. We said it with a great deal of deliberation, and it prompted an impassioned response from a reader that we want to share. Perhaps you share that reader's perspective.

6.4.1 THE QUESTION

The reader didn't like our statement that a non-significant result means that the research was just wasted time. They quoted the immense importance of null results in some circumstances – their example was the absence of a gender difference in intelligence. We can readily agree that this is important, and using our running example in this book, point to something very similar of real concern: whether there is a gender difference in exam grades.

6.4.2 THE ISSUE

What we have said about null hypothesis testing is unfortunately correct. When we fail to reject the null hypothesis, all those negatives are there to remind us that we have made no progress – *within the framework of null hypothesis testing*. The fundamental logic of null hypothesis testing is that we need an inconsistency between two propositions so that we can reject one of them – the hypothetical one. That logic is inextricably built into statistical testing.

6.4.3 A SORT-OF-SOLUTION

So null hypothesis testing is unsuited to show that there is no gender difference in exam grades. We will hold, for now, onto the logic of (hopefully) creating an inconsistency, but we will use it differently. We sit down and decide that, for all practical purposes, an effect size relating gender to exam grades that was less than 0.2 would be tolerable but an effect size greater would be very awkward: it would make exams quite an unfair way to test students.

We ask the question: is our sample inconsistent with a population effect size greater than 0.2? We have replaced the null hypothesis with this 'testing hypothesis'. We calculate the probability of getting our sample effect size or one further from the testing hypothesis. If that probability is low enough (less than 0.05), then we have our (hoped for) inconsistency and we can reject the testing hypothesis that the effect size is greater than 0.2.

This can be done – there is nothing wrong with it. Except, perhaps, that most software doesn't do it. Plus, it would take endless university committee meetings to decide on the value of 0.2 for the testing hypothesis.

6.4.4 A GOOD SOLUTION

Actually, we already have a better answer: **confidence limits**, which we looked at in Chapter 5. We take a sample of exam grades, calculate the sample effect size for gender *and its confidence limits* or even better the whole likelihood function. Suppose that we had the exam results from 120 students and we calculated the effect size for gender, then we would get a likelihood function similar somehow to that shown in Figure 6.6. We can convert the upper limit normalised effect size of 0.27 to the **BESD** effect size we looked at in Chapter 4 to see what impact it is having.

Using the BESD formula:

$$50 - (0.27 \times 50) : 50 + (0.27 \times 50)$$

$$36.5 : 63.5$$

What this means is that, despite having a normalised effect size as large as 0.27, gender affects the exam grades of no more than 13.5% of students: the difference between the observed count of 63.5 and the expected 'null hypothesis of no effect' of 50 is 13.5.

In truth, we would wish to see much more data than 120 exam grades and a correspondingly smaller range of possible population effect sizes to satisfy ourselves that there was no effect of gender (or that there was). The point here is simple, though: we use confidence limits to say that our data causes us to restrict the size of any possible effect.

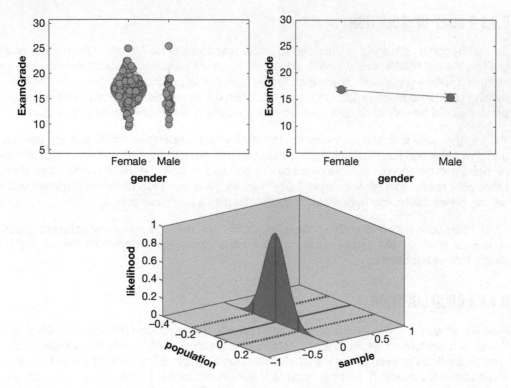

Figure 6.6   Sample showing the effect of gender on exam grades.

This graph illustrates some data showing the effect of gender on exam grades. The top half of the figure shows the sample graph and the descriptive statistics graph, where the effect can be seen. The effect is weak (it has an effect size of −0.103) with a small advantage to females. Beneath is the likelihood function for this sample. The central 95% comfortably includes 0, which means that a population effect size of 0 is quite plausible as an account of this data. The confidence limits are [−0.27 and +0.07].

6.4.5 THE QUESTION AGAIN

We have just reached this point: that a sample that fails to reject the null hypothesis can be used to set an upper limit on how big the population effect could be. Under strict null hypothesis testing, that is irrelevant. In practice, it is how researchers have managed to answer these no-effect questions. It isn't often appreciated that doing so means coming out of the null hypothesis testing system.

6.5 SUMMARY

We conclude this chapter with a quick look back at null hypothesis testing. The story is told in Figure 6.7.

The key point of Figure 6.7 is that by choosing 42 participants, we have created a situation where our sample needs an effect size of at least 0.3 to be statistically significant. If the population effect size is small, that is unlikely; if the population effect size is large, that is likely.

6.6 AN EVEN BIGGER PICTURE

It is important to see the bigger picture here. Sampling a population creates a sampling error, which cannot be known and cannot be avoided, and which we are characterising as an uncertainty in what we know about the population. We use statistics to estimate the magnitude of that uncertainty. However, it seems that collectively researchers cannot cope with that idea of uncertain conclusions, so then we have to bring in a new step – null hypothesis testing – to convert that uncertainty that exists into a definite (i.e. not uncertain) decision about what our data means. If that strikes you as being just slightly weird, then you are one of a growing band of researchers.

The consequence of null hypothesis testing is that for any given design (such as sample size), there is a fixed sample effect size that a sample must exceed in order to yield a statistically significant result. The larger the sample size, for example, the smaller the critical effect size to achieve statistical significance. So, the larger the sample effect size, the more uncertainty we are ignoring when we make a decision to reject the null hypothesis.

The shortcomings of null hypothesis testing are becoming apparent in psychology as the massive convenience it had in pre-computer days is lost. We really want a logic that has these features:

(i)   uses the likelihood function: what a sample tells us about the likely population

(ii) makes inferences about the hypotheses we are interested in, not artificial ones we are not interested in.

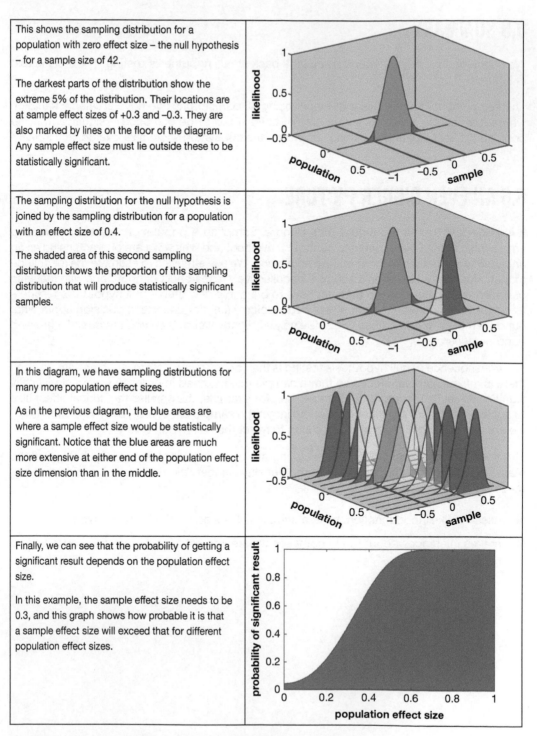

This shows the sampling distribution for a population with zero effect size – the null hypothesis – for a sample size of 42.

The darkest parts of the distribution show the extreme 5% of the distribution. Their locations are at sample effect sizes of +0.3 and –0.3. They are also marked by lines on the floor of the diagram. Any sample effect size must lie outside these to be statistically significant.

The sampling distribution for the null hypothesis is joined by the sampling distribution for a population with an effect size of 0.4.

The shaded area of this second sampling distribution shows the proportion of this sampling distribution that will produce statistically significant samples.

In this diagram, we have sampling distributions for many more population effect sizes.

As in the previous diagram, the blue areas are where a sample effect size would be statistically significant. Notice that the blue areas are much more extensive at either end of the population effect size dimension than in the middle.

Finally, we can see that the probability of getting a significant result depends on the population effect size.

In this example, the sample effect size needs to be 0.3, and this graph shows how probable it is that a sample effect size will exceed that for different population effect sizes.

132

Figure 6.7   The basic action of null hypothesis testing.

THE BIG PICTURE

A common approach that partly deals with the uncertainty in statistical inference is called null hypothesis testing.

WHAT IS NULL HYPOTHESIS TESTING?

1. Null hypothesis testing calculates the probability that the sample effect size (that we actually have) or one that was even stronger could have come from a (completely hypothetical) population with an effect size of zero.

2. Typically, the null hypothesis can be rejected when p (the probability value) is less than 0.05. The value of 0.05 is called alpha.

3. When p is greater than 0.05, we have failed to reject the null hypothesis.

INFERENTIAL ERRORS IN NULL HYPOTHESIS TESTING

1. When we reach a conclusion with null hypothesis testing, we may have made one of two different errors because of sampling error:

    a. Type I error: a false positive when we reject the null hypothesis even though there is no effect in the population.

    b. Type II error: a false negative when we fail to reject the null hypothesis even though there is an effect in the population.

2. Neither Type I nor Type II errors can be identified. It is not possible to know whether we have made an error or not. They are risks that are always taken with null hypothesis testing.

PROBABILITY OF MAKING AN INFERENTIAL ERROR

1. Before we begin a piece of research we could be about to make either a Type I or a Type II error:

    a. We can expect that there is a 5% chance of making a Type I error.

    b. We cannot know what the chance of making a Type II error is.

2. After we have done a piece of research, we can only have made either a Type I error or a Type II error, never both.

    a. The likelihood that we have made a Type I error is the p-value from our test.

    b. We cannot know the likelihood that we have made a Type II error: it would require knowledge of the whole population, which we almost never have.

IT IS A TEST OF THE EXISTENCE OF AN EFFECT, NOT THE STRENGTH OF AN EFFECT

1. The first point to be clear about is the question that null hypothesis testing answers. The question, in its broadest sense, is about the existence of a relationship between two or more variables. We use the word effect as a shorthand for the existence of a relationship between variables. Null hypothesis testing asks: 'Can we be fairly sure that there is an effect?'

IT IS ONLY A TEST OF THE NULL HYPOTHESIS, NOT OUR CHOSEN ALTERNATIVE HYPOTHESIS

1. Null hypothesis testing considers the view from the population, not the view from a sample.

2. It focuses on just one specific hypothetical population: the population of the null hypothesis, where no effect exists, so where the population effect size is zero.

    a. It is the opposite of the hypothesis we are really interested in, which is that there is a relationship (in statistical terms, this is called the alternative hypothesis). This is the point to be clear about: we are testing the null hypothesis, not our alternative hypothesis.

THE ANSWER IS STILL UNCERTAIN, EVEN THOUGH IT APPEARS DEFINITE

1. Up until this point, we have been talking about the uncertainty that comes with a sample.

    a. Suddenly, we are making a black or white decision. Think of it as a method that exists because researchers cannot tolerate the idea of uncertainty and the somewhat indeterminate results that means.

    b. Therefore, various statisticians decided to define a completely arbitrary rule to provide a definite outcome.

    c. The uncertainty is still there: we may have made a Type I or Type II error and we cannot know. But the rule allows us to hide the uncertainty. We hope you think this is unsatisfactory.

ONLY ONE OF THE TWO POSSIBLE OUTCOMES IS AN ANSWER

1. Null hypothesis testing leads to two outcomes: reject or fail to reject the null hypothesis.

    a. Reject the null hypothesis: we are making an inference.

    b. Fail to reject the null hypothesis: we are not making an inference. The word fail is correct here: we have failed to infer anything.

YOUR TURN

DEFINE THESE KEY TERMS IN THE SPACE PROVIDED:

1.   Null hypothesis

2.   P-value

3.   Type I error

4.   Type II error

FILL IN THE GAPS IN THESE SENTENCES:

1.   If you find a statistically significant result, using the most common value for alpha, your p-value must be less than ------------------

2.   If you do not find a statistically significant result, you cannot ------------- the null hypothesis.

ANOTHER ACTIVITY AND ANSWERS ARE AVAILABLE ONLINE

YOUR SPACE

📖 REFERENCES AND FURTHER READING

Cumming, G. (2012) *Understanding the New Statistics*. New York: Routledge.

Intended for a wide audience.

Harlow, L.L., Mulaik, S.A. & Stegier, J.H. (eds) (2016) *What If There Were No Significance Testing?* New York: Routledge.

A classic edited collection examining the strengths and weaknesses of null hypothesis testing.

THERE ARE MORE ACTIVITIES AND A SHORT
SUMMARY VIDEO FOR THIS CHAPTER AVAILABLE AT:
HTTPS://STUDY.SAGEPUB.COM/STATISTICSFORPSYCHOLOGY

CHAPTER

07

STATISTICAL TESTS FOR ONE INDEPENDENT VARIABLE

ANYONE WHO TELLS YOU
THIS BIT IS DIFFICULT
IS LYING TO YOU

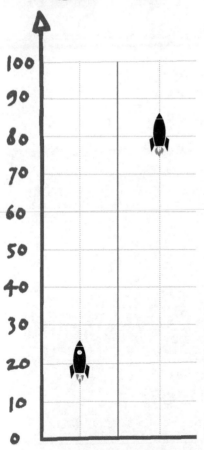

BUILDING   USING

We have learned in Chapter 6 what the p-value in a null hypothesis test actually is: the probability of the null hypothesis producing the effect size in our result or a stronger one. The smaller the p-value, the less likely it is that the null hypothesis did give rise to the sample. The actual calculations of the p-value done by various pieces of statistical software use some short cuts that are useful to know about.

Note: we have not included step-by-step procedures for conducting these tests using statistical software, partly because different readers will have different software preferences, and partly because we think it more important to understand what is being done than learning one specific application. Instead, our Chapter 7 online resources contain clear instructions for you.

There are SPSS walk-through guides and APA format resources available online

7.1 THE LOGIC OF A STATISTICAL TEST

Before computers, it was impossible to write down a formula that directly converted a **sample effect size** into a p-value. However, there is a way round this that is still used. We can convert the effect size, and its associated **standard error**, into a new quantity called a **test-statistic**. That test-statistic can be more easily converted into a p-value, taking the **sample size** into account.

7.1.1 AN EXAMPLE

We are going to use our basic **hypothesis** to demonstrate the theory behind statistical testing, using these specific variable types: RiskTaker? as a **Categorical variable** and ExamGrade as an **Interval variable**, pictured in Figure 7.1.

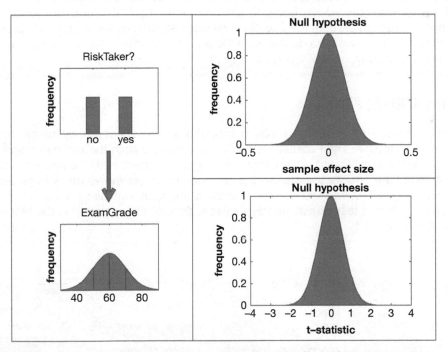

Figure 7.1   A reminder of our basic hypothesis, treating RiskTaker? as a Categorical variable.

On the right of the figure we show the sampling distribution for the null hypothesis, and beneath it the corresponding distribution of expected t-statistic values.

Imagine taking a sample from the population where the null hypothesis is true and calculating two quantities: the sample effect size and its standard error. Both of these are familiar concepts already. Then, in a new step, divide the effect size by its standard error and call the result a **t-statistic** ('t' simply stands for 'test'). Take note here that this particular t-statistic is one of several that are used in different situations. Its use here is the consequence of the variable combination we have in our hypothesis: other variable combinations will produce their own named test statistics (most creators of statistical tests were a little more creative than just abbreviating the word 'test'). Other test statistics will be covered in Section 7.2. All the possible expected values of this new quantity, t, that are drawn from the null hypothesis population (where there is no difference between the two groups) would have a specific distribution called the 'Student's t distribution'. There's no real reason for the 'Student' element of the name – this particular statistical test isn't reserved for students. It was just created by someone who decided to use Student as his pseudonym.

Now we can convert our actual sample effect size and its standard error to a t-statistic in just the same way. Then, instead of asking how often the null hypothesis produces our sample effect size or stronger, we are going to ask how often the null hypothesis produces our t-statistic or larger. Apart from the quantity involved, t-statistic rather than the effect size, this process is exactly as we have described in the previous chapter. The only reason for using t is pre-computer convenience: the student's t distribution was easier to work with.

7.1.2 THE GENERAL PROCESS

What matters here is a simple principle: dividing the sample effect size by its standard error produces a t-statistic. The t-statistic is a balance involving both the estimated strength of the effect and the estimated uncertainty: the bigger the effect size, the larger the value of the t-statistic; the smaller the standard error, also the larger the value. A large t-statistic indicates a large effect size and a small uncertainty and then a smaller p-value. While we will see several different test statistics, only this specific calculation provides *the* test-statistic that is simply called 't'.

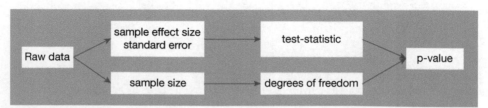

Figure 7.2   The basic sequence of operations that go from a sample through to the p-value for null hypothesis testing.

The exact nature of the test-statistic and the degrees of freedom depend on the variable types that are in use. It is always the case that the p-value becomes smaller as the effect size or the sample size increases.

A t-statistic is converted to a p-value with the use of **degrees of freedom** (abbreviated to '*df*'). The degree of freedom is a count of how much explaining we have left available to us. If our sample only has two participants, one in each category, then the two group means completely describe the sample and we would say that there are no degrees of freedom left or the degrees of freedom equals zero. Specific to our RiskTaker? → ExamGrade idea, if we have *n* (remember that *n* = number of participants) and we have so far explained them as two different group means, then we have *(n–2)* degrees of freedom left.

The sequence of operations to reach the p-value is always the same, subject to minor differences to suit different variable types. It is shown in Figure 7.2. This sequence is used in all the statistical tests that we look at in this chapter and the next. The test-statistic may instead be a **chi-square statistic**, or an **F-statistic**, depending on the variable types involved and each with its own degrees of freedom, but the logic is essentially the same. You can think of the *t* value and the degrees of freedom inside this as a bit of the machinery: it isn't very important to us, except that when we report a statistical test, we are expected to say what the value of the test-statistic and the degrees of freedom are (primarily for historical reasons).

The most common way to report the outcome of a statistical test in psychology is using **APA format**, which is simply a standardised style that makes results easy for all researchers to understand. We very briefly mentioned it in Chapter 2, and you will find examples in this chapter in each test section, and online. APA stands for American Psychological Association, and the intention behind the APA format is to ensure that all research publications in psychology have enough details about the statistical analysis and results. It is an evolving format, as notions of what statistics are most important to report are changing.

7.2 THE SPECIFIC STATISTICAL TESTS

As we saw in Chapter 3, there are three fundamentally different types of variable (**Categorical**, **Ordinal** or **Interval**). The case of Ordinal variable is slightly anomalous. If the Independent variable (IV) is Ordinal, then it is perfectly safe to treat it as if it were an Interval variable. It is only when the Dependent variable (DV), the variable we are trying to explain, is an Ordinal that we need to take it into account.

Therefore, there are 2×3 different combinations of two variables, shown in Table 7.1. Each of these leads to a different measure of central tendency, a different set of graphs and, as we see now, a different statistical test. However, there is still a simple unity in the system.

- If the DV is Interval, then the IV has the role of predicting the mean value of the DV.
- If the DV is Ordinal, then the IV has the role of predicting the median value of the DV.
- If the DV is Categorical, then the IV has the role of predicting which category is most likely.

Now, we just need to look at the different cells in Table 7.1 and see what the name of the test is for each combination of variables. Each test follows very simple rules.

Table 7.1   Variable combinations and statistical tests.

There are five typical statistical procedures or tests that are used for two variable hypotheses, plus extras for Ordinal DVs. Cat2 is used as shorthand for Categorical variable with two groups. Cat3+ is used as shorthand for Categorical variable with three or more groups.

		IV		
		Categorical		**Interval**
DV	Interval	t-test (*Cat2*) ANOVA (*Cat3*+)	***Between or within*** ***Between or within***	Pearson correlation
	Ordinal	Mann-Whitney U (*Cat2*) Wilcoxon signed rank (*Cat2*) Kruskal-Wallace (*Cat3*+) Friedman (*Cat3*+)	***Between*** ***Within*** ***Between*** ***Within***	Spearman correlation
	Categorical	Chi-square test of independence		Logistic regression

7.2.1 CATEGORICAL (TWO CATEGORIES) → INTERVAL (T-TEST)

First, we consider the case of a Categorical variable (with two categories) predicting an Interval variable. All the details that are needed are placed in Table 7.2. This is the test that suits our RiskTaker? → Exam Grade example in Section 7.1.

Table 7.2   The details for a t-test.

Note that n = sample size. Results should also quote the mean (M) and standard deviation (SD) for each group.

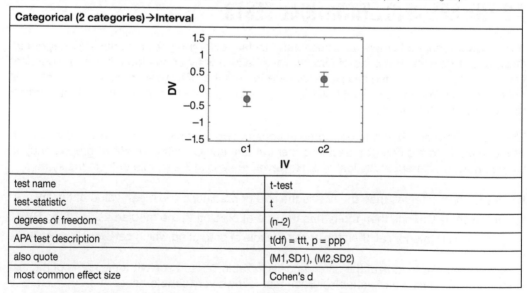

Categorical (2 categories)→Interval	
test name	t-test
test-statistic	t
degrees of freedom	(n–2)
APA test description	t(df) = ttt, p = ppp
also quote	(M1,SD1), (M2,SD2)
most common effect size	Cohen's d

When the Categorical IV has only two different categories the route to the p-value is via the t-statistic and the degrees of freedom. This procedure is called a t-test.

EXAMPLE

For our RiskTaker? → ExamGrade idea, imagine we are looking back at our sample with 42 participants, and with the result of effect size r=0.12, t=−0.473, p=0.639. To present this in the typical APA format, it should be written in a similar form to this (the APA format has been underlined):

An independent samples t-test found no significant difference of exam grades between non-risk-takers (M=66.7, SD=7.18) and risk-takers (M=65.6, SD=7.38), t(40)=−0.473, p=0.639.

Note that the APA specifies that the p-value is given without the first zero (i.e. p=.639). We find this an unnecessary confusion.

WHAT IS THE T-STATISTIC?

We saw that the t-statistic is a combination of the sample effect size and the standard error of that effect size. The normal way to do this is to use the difference in means for the two groups as the effect size (this is the natural effect size). The difference in means is twice the **standard deviation** of the group means. The standard error of the effect size is found from the standard deviation within the groups (differences between each data point and its respective group mean) and the square root of the number of data points.

So, the t-statistic is

$$\frac{\textit{difference in means}}{\textit{standard error}\,(\textit{difference})}$$

which becomes:

$$\frac{sd\,(\textit{group means})}{sd\,(\textit{residuals})} \times sqrt\,(n)$$

This new formula for t-statistic will be useful later on. It involves a ratio of two standard deviations: the top one being the effect of the IV, and the bottom one being what is left over in the data.

NOTES ON T-TESTS

The t-test is used when you have a Categorical IV with two groups. However, recall that with a Categorical IV we can divide participants into two separate groups (a **between-participants design**), or sometimes we can use all participants in both groups (a **within-participants design**). For example, our typical RiskTaker? hypothesis uses a between-groups design with

Table 7.3   The details for a one-way ANOVA.

Note that n = sample size; ng = no. of groups. Results should also quote the mean (MN) and standard deviation (SD) of each group. See that the test creates a test-statistic, which has been given its own unique name of 'F'. This isn't a maths thing; it's named after Sir Ronald Fisher, who came up with the test in the first place.

Categorical (3+ categories)→Interval	
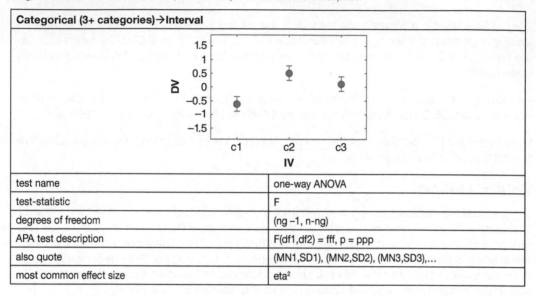	
test name	one-way ANOVA
test-statistic	F
degrees of freedom	(ng −1, n-ng)
APA test description	F(df1,df2) = fff, p = ppp
also quote	(MN1,SD1), (MN2,SD2), (MN3,SD3),…
most common effect size	eta^2

a 'yes' group and a 'no' group. This is a small thing to take note of when doing a t-test, as the procedures differ very slightly. When using statistical software, opt for the *independent* t-test if there are two separate groups, and the *paired* t-test if you are comparing data from the same participants tested in both situations. The paired t-test takes into account the reduced unknown **variability** (individual differences) of using the same participants in each group in its calculations.

7.2.2 CATEGORICAL (3+ CATEGORIES) → INTERVAL (ONE-WAY ANOVA)

Now we consider the case of a Categorical variable (with more than two categories) predicting an Interval variable. All the details that are needed are shown in Table 7.3. This would suit our RiskTaker? example if we used three possible values for RiskTaker?: yes, no, or sometimes.

For the case where the IV has more than two categories or groups, the t-test isn't helpful because it is designed to compare two groups. In theory, we could do t-tests between each possible pair of groups in the data. That is unsatisfactory, partly because it is just too much effort and partly because each time we do a t-test, we have a fresh chance of making a **Type I error** (getting a false positive). If we have four groups, then there are six different combinations of groups that we could test using t-tests. On each of those six tests there is a separate chance that we will make a Type I error. So the chance that that there is a Type I error somewhere in among those six tests is much higher than 0.05. In fact, it is 0.265 – more than five times as high.

To avoid multiple t-tests, we do an **omnibus test** of the null hypothesis that all group means are the same. It is called an omnibus ('for all') test because it is a test that looks at all the group means together. If that test turns out to be statistically significant, meaning there is a significant difference somewhere, then we can go back and do individual t-tests to see which group means are different from which. These are called **post hoc** tests: they are typically just an additional output you can choose when using statistical software. We've got more information about post hoc testing in our online resources.

This is explained in further detail online

The procedure for the omnibus test is called a **one-way ANOVA** (analysis of variance). As with the t-test, there is a computationally convenient route to the p-value. This time the test statistic is called the F-statistic, to distinguish it from the t-statistic of a t-test.

WHAT IS THE F-STATISTIC?

We can see the data points in our sample as a product of two types of effect: one due to the group mean for the group they belong to (and therefore due to the IV) and one due to random factors within their group (i.e. the **residual**). In doing this, we are splitting the **variance** of the whole sample into two independent types: part of the variance that we can attribute to the IV and the part that we cannot.

Variance is the square of the standard deviation, which we very briefly mentioned in Chapter 3 – so it is a measure of how much variability there is. Variance is also the sum of squared deviations divided by the number of data points. If we have two or more independent sources of variance (variability) combined in our sample or population, then their joint effect has a variance that is just the sum of the separate variances.

At its heart, the ANOVA is just a comparison of those two parts of the variance in the DV, taking into account how many participants there are and how many different groups they are split into. If our variance that is attributed to the IV is high, then we have a strong effect, a large value for our F-statistic and, depending on our sample size, perhaps a small p-value.

To understand how we compare these types of variance, consider these three points:

1. Total variance: the set of data points we have in our sample have a variance. This is called the total variance.

2. Variance explained: imagine that each data point is set to the value of its group mean: these new data points have a new variance, which will be less than the original data points. This new variance is the variance explained by the effect of the IV.

3. Variance unexplained: now we can look at just the difference between these new data points and the original data. This set of values has a variance, which is also less than the variance of the original data points. This third variance is the variance unexplained, which is also called the variance of the **residuals**.

The F-statistic is proportional to the ratio of variance explained divided by variance unexplained. There is a corresponding F distribution that shows how the values of F are distributed for the population of the null hypothesis, in the same way there is a t distribution. This F distribution can be used to find the p-value. To convert the F-statistic to a p-value we need two different degrees of freedom (number of groups − 1, number of participants − number of groups).

Recall from the previous section that the t-statistic involved the ratio of two standard deviations: due to IV and residuals. *If we squared the t-statistic, it would involve the same ratio of variances as is the F-statistic.*

NOTES ON ONE-WAY ANOVA

The one-way ANOVA is used when there is a Categorical IV with three or more groups. In the same manner as t-tests, there are slightly different tests for a between-participants design versus a within-groups design. A within-participants design is called a one-way *repeated measures* ANOVA.

The most commonly used **effect size** for a Categorical IV (three or more categories, or Cat3 in shorthand) → Interval DV situation is η^2 (pronounced eta squared: η is a Greek letter). It is equivalent to the normalised effect size squared and so gives a simple proportion of the amount of variance explained by the IV. Typically, anything less than 0.04 suggests a very small effect (low variance explained) and anything above 0.36 suggests a large effect (more variance explained). Sometimes a cousin, partial η^2, is quoted. This is a version of η^2 that is closer to the standardised effect size.

7.2.3 INTERVAL → INTERVAL (CORRELATION)

There is one more case where the DV is an Interval variable: where the IV is also Interval. All the details are summarised in Table 7.4.

As with the t-test and ANOVA, there is a computationally convenient route to the p-value. This time the test-statistic is called the **r-statistic** and the procedure is called **Pearson correlation** (which is often shortened to correlation, but there are actually many different types of correlation).

Table 7.4   The details for a Pearson correlation.

Note that n=sample size. Results should also quote the mean (M) and standard deviation (SD) of each variable.

Interval→Interval	
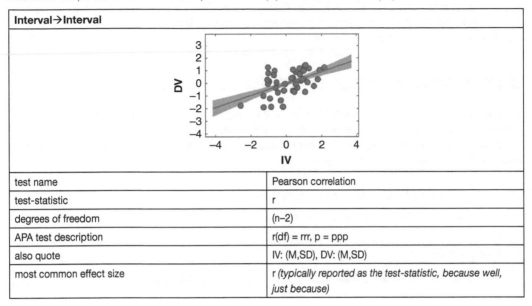	
test name	Pearson correlation
test-statistic	r
degrees of freedom	(n–2)
APA test description	r(df) = rrr, p = ppp
also quote	IV: (M,SD), DV: (M,SD)
most common effect size	r *(typically reported as the test-statistic, because well, just because)*

WHAT IS THE R-STATISTIC?

We saw that the ANOVA split the variance in the data into some due to the IV and some left over (the variability within the groups). The same idea can be used here, just with a modification because the IV is continuous: the regression line allows us to calculate an expected value for each participant based on the value of their IV. The variance of these predicted values is the variance explained by the IV.

As we think about the variance in our sample, we have again our three familiar quantities: total variance; variance explained from the value predicted by the IV; and variance unexplained by the prediction from the overall mean. We could therefore calculate F or t in the same way as we did for a Categorical IV and get our value of p. By convention, however, we do something a little different, but the idea is similar. Instead of comparing variance explained with variance unexplained, we compare it with the total variance. The ratio of variance explained to total variance is a quantity that goes from zero (no variance explained, i.e. no relationship) to one (all the variance is explained). The square root of this quantity is called the **correlation coefficient** and is given the symbol r.

If you have been following the pattern so far, you will be expecting an *r* distribution to go along with the *t* distribution and the *F* distribution. There isn't one. The r-statistic isn't actually the test-statistic; it is converted to *t* which is then used as the real test-statistic. It is converted to *t* by dividing it by its standard error. However, conventionally *r* is reported as the final outcome – just one of those traditions.

7.2.4 CATEGORICAL CATEGORICAL (CHI-SQUARE TEST OF INDEPENDENCE)

We now switch to the situation where the DV is a Categorical variable. This brings an important difference to the situation. With an Interval DV which has scale values, we could work in terms of the difference between the value for each individual and the mean value or regression value. Now, we think in terms of frequencies.

Table 7.5   The details for a chi-square test of independence.

Note that df = (ng1–1) × (ng2–1) and ng1 = no groups in IV; ng2 = no groups in DV. The contingency table (an example is given in this section) should also typically be provided.

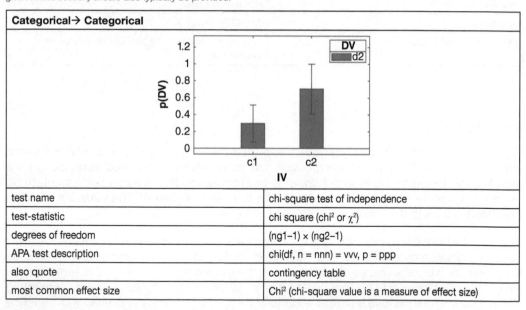

Categorical→ Categorical	
test name	chi-square test of independence
test-statistic	chi square (chi^2 or χ^2)
degrees of freedom	(ng1–1) × (ng2–1)
APA test description	chi(df, n = nnn) = vvv, p = ppp
also quote	contingency table
most common effect size	Chi^2 (chi-square value is a measure of effect size)

The procedure for null hypothesis testing a Categorical → Categorical hypothesis is called a chi-square test. This time the test-statistic is called the chi-square statistic (typically just referred to as the chi-square, or chi-square value and often given as the Greek symbol χ^2).

The null hypothesis is that there is no effect of the IV on the DV. Converted into frequencies, this says that the relative frequencies of the different categories of the DV are the same in all the different categories of the IV: we wouldn't expect to see a noticeable pattern if we plotted a graph if the null hypothesis was true.

Let's use a concrete example: IV=RiskTaker? and DV=Pass?, both with values yes or no. We are asking the question: is the proportion of people who pass the exam different among risk-takers than it is among non-risk-takers? Note that we are not asking anything about the proportion of people who pass, just about whether that proportion depends on whether you are a risk-taker or not.

If there is a relationship between the IV and the DV, then the relative frequencies of the various categories of the DV will be different for different categories of the IV. If we treat our two variables as Categorical (RiskTaker? and Pass?), then a relationship between these two would result in a higher proportion of people in the yes RiskTaker? category belonging to the yes Pass? category than is found in the no RiskTaker? category. Visualise this as a set of cells with the count of participants in each – see Table 7.6. This table of cells is called a **contingency table**. In this case it is 2×2, but it would have other sizes if either of the variables had more categories.

Table 7.6   Contingency table 1.

This table has the counts for each combination of the categories of the two variables. It is called a contingency table. For this example, n=63.

Observed data	RiskTaker? no	RiskTaker? yes
Pass? yes	17	31
Pass? no	8	7

The null hypothesis is that the proportions of exam passes in the two columns are the same – both at 76%, which is how many students passed the exam regardless of their value for the IV. That means that we can calculate a new table that has the counts we should expect if the null hypothesis is exactly true. This is shown in Table 7.7.

Table 7.7   Contingency table 2.

This is a contingency table for expected data (to be distinguished from the observed data in Table 7.6). These values come from the percentage calculated above: if the null hypothesis was true, 76% would be expected to pass from each group of RiskTaker?: 76% of non-RiskTakers is 19, and 76% of yes RiskTakers is 28.9. While physically you can't have 28.9 of a person, mathematically speaking, this is what the calculations require.

Expected data	RiskTaker? no	RiskTaker? yes
Pass? yes	19	28.9
Pass? no	6	9.1

Then the question becomes this: are the observed frequencies (Table 7.6) sufficiently different from the expected frequencies (Table 7.7) that we should reject the null hypothesis? As before, we can use a computationally convenient route, this time with a chi-square statistic, often denoted with the Greek symbol χ^2.

WHAT IS THE χ^2 STATISTIC?

The χ^2-statistic compares the observed counts in the contingency table with the counts we would expect if the null hypothesis were true (so very often the expected value is simply equal counts per category), using this formula:

$$\chi^2 = \sum \frac{(observed - expected)^2}{expected}$$

The bigger this number, the stronger the effect is. If everyone is in the top right or bottom left cell, then the theoretical maximum value of χ^2 is reached, which is just the number of participants (when they are evenly divided in the individual categories).

The χ^2 value that we calculate from our sample is then compared with the distribution of χ^2 values that are expected from the null hypothesis and a value for p is obtained. To make this comparison we have to say how many degrees of freedom are left. When we are dealing with counts, then what matters for the degrees of freedom is the number of categories, not the number of participants. We have two categories for RiskTaker?, and so if we only need to say how many one of the two categories has.

The degrees of freedom for a contingency table and a chi-square test is this:

   (number of rows – 1) × (number of columns – 1)

The chi-square test needs the χ^2 value, the degrees of freedom and the total number of participants – then it can calculate a p-value. When we report a chi-square test, we must give all of these quantities: for example in APA format, χ^2 (1,n = 42)= 6.11, p = 0.0134.

Although the details are quite different, especially that we are using counts not means, the process is a direct parallel to the process for a t-test.

7.2.5 INTERVAL $\rightarrow$ CATEGORICAL (LOGISTIC REGRESSION)

The final case we must attend to is an extension of the ideas in Categorical→ Categorical, but for an Interval IV.

When the IV is Interval and the DV is Categorical, the null hypothesis test is called **logistic regression**. The test-statistic is once again χ^2. Logistic regression is a blanket term for Interval → Categorical testing, and you will find some variations on the internet

Table 7.8   The details for a logistic regression.

Note that k = (n2–1) and n2 = no groups in DV.

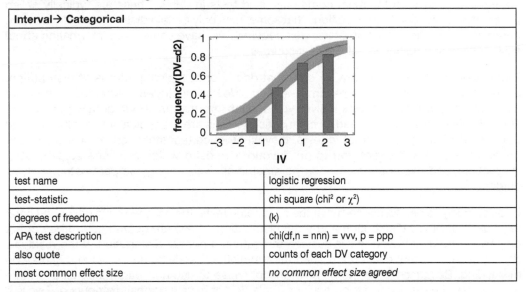

Interval→ Categorical		
test name	logistic regression	
test-statistic	chi square (chi² or χ^2)	
degrees of freedom	(k)	
APA test description	chi(df,n = nnn) = vvv, p = ppp	
also quote	counts of each DV category	
most common effect size	*no common effect size agreed*	

for different numbers of categories (all of which contain logistic regression in the name somewhere). We use the term here to describe a Categorical DV with any number of categories (two or more).

In the Categorical → Categorical section previously, we compared a set of observed and expected frequencies. We used a chi-square test to reveal whether or not the proportion varied significantly between categories of the IV. In this case, we have an Interval IV which is continuous. The idea is the same in principle: we are interested in the proportion of participants falling in different categories of the DV – and specifically whether that proportion varies with the IV. Logistic regression uses the IV to predict the probability that the DV is one or the other category. So, although it may have been that a person had a 75% chance of passing the exam because of their relatively high risk-taking score, the only thing we can observe is whether they did pass or not.

It is still possible to find a best-fitting S-shaped line for the data. That best-fitting line is compared with the null hypothesis by using the χ^2 again. The line tells us what the expected frequency of each category should be for any value of the IV we need. Our data tell us what the observed frequency is for the values of the IV in our sample. So, we have expected and observed counts as before and we use these two to get χ^2 as before. And we report it in just the same way.

7.2.6 NOTES ON ORDINAL TESTS

You can find guides for non-parametric tests alongside the guides for parametric tests

We have now covered the most commonly used tests in detail. These are typically called **parametric** tests, due to assumptions that sometimes only certain distributions of data were appropriate – particular 'parameters' were required. We have some more information about assumptions and testing in our online resources.

Tests designed for ordinal data, or data that does not fit typical patterns of distribution, are historically known as **non-parametric** tests. We have included the names of the most common ones in Table 7.1, which gives you enough information about them to get started. They all rely on medians instead of means, as medians are the typical value for an ordinal data set. And just like parametric tests, they all produce test statistics and p-values. Our online resources will direct you to our favourite website which provides step-by-step instructions and explanations for non-parametric analysis, alongside parametric analysis guides.

It has sometimes been a concern that the parametric tests (the ones we have described here) rely heavily on the t distribution and the F distribution. These are guaranteed to be correct only when the distribution of residuals in the data is a normal distribution. If the residuals do not have a normal distribution, then the t-statistic, F-statistic and p-value might all be misleading. Because of this, it has been thought wise to use non-parametric tests if there is a risk that the residuals in a particular sample do not have a normal distribution. This is a shame, because non-parametric tests typically give a larger p-value than parametric tests when given the same data.

Actually, in practice the effects of a non-normal distribution of residuals rarely has any noticeable consequence and the advice is nearly always a little too cautious. Moreover, since the distribution of values for the residual depends much more on the distribution of values for the DV than it does on the IV, it is really only the DV that needs some attention. And, it is quite possible for the DV itself to be skewed or not normal in some other way, but the residuals to be perfectly normal. If you are considering a non-parametric test because you are concerned about distributions of values, then you may find it is actually fine to choose a parametric option.

7.3 A LITTLE EXTRA KNOWLEDGE

If you take data that would normally go into a t-test and by accident (or on purpose) put them into an ANOVA, you will get the right p-value. Why? Because the F-statistic is just the t-statistic squared.

Actually, if you code the two categories in the IV for a t-test as two different numbers (say 42 and 65), then a correlation between a column of those 42s or 65s and a column with the DV values will also give you the right p-value. Why? Because correlation uses the t-statistic behind the scenes.

You will also see that in every table for a statistical test we have included the most commonly reported effect size. We are still of the opinion that r is the most useful effect size, and most of the other values provided could be converted to r to make results easier to compare and translate to an audience.

THE BIG PICTURE

We have kept the details in this chapter to a minimum for you to understand. Once upon a time, researchers had to calculate all these test values by hand or use books of tables to get there. Those days are gone now and we can rely on software to do all the work. So, it is now much more important to understand what a t-test is (for example), so you will know what it tells you.

SELECTING A TEST IS EASY

1. Use the IV versus DV 2×2 table to look it up: we have included the most basic one below (see Table 7.9), or you can refer back to Table 7.1 earlier in this chapter.

2. This is not a decision that requires any kind of work: the type of your variables completely determines what test to do. It is just a case of looking it up. Literally.

3. Often non-parametric tests are the result of over-cautiousness: even if your data do not look normally distributed, often the pattern of the residuals still is.

DOING A TEST IS EASY

1. We need a test-statistic (such as t, F, χ^2). This is just an intermediate calculation to get to the p-value.

2. We also need the degrees of freedom.

   a. Degrees of freedom are a count of how much explaining of the data remains. To start with, we have n data points to explain. Each time we calculate a new statistic, such as a group mean, we have done one piece of explaining and the degree of freedom goes down by 1.

REPORTING RESULTS IS EASY

1. In psychology the 'APA' style is normally used. We have included the relevant resources here, which can also be found all over the internet.

2. It should be said that we, the authors, think that the APA have actually got this wrong and that it is more important to write down what should be the r-family effect size, sample size and (maybe) the p-value. However, it is straightforward enough to include effect sizes with your results, alongside an APA-style write-up of your null hypothesis tests, to keep everyone happy until psychology moves forwards…

Table 7.9   Cheat sheet for two-variable tests – a summary of the specific details for the tests for each type of two variable hypothesis.

		IV	
		Categorical	Interval
DV	Categorical	Bar chart Contingency table chi-sqr independence chi2(dof,n = ??) = ??, p = ??	Bar/line hybrid logistic coefficients logistic regression chi2(dof,n = ??)= ??, p = ??
	Interval	Line graph Group means and sds t-test or ANOVA t(dof)= ??, p = ?? or F(dof1,dof2) = ??, p = ??	Scatter plot regression coefficients correlation r(dof) = ??,p = ??

YOUR TURN

FILL IN THE GAPS IN THESE SENTENCES:

1. A Pearson correlation is used when the IV is .... type and the DV is .... type

2. A t-test compares two ....

3. An F-statistic is the result of a ....

4. A Categorical IV (3 categories) and a Categorical DV lead to a .... test.

5. APA format is used to ....

ANOTHER ACTIVITY AND ANSWERS ARE AVAILABLE ONLINE

YOUR SPACE

 **REFERENCES AND FURTHER READING**

Nuijten, M.B., Hartgerink, C.H.J., van Assen M.A.L.M. et al. (2016) The prevalence of statistical reporting errors in psychology (1985–2013). *Behavioural Research Methods* 48: 1205.

This paper is easy to read. It shows how often statistical analyses are published with errors in them. We thought you might enjoy this.

THERE ARE MORE ACTIVITIES AND A SHORT
SUMMARY VIDEO FOR THIS CHAPTER AVAILABLE AT:
HTTPS://STUDY.SAGEPUB.COM/STATISTICSFORPSYCHOLOGY

INTERMEZZO 2

Tails — One, Two or Many?

We saw in Chapter 6 that the sampling distribution for a population with zero effect size allows us to know what the distribution of hypothetical sample effect sizes should be, if the null hypothesis were true. We then say that if our actual sample effect size is far enough out into the tails of this distribution of null hypothesis effect sizes (and therefore making it unlikely to have come from this population where the null hypothesis is true), we can reject the null hypothesis. The default approach is where we just require our sample effect size to be far enough out to be satisfied with the result.

IM2.1 EXPLAINING TAILS

IM2.1.1 T-TESTS

Some combinations of variables result in a t-test. In these cases, the sample effect size is converted to a **t-statistic** and that is compared with the Student's *t* distribution to calculate the p-value. If the t-statistic lies in the extreme 5% of the distribution, then we can reject the null hypothesis (as seen in Chapter 7). We will call this 5% area of the distribution the critical 5%. This happens in two specific cases that we have looked at so far:

1. IV is a Categorical variable with two categories, DV is Interval.

2. IV is an Interval variable, DV is Interval.

Recall from Chapter 7 that despite two Interval variables commanding a Pearson correlation, the *r* outcome technically becomes a *t*-statistic – people just don't report this step. For both of the combinations of variables listed above, both the effect size and the t-statistic will have a clear and unambiguous sign: positive or negative.

The Student's *t* distribution has two tails, corresponding to the two signs that *t* can have. In the default approach, called **two-tailed testing**, if the t-statistic we calculate from our sample lies far enough out *in either* tail, then we reject the null hypothesis. This means that the t-statistic must lie in either the most extreme 2.5% of the positive tail or the most extreme 2.5% of the negative tail.

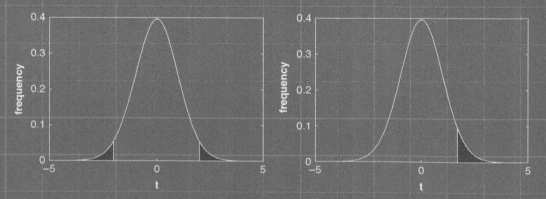

Figure Im2.1   The Student's *t* distribution.

This figure shows the Student's t *distribution for the case where the sample size is 42. On the left, it is set up so that the critical 5% covers both tails (two-tailed testing); on the right, it just covers the positive tail (one-tailed testing).*

Sometimes, we can have good reason for not expecting and not being interested in one of the two effect size signs. We may have strong reasons for expecting that the effect we are studying will have an effect size with a positive sign. We may have a hypothesis that only makes sense for a negative effect size. In these cases, we can decide to switch to **one-tailed testing** *before we collect the data*. When we do this, we move all of the critical 5% into the relevant tail of the distribution. When we do this, we are committing ourselves to a very particular situation. If we use a one-tailed test for a positive sign and our sample effect size is strongly negative, so negative that with a two-tailed test we would get a tiny p-value, then we must now regard it as a failure to reject the null hypothesis.

This is exactly like betting: you have your 5% and you can go for the relatively non-committal two-tailed test (where an outcome in either direction is acceptable) or you can be specific and go for a one-tailed test. In the one-tailed case we place the whole 5% where we expect the sample effect size to lie, increasing our chances of getting a significant result if our expectations are right.

IM2.1.2 F-TESTS

If we have a Categorical IV with three or more categories, then it is not so clear what would count as a positive or a negative effect. To have a sign of effect size here we need to find a way of ordering the categories. The F-statistic that we calculate in this situation has no sign: it is just a measure of how different the group means are, not which is the largest or smallest. This is why the F-test in an ANOVA is called an **omnibus** test: all possible patterns of effect are treated equally. It is the equivalent to a two-tailed test. As a side note, the *F* distribution only has one tail anyway (Figure Im2.2), so we can't pick our preferred tail.

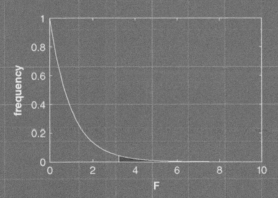

Figure Im2.2   The *F* distribution.

The extreme 5% is shaded. Any result falling in this region would be considered statistically significant.

This suggests that the benefits of one-tailed testing are not available for hypotheses that involve Categorical variables with three or more categories. In the next section, we will see how that can be overcome.

IM2.2 CONTRASTS: DIRECTIONAL TESTS

One way of thinking about the one-tailed t-test is that it determines a specific direction that the effect should go in. For example, a one-tailed test might test the hypothesis that risk-takers do better than non-risk-takers in exams. We would call this a directional hypothesis: we are saying what direction the effect is hypothesised to go in. With this thought, we can see that there are only two directions when the Categorical IV has only two categories: the effect is either positive or it is negative, and the two tails of the t distribution correspond to these two directions. One-tailed testing is directional testing.

We can start with a Categorical variable with two categories, which we will call C1 and C2. Now look at this expression:

$$\text{mean(DV} \mid \text{IV} = \text{C1)} > \text{mean(DV} \mid \text{IV} = \text{C2)}$$

where the vertical line can be read as 'when'. So, in plain language this says:

the mean value of DV when the IV equals C1

is greater than (>)

the mean value of DV when the IV equals C2

This is a one-tailed hypothesis, spelled out very laboriously. We are going to massively abbreviate it to:

C1 > C2

now that we have explained what it means. Now the two possible directions or tails can be written down as:

C1 > C2

C2 > C1

This way of thinking can be applied to Categorical IVs with three or more categories. Consider the case with three categories. If we call the three categories C1, C2 and C3, then there are six possible directions:

C1 > C2 > C3

C1 > C3 > C2

C2 > C1 > C3

C2 > C3 > C1

C3 > C1 > C2

C3 > C2 > C1

It is as if this hypothesis, where the IV has three categories, has six possible tails. However, as we have just discussed in Section Im2.1.2, we can't just pick a direction with the F-test as it is essentially directionless – it only has one tail to start with. So we need to do something to modify our data first.

IM2.2.1 DIRECTIONAL TESTS AS CORRELATIONS

Let's suppose that the direction we are interested in is specifically this one (just chosen randomly):

$$C2 > C1 > C3$$

Now let's imagine that in our data we replace the occurrences of the value C2 with the number 3, C1 with the number 2 and C3 with the number 1. To make it clear:

$$C2 = 3$$

$$C1 = 2$$

$$C3 = 1$$

Before doing this, the value for each participant was one of C1, C2, C3. Now, after we have done this, the values are one of 2, 3, 1. The numbers we are substituting in are just the order we expect the group means to follow, with the highest value assigned to the group that we think has the highest mean. Notice that we have converted our Categorical IV into a numeric DV by turning the categories into ordered numbers based on how we expect their effect on the DV to be ranked. C2 gets a 3 because we expect it to have the greatest effect on the DV, and so on.

We can then do something very simple. We just do a correlation between this new variable and the DV and subject the outcome to a one-tailed test. If the correlation is positive and that test is significant, we can reject the null hypothesis. If the order of the means for the different categories is different from the one we are interested in, the correlation won't be strongly positive. This conversion and correlation process is called a **contrast test** and it is how we do a directional test when we don't have a t-test.

IM2.3 SUMMARY

Sometimes we have a good reason for expecting the effect we are studying to go in one specific direction. In that situation, we can build a directional hypothesis: one that includes the effect sign. When we do so, we are duty bound to treat any result that doesn't conform to the direction as a failure to reject the null hypothesis, even if it would be wildly significant.

The benefit of one-tailed testing is quite dramatic: the p-value is halved. The reason for this is simply that we are able to ignore one of the tails. Let's say, for example, we have an effect size of 0.3. When we do a two-tailed test, then we are asking what the probability is of the null hypothesis producing sample effect sizes that are *either* (i) greater than +0.3 *or* (ii) less than -0.3. When we do a one-tailed test we are only asking about one of the two – so half the probability.

We can do this when we are using the t-test but not when we are using the F-test. However, we can always convert a Categorical variable into an Interval or Ordinal one by choosing a direction for the effect. Then we can use correlation (which is based on the t distribution) to achieve the same benefit as one-tailed testing.

REFERENCES AND FURTHER READING

Rosenthal, R., Rosnow, R.L. & Rubin, D.B. (2000) *Contrasts and Effect Sizes in Behavioral Research: A Correlational Approach.* Cambridge: Cambridge University Press.

The classic text.

CHAPTER

08

MINIMISING UNCERTAINTY: RESEARCH DESIGN

RESEARCH DESIGN: I DID IT MY WAY (AND HERE'S WHY)

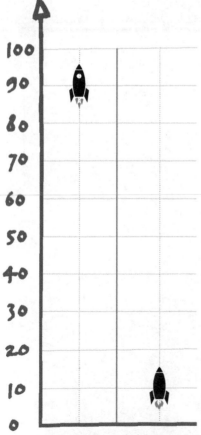

When we are trying to answer a research question, we must use evidence – for our purposes that is data. A sample doesn't simply happen and give us data: we need to go out and actively get it. In order to collect that data and make sure that it answers our research question, we use a research design to plan the process. The research design is a set of decisions that we make about how to obtain our data.

It may seem like we are coming to the question of how to obtain data quite late in the day: after all, the data we were analysing in the previous chapters had to come from somewhere. However, in order to create a good design, it is important to understand how the decisions we must make matter. All the previous chapters provide key building blocks that we will use now to explore how they shape research design.

In Chapter 5, we examined the concept of uncertainty in research: the gap between the knowledge about our sample and the knowledge it gives us about the population. As we saw, uncertainty always exists when we take a sample and use it as a guide to the population, and we use statistics to estimate that uncertainty. The amount of uncertainty is strongly influenced by the way in which we get our data: our research design.

Once we have data, the outcome is fixed: there is nothing further we can do to reduce the uncertainty. For that reason, it is very important to develop the research design carefully before beginning to collect data. We will look at research design in depth in this chapter and the next two chapters. Just like Chapter 5, this chapter begins with theory that will help you understand *why* your research decisions are important.

There is really only one new idea in this chapter. We have already seen in Chapter 5 how we can calculate how much uncertainty a result has. We are now going to take that a step further and compare the uncertainty that would be produced by different research designs, *before* we do the research, to see which design is likely to lead to the lowest uncertainty.

Because we are building a further understanding of uncertainty in this chapter and the next two, just like Chapter 5 there are lots of diagrams and graphs that illustrate uncertainty using various formulae. These are not something you would expect to produce for yourself. However, if you are interested, you will find details online.

8.1 A BRIEF RECAP OF UNCERTAINTY

The purpose of doing research is to find out something new and useful, and then to persuade others to accept it. We know that the process of using a sample from a population introduces an unavoidable uncertainty – called **sampling error** – and that uncertainty can, if large enough, mean that either we don't succeed in finding out something new and useful, or we fail to persuade others. This is the fundamental reason it is important to care about research design: it is how we manage the uncertainty as much as possible.

For example, suppose we had done the research and we had found that there is a 50–60% chance that risk-taking affects exam grades. This would mean that there is a 40–50% chance it doesn't. With high uncertainty, we are very unlikely to persuade anyone else that we have found something that is worth knowing. We would probably be looking at our data with hindsight saying 'if only…' about all the things we could have done better. So, we need to approach the research with an understanding of which decisions we can make to help avoid such an uncertain outcome.

Even before we do any research, we can explore the range of possible outcomes to refine how we do our research. Doing this, we will make sure that our result is not more uncertain than necessary. It's quite like having the hindsight before the event. A bit of careful thought and planning can considerably improve our chances of having a clear result that will persuade others.

8.2 PLANNING AHEAD: PREDICTIONS

The first and most important ingredient we need to make a research design is a good prediction. Let's start with our RiskTaker and ExamGrade scenario. In Chapter 5 we simply said that the population had an effect size of 0.3 and explored what that would mean for samples. This time we are going to make a prediction about the relationship between the variables RiskTaker and ExamGrade: we predict that the effect size will be 0.25 and we will call this the predicted effect size. Prediction is just a formal word for our expectation of what may turn out to be true. We may have reached this prediction because of a string of published research that leads us to it, or it may be a wild guess. The difference between making a prediction and what we were doing in Chapter 5 isn't very much. Before, we were just saying what the population effect size was; now we are saying what we predict it is.

Much more importantly, in Chapter 5 we just said that the design for the sample was going to be 42 participants obtained randomly from the population (for no particularly good reason). Now, we are going to ask what design would be best. To do that, we will look at uncertainty just as in Chapter 5, but for the purpose of finding out what design gives us the best outcome. This is using our prediction to plan ahead: to make sure that whatever result we get is as good as we can feasibly achieve.

Table 8.1   Two different types of research question.

Research asks two different sorts of question and the approach to uncertainty and design reflects the differences. For both questions, our principle objective must be to find an accurate and correct answer. Although null hypothesis testing often generates a desire to get a statistically significant result, we must try to avoid being controlled by that desire – even if that means our p-value isn't below 0.05.

	Effect existence?	**Effect strength?**
Two types of question	Research commonly asks a question about whether an effect exists or not (does RiskTaking? affect ExamGrade?).	It's much more interesting to ask to what extent one variable affects another.
Two types of answer	This is answered with null hypothesis testing to say whether the sample effect size is large enough.	The sample effect size is used to estimate the population effect size.
Two types of uncertainty	We saw in Chapter 6 that the uncertainty in our result is whether we have made a Type I or Type II error.	We saw in Chapter 5 that the uncertainty is how wide the likelihood function is.
Two types of tool		
	Sampling distributions shows us what samples we should expect from a population. The sampling distribution from the null hypothesis population (behind), and the real population (in front), combined show us what to expect. The null hypothesis distribution divides the full range of sample effect sizes into two: significant (shaded) and not significant (unshaded). A Type I error is when our sample falls in the shaded area of the back distribution. A Type II error is when our sample falls in the front shaded area. Our uncertainty in this case corresponds to the combined shaded areas in the two sampling distributions.	**Likelihood functions** show us what populations could have given us our sample. The likelihood function for a sample effect size. Our uncertainty in this case is just the width of the distribution.

We start with our prediction and then explore what research design will give us the lowest amount of uncertainty in our result. This means that our focus is now not on what the uncertainty will be, as it was in Chapter 5, but on what we can do to reduce it.

8.2.1 UNCERTAINTY ABOUT EFFECT STRENGTH

If we are asking a question about the strength of an effect, then we are interested in the sample effect size and the amount of uncertainty associated with that as an estimate of the population effect size. Once we have a sample, we can use it to make a likelihood function that shows us how likely different population effect sizes are: it encapsulates all the information we have in our sample about the population effect size. Our uncertainty here is measured by the spread of the likelihood function: a wide function would mean much uncertainty about the population, like the left panel of Figure 8.1, whereas a narrow function would mean little uncertainty, like the right panel.

Recall that the **standard error** is the standard deviation (width) of the sampling distribution: the wider the sampling distribution, the larger the standard error. Because the likelihood function is built up from many sampling distributions, the size of the standard error also determines how wide the likelihood function is: a bigger standard error would result in a wider range of potential population effect sizes and more uncertainty.

A good design will try to keep the width of the likelihood function small by making decisions that will lead to a small standard error. In the next two chapters, we will be exploring specific decisions about research design that influence the size of the standard error and therefore the width of the likelihood function.

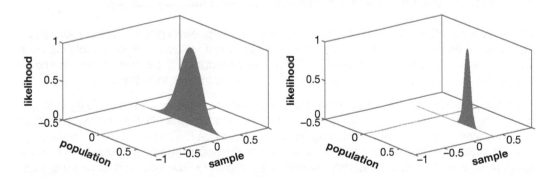

Figure 8.1   Two examples of likelihood functions with very different widths.

The right version has much less uncertainty than the left version. There is less uncertainty because we have tried to minimise the standard error by using a larger sample size.

How can we make the standard error smaller? When we are using normalised effect sizes (the r-family), as we do throughout this book, the standard error of a sample effect size has a simple formula that applies in most cases:

$$se(r) = sqrt\left(\frac{1 - r^2}{n - 2}\right)$$

where r is the sample effect size and n is the sample size (number of participants)

Don't worry about this formula: it's only here so that we can use it to understand how to reduce our standard error by looking at the various elements of it. These are the important things about the formula:

- The first thing is that we can ignore the square root part of it. Anything that makes a number smaller also makes its square root smaller. This means we can just focus on the bit inside the brackets.
- Inside the brackets there is a fraction with a top part $(1 - r^2)$ and a bottom part $(n - 2)$.
- There are two ways we can make a fraction smaller: we can make the top smaller (1/3 is smaller than 2/3) or the bottom larger (1/10 is smaller than 1/3).

So, if we want to make the standard error smaller (meaning our uncertainty is reduced), we must try to make the top part of the fraction smaller or the bottom part larger.

- Making the top part smaller would mean making r^2 larger but r, the sample effect size, isn't really under our control in any direct way. We can, however, certainly try to ensure that we don't inadvertently make it smaller than it should be – that we don't underestimate the effect size by making poor design choices.
- Making the bottom part larger means making n, the sample size, larger.

Uncertainty for effect size estimation is reduced if we happen to get a larger sample effect size, but we can't usually plan for that; it is also reduced if we use a larger sample size that we can plan for. The effectiveness of each of these for reducing the standard error is shown in Figure 8.2, which shows that sample size has a bigger impact than the effect size.

From this, we can choose our priorities for a good research design. A high priority is to use a suitably large sample size – this is explored in detail in Chapter 10. For the sample effect size, it is less clear-cut. Our priority regarding the effect size is to make sure that our design choices don't lead to a sample that underestimates the population effect size. For example, imagine we are interested in whether risk-takers are more confident about their exam grades, so we have a variable ExamConfidence. If our ExamConfidence is measured so that each person chooses one of three categories ('certain to fail', 'neutral', 'certain to get full marks'), then nearly everyone is going to choose the middle category. This will mean a sample effect size near to zero, regardless of how strong the effect is in the population, which in turn would mean a large standard error. We will look at all the issues like this in Chapter 9.

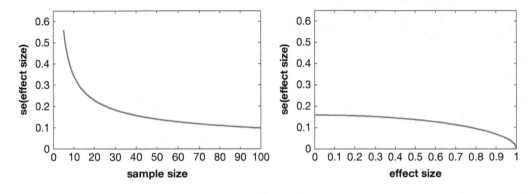

Figure 8.2   Standard error of the effect size is altered by changes in the sample size (left) and effect size (right).

Table 8.2   Minimising uncertainty for effect size estimation.

This is a simple summary of the factors that are involved in minimising uncertainty for effect size estimation. We want to choose a design that won't lead us to a sample effect size that is smaller than what really exists.

Parameter	Minimise SE
Sample effect size	Avoid underestimation
Sample size	Increase

8.2.2 UNCERTAINTY ABOUT EFFECT EXISTENCE

The other possible question we might be asking is whether the effect exists or not in the population we are interested in, which would require the process of null hypothesis testing to get an answer. This leads us to make the binary significant/not significant decision and we are open to the chance that our decision will lead us to a conclusion that is at odds with reality. Table 8.3 reminds us of the outcomes from null hypothesis testing.

Table 8.3   A reminder of the outcomes from null hypothesis testing.

	Population has effect	Population has no effect
$p \geq 0.05$	Type II error (false negative)	Correct
$p < 0.05$	Correct	Type I error (false positive)

A Type I error is the situation where we get a statistically significant result even though we should not (a false positive). A Type II error is the opposite scenario, where we get a result that is not statistically significant even though the population has the effect we were looking for (a false negative). The uncertainty we have with regards to the effect's existence or not

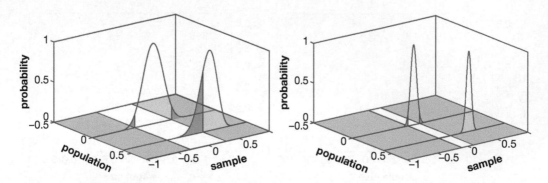

Figure 8.3   Sampling distributions and Type I/Type II errors.

Minimising uncertainty in null hypothesis testing involves the issue of how likely it is that we will make a Type I or a Type II error. This means that we are really considering two possible populations: the two shown in this figure, which are the null hypothesis (effect size = 0, shown as the back distribution) and the real population (shown as the front distribution). Type I errors correspond to the shaded areas on the sampling distribution behind and Type II errors correspond to the shaded area on the sampling distribution at the front. The figure shows how reducing the width of the sampling distributions can reduce the chance of a Type II error but leave the chance of a Type I error unchanged.

is just how likely it is that we have made either a Type I or a Type II error once we have done our null hypothesis test.

At this planning stage, before we have data and a test outcome, we must be aware that when we come to examine our result we could make either a Type I or a Type II error. We can be confident about what our result tells us about the existence of an effect if we have built a design that will result in suitably low probabilities of making Type I or Type II errors.

Figure 8.3 shows what would help to reduce Type I and Type II errors. A Type I error happens when the population has an effect size of zero (so our sample comes from the back-sampling distribution in the figure) and the sample effect size is far enough left or right to lie in the shaded tails of that distribution. Those tails always contain 5% of all the possible samples regardless of the width of the sampling distribution itself: on the right of the figure is a narrower sampling distribution but the (narrower) tails are still 5% of that (narrower) distribution. This means that normally the chances of us making a Type I error are 5% and are not affected by anything we do. If, however, we pretend we have more participants than we really have, or

Table 8.4   Summary of minimising uncertainty.

A simple summary of the factors that are involved in minimising uncertainty for effect size estimation and minimising inferential errors in null hypothesis testing.

Parameter	Minimise SE	Minimise Type I errors	Minimise Type II errors
Sample effect size	Avoid underestimation	Avoid overestimation	Avoid underestimation
Sample size	Increase	Count accurately	Increase

do something that leads to an overestimated effect size, then the chance of making a Type I error is increased, so we should avoid anything that might do these. It is important to notice here that increasing the sample size *does not* change the chances of making a Type I error.

A Type II error happens when the population has an effect (so our sample comes from the front sampling distribution), but the sample effect size lies inside the unshaded central 95% of the null hypothesis sampling distribution (the back distribution): the effect size isn't large enough to allow us to reject the null hypothesis. Figure 8.3 now allows us to see how to reduce the chances of a Type II error: we just need to get as much of the front sampling distribution out of the unshaded area as possible. If we ask what can achieve these, then it comes down to three things:

(i)   Making the width of the null hypothesis sampling distribution small.

(ii) Making the width of the sampling distribution that the sample comes from small.

(iii) Making the effect size of the sample large.

The first two of these are easy: we can reduce the width of the sampling distributions by taking steps to reduce the standard error, which we explored in Section 8.2.1. This time there is a double gain from increasing the sample size: the width of the null hypothesis sampling distribution shrinks, and the width of the actual sampling distribution also shrinks, so the overlap between them is much reduced. The third way to reduce Type II errors, increasing the sample effect size, is out of our control, although just as above, we should avoid anything that will cause us to underestimate it.

8.3 USING EXPECTED OUTCOMES TO CHECK A DESIGN

Once we have produced a design and a prediction, we can use these to see whether the design is good or not. This can be done for both questions of 'How strong is the effect really?' and 'Does the effect really exist in the population?'.

We are going to use our specific prediction in this section as an illustration, $r=0.25$, plus a specific design ($n = 42$, random sampling). We already know from Chapter 5 that the sampling distribution shows us the range of samples that we expect from our predicted effect size and this design. It is shown in Figure 8.4.

8.3.1 HOW STRONG IS THE EFFECT? EXPECTED STANDARD ERROR

For effect size estimation, the example design we started with ($n = 42$, random sampling) leads to a wide range of potential sample effect sizes, and therefore a wide range of over- or underestimates of effect size. Figure 8.4 shows that 50% of samples will have a sampling error greater than 0.1. Using the formula that we gave above in Section 8.2.1, we can calculate

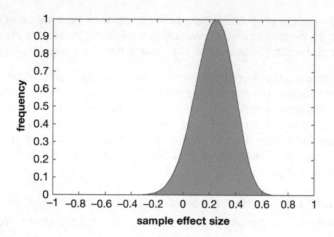

Figure 8.4   Sampling distribution for a sample with *n*=42 and random sampling for a predicted population of *r*=0.25.

This is the distribution of expected sample effect sizes that is produced from that population and design. In this case, the distribution is quite spread out: 50% of samples will be outside the 0.15–0.35 range.

that the standard error for sample effect sizes for this design is 0.15. If we judge this to be adequate, then we can proceed. 'Adequate' sounds like a bit of a cop-out. Unfortunately, just like many other things in research, there isn't one hard-and-fast rule and it is more a matter of judgement. Is it a fairly small number? If yes, and you've made other sensible design choices, then get stuck into your research. If you wish to have a smaller standard error for lower uncertainty, then you must reconsider elements of your research design to see what can be changed.

8.3.2 DOES THE EFFECT EXIST? EXPECTED TYPE I AND TYPE II ERRORS

Given a prediction and a design, we can calculate what range of p-values we should expect (just like the sampling distribution is the range of sample effect sizes we should expect). The distribution of expected p-values for our prediction of an effect size of 0.25, and a design of 42 participants randomly recruited, is shown in Figure 8.5 as an example.

If our prediction is correct, then the distribution of expected p-values in this example shows us that:

(i)   we have a 36% chance of a significant result (despite knowing that our predicted population has an effect)

(ii)   we can reasonably expect both quite large p-values and very small p-values.

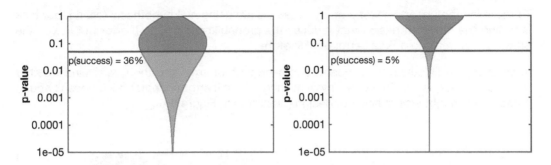

Figure 8.5   Distribution of expected p-values for our hypothesis (left) and the null hypothesis (right).

In this figure we show two distributions for expected p-values with n=42. On the left is our hypothesis and on the right is the null hypothesis. Note how spread out these distributions actually are. This indicates what a wide range of p-values can come from a fixed population and separate random samples.

The distribution of expected p-values is surprising the first time you see it. It tells us that the same population and the same design (in other words the same set of decisions) can lead to very different outcomes just by chance. In terms of uncertainty, this observation should be worrying. It also reiterates the limited value of the p-value as a measure of uncertainty: the range of expected p-values is very large.

The important feature of this distribution is not its spread but how much of it lies beneath alpha (0.05, marked with a line). If the population we are studying really does have the effect that we predicted, then any outcome with a p-value above 0.05 (where we failed to reject the null hypothesis) would be an error. Our design decisions will be focused on trying to create a situation where, if there is an effect in the population, we are likely to obtain a low p-value (and not if there isn't an effect in the population).

The expected p-value distribution in Figure 8.5 shows a 36% chance of a significant result. This means that there is a 64% chance (100% minus 36%) of not getting a significant result: of making a Type II error (if our prediction is correct). Remember that this is *only because we are predicting that the effect really exists* in the population we are examining, and that allows us, for now, to suppose that a non-significant result could be called an error. We are making a prediction and working out what to expect if that prediction is correct. We could be wrong in our prediction about a relationship existing in the population, which would mean that not getting a significant result would be a perfectly accurate conclusion.

To calculate the probability of making a Type I error, with this design, we need to get the equivalent distribution of p-values but for the null hypothesis population, not our predicted population. This is also shown Figure 8.5. If the null hypothesis were true, it would result in a p-value that is less than 0.05 on 5% of occasions. Normally, provided all is done properly, the chance of a Type I error is going to be the same as the alpha criterion for statistical significance: 5%.

To minimise the uncertainty of a study, when we are using null hypothesis testing, our task is to find the research design that reduces the probability of a Type II error but leaves the probability of making a Type I error at 5%: **alpha**.

In practice, we calculate the probability of each type of error and then determine whether that is adequate. Is a 64% probability of making a Type II error acceptable? It doesn't sound great, so we might well rethink our design (illustrated in Figure 8.6).

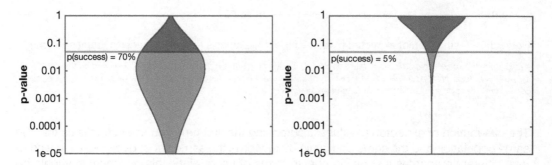

Figure 8.6   Comparison of expected p-values.

In this figure we show two more distributions for expected p-values, this time with n = 100. On the left is our hypothesis and on the right is the null hypothesis. Notice that the distribution on the left has many more significant results than Figure 8.5. The null hypothesis distribution, however, is unchanged by changing the sample size.

The prediction and design we have been using as an example (*r*=0.25, *n*=42) are fairly typical for psychology, so it seems many researchers are content to live with a 64% chance of a Type II error. If that strikes you as odd – you didn't know that psychology researchers were such gamblers with their findings – then all you need to know is that to reduce that chance of a Type II error to, say, 20% (which sounds better), the number of participants you need goes up from 42 to 121, which is nearly three times as many. We'll look at how to work out how many participants you need for this in Chapter 10.

Now here's the really interesting bit: consider two different strategies for a population with an effect size of 0.25. In both cases we have 120 participants at our disposal, but we can only use each person once.

Strategy 1 (*low* uncertainty):

• We use all 120 together.
• We have an 80% chance of getting a significant result with our one study (calculated using the maths we'll cover in Chapter 10).

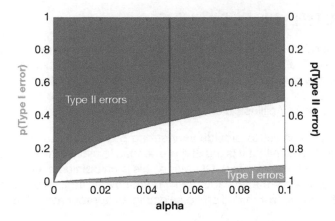

Figure 8.7   Illustration of what happens to Type I and Type II errors when we change alpha, the criterion value for calling a p-value significant.

This graph is a type we will use several times in this chapter and the next two. The probability of a Type I error (mid-blue) is shown upwards from the base of the graph; the probability of a Type II error (dark blue) is shown downwards from the top of the graph. In both cases a larger area means more probability of an error. Overall less grey means more chance of making an error. This graph shows that making alpha smaller than 0.05 does indeed lead to fewer Type I errors, but disproportionately leads to higher Type II errors.

Strategy 2 (*high* uncertainty):

- We split the 120 into three parts and try three times using 40 participants each time.
- We have a 36% chance for each time (calculated by that same maths), but we get three separate attempts. Over all, that gives us a 72% chance of getting at least one significant result from those three attempts.
- It also gives us 30% chance of getting at least two significant results.
- And a 5% chance of getting three significant results.

Now suppose that we play these two strategies 100 times. Strategy 1 (low uncertainty) will lead on average to 80 significant results. Strategy 2 (high uncertainty) will lead on average to 110 significant results.

And maybe even worse, if the real population has *no effect* and *any significant results are Type I errors*, then on average 100 uses of strategy 1 leads to five significant results but strategy 2 leads to 15 significant results. In principle, from the point of view of science, strategy 1 is always best. From the point of view of a researcher wanting significant results at all costs, strategy 2 is always best. Null hypothesis testing, in this sense, rewards working with higher uncertainty. We hope you find that more than a bit disorienting after all we have just learned about reducing uncertainty.

8.3.3 BALANCING TYPE I AND TYPE II ERRORS

It may seem a little odd that we are not looking for ways to reduce the probability that we will make a Type I error. There is a good reason: there is a balance between Type I and Type II errors. In practice, the only way we can reduce Type I errors is by reducing alpha, the criterion p-value. If we set alpha to a lower value to reduce Type I errors, then we automatically make Type II errors more likely. An illustration of this is shown in Figure 8.7.

As things stand, alpha is set to provide very strong protection against Type I errors. This reflects an unstated opinion that it is much more serious to claim that an effect exists when it doesn't than failing to find that effect. Of course, this is an opinion even if it is unstated, and can be challenged. There are a few authors who are now asking for some consideration to be given, as part of the research design, to selecting an appropriate value for alpha.

8.4 DESIGN FOR CAUSATION

As well as designing to minimise uncertainty, there is one type of design that is used for a different reason: to allow us to reach conclusions about causation. This design is called an **experiment** (look back at Section 3.1.3 for our brief comparison of experiments and observations). One of the main reasons for doing experimental research is that it helps to simplify arguments about causality. This is because we can state with full certainty how the values for the experimental variable were caused: we allocated participants to the different groups that form that variable.

The existence of a relationship between an IV and a DV is a *necessary* condition for causation, but not a *sufficient* condition. It is necessary but not enough on its own. If there is a relationship between an IV and a DV, then there are three explanations:

1. IV causes the DV.

2. DV causes the IV.

3. Something else causes both the IV and the DV.

The first and third specify how the DV is caused; the second and third specify how the IV is caused. If we know already for some other reason exactly how the IV is caused, then that would mean that the second and third explanations were invalid – leaving us only the first. Usually it is impossible to know exactly how a variable is caused. Knowing some of the causes of a variable is not enough; we need to know the full exact cause of the variable. There is really only one way to be sure: we deliberately cause the variable ourselves. In this situation, we can then make inferences about causation.

It is important to understand that the critical step here is randomly assigning participants to groups. It makes sense to have the two groups different in some way (such as by giving them different treatments), but the difference is not what matters; it is the random allocation that allows the inference about causation.

8.5 BASIC DESIGN ELEMENTS

A research design is like a recipe for how we will get our evidence: the data. It has two basic elements, each covering a small cluster of related decisions that we make when designing a piece of research. They are listed in Table 8.5. All are decisions we make *before* we collect our data. In the next few pages, we will see that these decisions have consequences for the amount of uncertainty that our result will have.

Table 8.5   Design decisions.

These are the decisions we must make when we design a piece of research. Each of these decisions will influence the outcome. We can make decisions that balance practicalities with the desire to minimise uncertainty.

	Design parameter	Question
Measuring variables	variable types	Does the variable have a natural ordering for its values?
	variable values	How many categories? what scale?
Sampling participants	sample size	How many participants?
	sampling method	How are they obtained?
	sample usage	How do we use each participant?

Some of these decisions can be made easily; some of them can only be done with a degree of guesswork (or hindsight). Variable types are often dictated to us by the nature of the variable or the way we plan to measure it. The ideal sample size, at least when we are doing null hypothesis testing, depends on us making an educated prediction about what effect size we are likely to find. In the coming chapters, we will examine measurements and sampling in more detail.

We go on next to explore the consequences of each of these decisions in more detail. Our plan is to see how important those consequences are and the guidance they suggest. We aren't going to tell you how to collect data: we are instead providing all the knowledge and understanding that will guide you towards making the best choices for yourself. It is up to you whether you run a laboratory experiment, deliver questionnaires, observe participants in a natural setting, and so on. You will find lots of inspiration in published papers relevant to your work; and the theory that you need to make educated decisions, in the next two chapters.

8.6 A GENERAL FRAMEWORK FOR DESIGN DECISIONS

This chapter has looked at the reasons why a researcher should examine their design decisions before they collect their data. While there is quite a lot of information in this chapter, really it comes down to this:

- Our sample gives us information about the population.
- The best outcomes arise when we have information that has high quality and is of sufficient quantity.

8.6.1 QUALITY OF INFORMATION

This is about getting data that are as precise as possible. The more precise our evidence is, the greater the quality of our information. In Chapter 9 we will look at how we should plan to make measurements to ensure we have the best quality of information we can.

8.6.2 QUANTITY OF INFORMATION

This is about getting data from as many independent sources (participants) as possible. The more independent sources we have, the greater the quantity of information. In Chapter 10 we will look at how to design research to ensure an adequate quantity of information.

THE BIG PICTURE

In this chapter, we have seen the start of something that changes everything. We have seen the possibility of taking control of the inevitable uncertainty by careful design.

UNCERTAINTY CAN BE MINIMISED

1. Uncertainty is unavoidable, but careful design decisions can minimise it.

2. The standard error depends on the sample effect size and the sample size:

    a. Larger effect sizes mean smaller standard errors.

    b. Larger sample sizes mean smaller standard errors.

    c. Smaller standard errors mean less uncertainty.

3. Accurate estimates of the standard error are crucial.

    a. These require accurate estimates of the effect size.

    b. Accurately counting the number of independent participants is important.

DESIGN FOR NULL HYPOTHESIS TESTING

1. The probability of Type I errors is unaffected by any design decisions. They are affected when *something has gone wrong*.

2. The probability of Type II errors is affected by almost every design decision.

3. Changing alpha, the criterion for significance, changes the probability of Type I and Type II errors in opposite directions.

PRACTICAL MATTERS

1. It may sound like we have provided a set of rules for you to follow in your research, but that is not true: it all comes down to adequate quality and quantity of information as a result of sensible forward planning.

2. Research is where the idealised world of hypotheses and theories meets up with the messy, complex world of realities.

3. Understanding what type of compromise is involved in using various types of measurement or sampling method, on the other hand, creates a researcher who can adapt a design to match what reality will allow, with awareness of what compromise costs.

YOUR TURN

SELECT THE CORRECT WORD/SET OF WORDS TO FINISH THESE SENTENCES:

1. Null hypothesis testing investigates where or not an effect size exists/is very big in a population.

2. The probability of a Type I/Type II error is not affected by sample size.

3. To reduce uncertainty, the standard error should be increased/decreased.

THE ANSWERS ARE AVAILABLE ONLINE

YOUR SPACE

 REFERENCES AND FURTHER READING

Cohen, J. (1988) *Statistical Power Analysis for the Behavioural Sciences*. New York: Psychology Press.

The classic text on power analysis.

THERE ARE MORE ACTIVITIES AND A SHORT
SUMMARY VIDEO FOR THIS CHAPTER AVAILABLE AT:
HTTPS://STUDY.SAGEPUB.COM/STATISTICSFORPSYCHOLOGY

CHAPTER

09

MEASUREMENTS AND UNCERTAINTY

OR WHY DOG-LOVER VERSUS CAT-LOVER ISN'T THE BEST WAY TO MEASURE PEOPLE

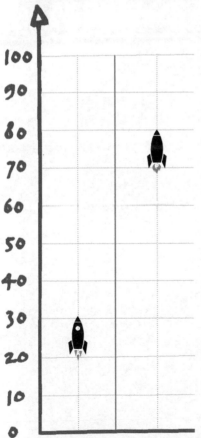

Now that we have seen just how important it is to minimise uncertainty through design, we can look at one of the practical ways of doing so: measurement decisions. This chapter is about variables and how the decisions we saw in Chapter 3 affect the results we will get.

As we plan a piece of research, we are making decisions about which variables to measure and how to measure them. Choosing what variables to measure is determined by our question and the hypothesis we are investigating, while choosing how to measure them is something we must always consider. Decisions about how to measure variables are essentially about what type of variable to use (Interval, Ordinal or Categorical) and, given that, what categories or scale to use. These decisions have small influences on the uncertainty in our result.

When we use experimental variables, then it is obvious that we have decisions to make about what values the categories will take. With observational variables, we should be aware that even though the variability we are measuring already exists, we have to make active decisions about how to capture that variability. There is nothing passive about measuring observational variables.

9.1 DECISION 1: MEASUREMENT TYPE

The choice of variable measurement type has implications for the amount and type of information we will be able to use in our data analysis. An Interval variable has the most information; an Ordinal variable type has less because it doesn't allow us to do more than rank values; a Categorical variable has less still because it only allows us to find differences between categories. Saying that someone is 50 years old (Interval type) says more than saying that they are the third oldest in the class (Ordinal type) and even more than saying they belong to a 'middle-aged' group (Categorical).

The key to understanding this is to recognise what the different variable types record about the differences between participants. All of them register the most basic information – the existence of differences: we can say that participant X has a different value from participant Y. With Categorical data, all that we know is that one participant is in the same category as or a different category from another. Interval and Ordinal also record the ordering of participants along a dimension: participant X has a higher value than participant Y. Interval data then have the added benefit of recording the amount of difference in a way that allows us to interpret how big a difference is between two participants: more information still.

The amount of uncertainty that we have in a result is reduced by having more information. This means that Interval measures, which have the most information, are also going to lead to the lowest uncertainty. Categorical measures, with the least information, lead to the highest uncertainty. This is shown in Figure 9.1, which shows how the probability of Type I and Type II errors depends on the variable type of the independent variable (IV). There is a small advantage in Type II errors for the Interval variable type.

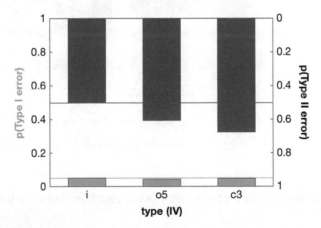

Figure 9.1   Effect of IV type on the probability of Type I and Type II errors.

Recall from Chapter 8 that the probability of a Type I error (pale blue) is shown upwards from the base of the graph; the probability of a Type II error (dark blue) is shown downwards from the top of the graph. In both cases a larger area means more probability of an error. This graph shows the effect of the type of the IV (where i=Interval, o5 = Ordinal with five levels, and c3 = Categorical with three groups) on the probability of Type I and Type II errors for a hypothesis with an Interval IV and an Interval DV. Similar effects are found with different types of measure for the DV. The results illustrate the benefits of using Interval variables wherever possible.

9.2 DECISION 2: MEASUREMENT VALUES

Once we have chosen what variable type we are going to use for each variable, then we can move on to consider what values we will use to describe our participants.

9.2.1 CATEGORICAL VARIABLES

When we choose to make a variable Categorical, we have to consider how many categories to use. This may be determined by the need to have a category that each participant can belong to, but sometimes we may have a choice.

In general, the more the categories, the greater the uncertainty in a result, as shown in Figure 9.2. The main reason for this is that more categories will mean fewer participants in each category, unless we also increase the number of participants, and fewer participants means more uncertainty about that category.

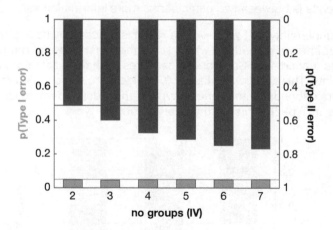

Figure 9.2   Effect of number of categories (for Categorical IV) on Type I and Type II errors.

Generally, fewer groups is better. This is mostly because each group will typically have fewer participants in it as the number of groups increases.

When considering the categories for a Categorical variable, there are two things we need to watch out for:

1. There must be a category for everyone. If we have two categories, such as dog-lover and cat-lover, then someone who doesn't like pets will end up in a category that doesn't really reflect them.

2. The categories mustn't overlap. Someone who has both cats and dogs will also end up in a category that doesn't really represent them.

9.2.2 ORDINAL VARIABLES

If you are going to use an Ordinal variable, then you only really have one important decision to make. The choice is between an odd number of levels (e.g. low, mid, high) or an even number (e.g. very low, slightly low, slightly high, very high). Unfortunately, no-one has the right answer to this decision. The question revolves around the psychology of what people do when there is or isn't a middle – neutral – level. If it is available, it is very easy to be non-committal and use the middle level. If there isn't a middle level, then people are forced to go one way or the other. All of which is avoided with a slider leading to an Interval measure (something we prefer using whenever we can) .... just saying.

9.2.3 INTERVAL VARIABLES

When we measure an Interval variable with a scale of values, although we may not think of it, we make a whole range of decisions about the scale. Many of them are completely irrelevant. It makes no difference to effect sizes or to uncertainty what units we use. We could measure exam grades on a 100-point scale; we could also use a 25-point scale, or a 200-point scale. The numbers for the values of this variable and the descriptive statistics that we calculate would differ, but the relationship with risk-taking and the uncertainty of a sample would be entirely unchanged.

One important choice we do make, nearly always without realising it, is whether to use a linear scale or not. A measure of risk-taking that counted up how many times a person undertook a risky activity would be an example of a linear scale. Linear just means that the score involves counting a standard unit. Nearly all common scales are linear because counting is so easy.

However, linear scales aren't always best for our purposes. We want differences on the scale to correspond to some consistent meaning. Think of a participant's age as a variable: a linear scale would just be how many years old they were, which is easy to calculate (by counting). However, the change in a person between the ages of 8 and 16 (8 years difference) is much greater than the change in that person between the ages of 40 and 48 (also 8 years difference). We could argue that for some variables, the meaning of a difference of 8 is not consistent. That would mean that age on a linear scale is not ideal.

Ideally, we would want a scale that aligned more closely with the consequences of age. In this situation, we might choose a scale that treated every doubling of age as the same – so the change between age 8 and 16 (a difference of times two) is the same as the change between 16 and 32 (also a difference of times two). This scale is not a linear scale – we can't get it by counting years – but it is potentially more useful to us because it recognises that as you get older things change more slowly.

Table 9.1   Comparison of a linear scale and a logarithmic scale.

A linear scale for age and a logarithmic scale compared. Many who are old enough to look back over long time scales would be inclined to agree that less changes as you get older (until bits start packing up and dropping off). The consequence of this is that time seems to pass quicker. You have been warned.

Ages	Linear step	Log(Ages)	Log step
16–24	8	4–4.6	0.6
24–6	12	4.6–5.2	0.6
36–54	18	5.2–5.8	0.6

Logarithms are explained in further detail online

This scale is called a **logarithmic scale**, which only matters because it has the useful property of stretching the differences between low values and compressing the differences between large values. Logarithm is a mathematical transformation: it gives us a new value to replace the old one for each participant. It is used in this case so that the values make more sense to interpret. Table 9.1 shows an example for age; we have split age up into three ranges on the left and beside them we have their linear (ordinary) steps from one range to the next, which increase steadily. The logarithmic age is shown next and, beside that, the steps in this scale, which are now equal because of the log transformation.

Because this is quite important, but also quite unusual, we will look at another example, which helps us to understand more. To measure someone's value on a risk-taking variable, we could count up the number of risks they have taken. This linear measure of risk-taking sounds sensible: the more risks you take, the higher your score. However, that scale may well result in a distribution of values that were strongly skewed: a few people with very high values compared to the majority. This **skew** means that the mean value is not quite as representative of the population as we might desire. The distribution we have in mind is shown in the left panel of Figure 9.3.

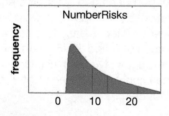
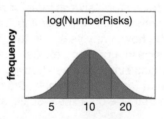

Figure 9.3   How a logarithmic scale can reduce or remove skew.

Here are two possible measures of risk-taking. Both are a count of number of risks taken, and each has a mean of 10. In the left case, we use a linear scale and the distribution of values is highly skewed. In the right case, we use a logarithmic scale and the distribution is much more normal. In both cases, the actual number of risks each person takes is the same, but the application of different scales leads to distributions that have different shapes. Notice that on the right, equal spaces along the x-axis correspond to a doubling of the number of risks taken: this is the effect of the logarithmic scale.

The measurement we are making of risk-taking is our choice and could be different. Imagine that we had a reason for thinking that every increase in the internal, natural tendency to take risks resulted in a doubling in the number of risks taken. Just like with the age example above, this circumstance would lead us to consider that the relationship between the internal tendency, which is what we are really interested in, and the number of risks taken is not linear. In this situation, just like age above, we might choose to use a logarithmic scale of the number of risks because we think it might be more meaningful. The distribution this would lead to is shown in the right panel of Figure 9.3. If you'd like to learn a little bit more about logarithms, you'll find some information in our online resources.

While we have presented logarithms as a way to remove skewed values, it is actually important to tell you now that the skew doesn't really matter for uncertainty about the relationship between variables. The only thing that skew impacts is the measures of central tendency: the mean of a skewed distribution probably isn't a very useful typical value – it certainly isn't the most common value. Let us go on a brief tangent to discuss skew – stick with us if you're interested or skip to Section 9.3 if you so wish.

The basic statistical tests (t-test and one-way ANOVA) work by comparing a measure of effect size with the size of the **residuals**, by comparing the variability in the dependent variable (DV) that is explained by the IV (the effect) and the remaining variability that isn't explained by the IV (the residuals). When these tests were developed, it was necessary to prove that they work properly – that the p-value they calculate is correct. To do this, mathematicians found it necessary to assume that the distribution of residuals was normal and not, for example, skewed; they couldn't make the proof work without this assumption. When mathematicians make assumptions, these are required to help their work along but aren't necessarily to be taken as strict conditions by ordinary users. In this case, mathematicians are fairly comfortable with users ignoring skew. In their language, the t-test and F-test are robust to skew.

We have run simulations of situations where the DV has various different amounts of skew and we have looked to see how this affects Type I and Type II errors. We have used a sample size of 42 and a population effect size of 0.3, both very characteristic of psychology. The result is shown in Figure 9.4, and as you can see, skew doesn't noticeably affect either type of error.

Skew is explained in further detail online

9.3 ACCURACY OF MEASUREMENTS

Once we have decided on variable type and values, we need to make sure our measures are as accurate as possible. Any inaccuracy in measurements we make will result in smaller sample effect sizes and higher uncertainty. It is sensible to keep inaccuracies to a minimum.

Let's start by supposing that there is real internal variable (a **latent variable**) inside each person and we are trying to make an external measurement of it based on **self-report**: we ask each participant to tell us about themselves.

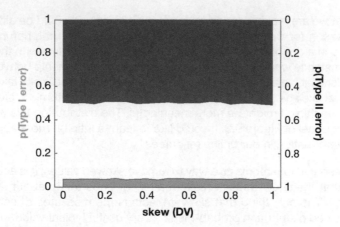

Figure 9.4   Effect of increasing skew (left to right) on the probability of Type I or Type II errors.

Essentially there is no effect. The result shown here was produced by computer simulation of the statistical process, which is explained in more detail in Chapter 10 where it is used more frequently.

Self-report is a key method in psychology. We can't readily observe someone's mental state, and so we ask them to report it to us. It is easy to see that self-report can be susceptible to all sorts of biases. Some of these will be conscious on the part of the participant, but others will be quite involuntary. Participants usually comply with requests for self-report, of course, otherwise we would not be able to do much psychological research. But they do more than that. They will usually try to fulfil the researcher's wishes, maybe without even realising it, and this distorts the measurement.

Think about asking someone to 'Please think of a time when, as a child, your parents were proud of you. Indicate, using the scale below, how happy you felt'. That isn't a normal thing to ask a person, especially if we don't know them. It probably pushes them to consider how much they are willing to reveal about themselves, which will depend on how they view the intention of the researcher.

Many researchers hide the true intention of their research – while providing as much information as possible and minimising participant risks as far as possible – to try to obtain the most honest set of responses they can find.

9.3.1 ISSUE 1: BIAS

If we ask participants how much they enjoy taking risks, and we are standing on the roof of a very tall building, there is probably a higher chance that they will say they don't like risks, because we may be putting them in an uncomfortable situation that is influencing what they say. This is a bias. In this case, it would be a bias towards disliking risks.

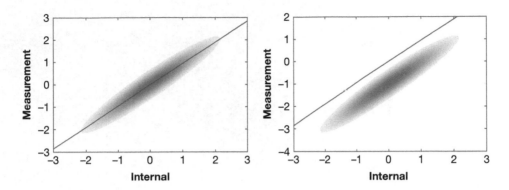

Figure 9.5   An illustration of bias.

This figure illustrates bias. On the left, the measurements correspond closely to the internal states. On the right, however, there is a negative bias: measured values are systematically lower than the internal states. However, all participants appear to have been influenced by bias equally in this example, which causes less problems when looking for an effect.

There are plenty of situations that can lead to bias; for example, asking people about their self-esteem just after they have spent 2 hours trying on clothes that don't fit; or asking people to meditate in a room full of brightly coloured posters and distracting photographs of a busy Times Square in New York City. Neither of these scenarios would give us a very accurate measure of what we are interested in. For the former case, the bias arose because we didn't plan our timing well enough; with the latter, the bias arose as the result of us not taking care of our research environment. Bias coming from any influence should always be minimised.

Fortunately, bias is often irrelevant for research; for example, by asking participants to participate in one simple activity, such as eating hot chillies to determine a risk score, and then collecting all their exam grades, the bias that may creep in will affect everyone equally and won't change the effect of risk-taking on exam grades. This is illustrated in Figure 9.5.

9.3.2 ISSUE 2: RANDOM VARIABILITY

If we ask that same risk-taking question again, but instead of being on one roof our participants are spread across different roofs of varying height, with varying levels of safe-looking walls and fences around the edges, then each person will be personally biased but to a different extent from everyone else. This will amount to a random variability in the sample we have taken, shown in Figure 9.6. For some people our measure of RiskTaking will provide an accurate value, and for others, their answer would be wildly different from their real attitude to risk.

Random bias leading to random variability will reduce the sample effect size and this will increase uncertainty. Anything we can do to ensure that random variability in the measurement

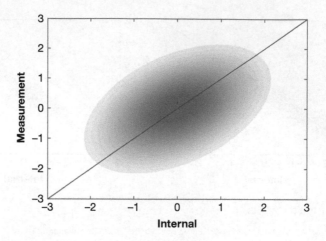

Figure 9.6   An illustration of random variability in a sample.

The consequences of random variability in the sample is that the relationship between the internal state and the measurement that we make becomes weaker.

process is avoided will be very beneficial. Note that this is *not* the same as the real variability in the things we are measuring.

The best way to handle random variability is to minimise the irrelevant differences between participants: for example, using the same research environment for all of them, including as many factors as we think important. Of course, if you are delivering a questionnaire online, there is very little that you can really to do minimise random variability.

9.3.3 ISSUE 3: SUPPRESSION

There is a third issue for measurement accuracy. It is due to the way in which participants have a tendency to avoid using extreme values in self-report. If I ask people how much they are enjoying themselves, they will feel a degree of preference to use moderate rather than extreme responses, even if they are having an extreme time. We call this suppression: participants tend to suppress extreme values for self-report. We've provided an illustration in Figure 9.7.

We can think of suppression as a variable bias: the bias shown depends on the internal state. Where it exists, there is the chance that any effect size we measure will be reduced and uncertainty increased.

The basic problem with suppression is that participants need some encouragement to use the extremes of a scale. This isn't restricted to Likert scales – it applies to sliders too. A scale measurement that has end values that are clearly for extreme cases but that has plenty of opportunity for participants to provide different responses without (usually) using the extreme values would usually work well. An example of a good scale and a bad one is shown Table 9.2.

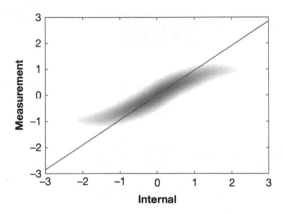

Figure 9.7   An illustration of suppression.

Participants often have a preference to avoid extreme response values. This means that the measurements that we make might be closer to the central value than the extremes of the scale.

Table 9.2   Two possible measurement scales.

The top one is very poor and will lead to lots of suppression. The lower one is much better: although people will still avoid the extremes, there is room for them to indicate a range of feelings.

How are you feeling?	very bad			OK			very good
How are you feeling?	very bad	bad	slightly bad	OK	slightly good	good	very good

9.4 ETHICS OF MEASUREMENTS

Something that we haven't given any attention to yet in this book is ethics, and this is a good place to fit it in. Whether your participants are people or animals, the number one rule of research is to protect them from harm. That may sound very easy, such as not making them run across busy motorways, or not asking them to ingest strange liquids, but there are finer details in measurement decisions that also require ethical consideration. Really, the relationship between ethics and uncertainty is that ethics are in place to make participants comfortable (to as great an extent as possible), and comfortable participants will be more helpful and honest: you will get much better and much more accurate data this way.

In terms of how to be ethical in your measurements, do this: every time you design a study, go back and read it again. Are you asking a participant to invoke memories that might be distressing? Are you asking them to report on something that makes them uncomfortable? Have you used any language that might be upsetting in some way? Make sure you provide resources such as helplines and disclaimers if your research strays into particularly uncomfortable territories.

THE BIG PICTURE

Although the choices that we make about variables do not have a large effect on the outcome, they are nonetheless important.

DESIGN CHOICES ABOUT VARIABLES

1. Decide what sort of information is available about a variable.

   a. If we can only identify differences between people, then we use categories as values and a Categorical variable.

   b. If we can place people in an order by their differences, then we use a scale for values and an Interval or Ordinal variable.

2. We make our measurements so that they capture differences between people that might matter for our hypothesis.

   a. If we are using categories, make sure they are suitable ones and that everyone can go into one of the categories. Categories that end up empty are not helpful and variables where everyone goes into the same single category are also not helpful.

   b. If we are using scales, then we should make sure that the values we get are well distributed across the scale.

YOUR TURN

DEFINE THE FOLLOWING KEY TERMS:

1. Biased measurements

2. Suppression

3. Skew

FILL IN THE GAPS TO COMPLETE THE SENTENCES.

1. With Categorical variables, more categories increases Type ..... errors.

2. The presence of skew usually .... Type I errors.

3. Random variability in a measurement .... the measured effect size.

THE ANSWERS ARE AVAILABLE ONLINE

YOUR SPACE

 REFERENCES AND FURTHER READING

Barford, N.C. (1985) *Experimental Measurements: Precision, Error and Truth* (2nd edition). Chichester: Wiley.

The best book, now out of print.

Rosnow, R.L. & Rosenthal, R. (1997) *People Studying People: Artefacts and Ethics in Behavioural Research*. New York: Freeman and Co.

A classic text.

 THERE ARE MORE ACTIVITIES AND A SHORT SUMMARY VIDEO FOR THIS CHAPTER AVAILABLE AT: HTTPS://STUDY.SAGEPUB.COM/STATISTICSFORPSYCHOLOGY

CHAPTER 10

SAMPLING AND UNCERTAINTY

KEEP YOUR FRIENDS CLOSE,
AND YOUR OUTLIERS CLOSER

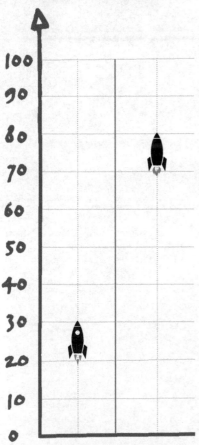

We need participants for our research, to provide us with data, but where do we find them? A **sample** doesn't just happen: we have to actively recruit the participants. If some thought is given to designing how to obtain and use participants, then the results of a study will benefit considerably. There are only three decisions to be made, but each of them can have strong consequences for how much uncertainty we are left with.

We will now look at how the decisions we make about sampling will affect the uncertainty in our results. We will assess uncertainty by changes in the standard error of an effect size and the probability of making a Type I or Type II error. Rather than just presenting these effects of sampling as bald statements, we will provide some understanding of why each decision affects uncertainty and indicate just how much impact various sampling decisions can have. Many of the figures are derived by simulating the statistical processes involved thousands of times on a computer. Check our online resources for videos of this.

There are three decisions involved in research design that relate to sampling. They are:

1. How we will recruit our participants.

2. How we will use them.

3. How many we will recruit.

In each case, what we will find is that we must reach a compromise between what is theoretically best and what is actually practical.

10.1 DECISION 1: RECRUITING PARTICIPANTS

The first decision we must make is the sampling method: how to recruit our participants. Recall that **sampling error** arises because of the difference between our sample and the population. Our intention when recruiting participants is therefore to reflect as many characteristics of the population as possible in our sample.

It is usually best to suppose that we don't know anything about the population. For example, we know that the distribution of IQ values has a mean of 100 and a standard deviation of 15 (because that is how it is defined by the inventors of the scale). However, if we are specifically interested in whether IQ scores affect exam grades, then we need to consider who takes exams and whether their IQ scores are distributed the same as the general population – and they are probably not. In this situation, it is better to suppose that we don't know anything about how IQ is distributed.

10.1.1 RANDOM SAMPLING

In **random sampling**, shown in Figure 10.1, we identify the whole population and then select our participants by an entirely random process. Random sampling is a form of sampling that is blind: we choose participants without any regard to what their characteristics might be. While this sounds counter-intuitive, as we want to know we have captured the characteristics of the population, it is actually a very good way to collect a representative sample.

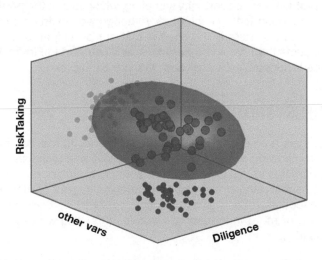

Figure 10.1   An illustration of random sampling.

We are interested in the variables of the left to right and bottom to top dimensions – and these are shown as the pale dots on the back of the graph. Random sampling gives a good spread in these variables and in any others.

Random sampling is difficult to achieve. We don't have practical access to every member of the population, so not all members are equally likely to be recruited. Any participant who opts not to be selected breaks the randomness: our sample is then comprised only of willing participants and this may mean that the sample is not representative of the population.

Random sampling, when done correctly, is reliable: it is least likely to introduce problems that will have an impact on uncertainty.

10.1.2 OPPORTUNITY SAMPLING

Normally, because random sampling is often impractical and requires participants always to say yes when asked, it is very common to use a compromise which is called **opportunity sampling** (or convenience sampling). The idea here is that we attempt to preserve some degree of random selection, but only within the participants we have ready access to and who are willing to volunteer. That means that opportunity sampling is a compromise between the ideal of random sampling and the practicality of the availability of participants.

Obviously, there are risks here in that the groups we have access to may not be entirely characteristic of the population we are studying. For example, if we only have access to university students, what we conclude with them may not apply to non-students. If the sample is not representative of the wider population because it is a specific subset, as illustrated by Figure 10.2, that will be a problem. Later on in this chapter we will look at the consequences of **patchy coverage** of this type.

There is a second problem with opportunity sampling, which is that the participants are quite possibly not entirely independent of each other. Although we would be careful not to recruit the same participant twice, there is the chance that our participants will be more closely related in some respects than would be desirable, as illustrated in Figure 10.3. This type of **non-independence** is serious, as we will see later in the chapter.

10.1.3 OTHER SAMPLING STRATEGIES

Beyond these two, there are several other methods of sampling that can be very useful, but that rely on us already knowing something about the population and the effect we are studying. In all these cases, participants are deliberately selected to match population characteristics. This comes close to a real danger: we might be pre-selecting our participants by what they may mean for our hypothesis. So, a safe rule is that we select participants only on the basis of their value on one or more Independent variables (IVs) and we never select using the Dependent variable (DV).

The most common sampling method that falls into this category is **stratified sampling**. This is where we choose people by their values on one or more IV, aiming to reproduce the distribution of values we know the IV to have. An example would be where we choose

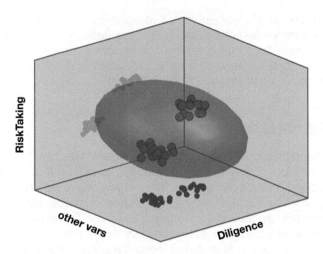

Figure 10.2   A non-representative sample.

Imagine our population is all the students attending a particular university, shown as the whole of the big blue shape. We use a method of opportunity sampling: we wait in a corridor and approach each person who passes by. At the time we are doing this, the majority are psychology students going to a lecture around the corner from us and philosophy students leaving the same lecture theatre. We get plenty of participants, but their characteristics are likely to be rather clustered and not representative of the whole university student population.

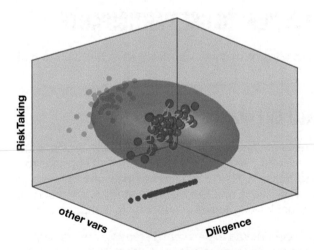

Figure 10.3   Too many connected participants in a sample.

Recruiting participants with opportunity sampling via social media can lead to a sample of participants who share far too many similarities. This diagram represents the effect of using social media to recruit. Each person is invited by somebody that they are connected to (shown by the pale lines) who was also invited. Overall, nearly everybody in this sample is connected to at least two other people in the sample.

people so that we have equal numbers in our two groups: risk-takers or non-risk-takers. Another might be where we select people so that we get a normal distribution of values for IQ, or where we select the same spread of ages that we know exists in the population. Stratified sampling is safe, as we are trying to produce the most representative sample possible, and in some circumstances is worth the effort.

10.1.4 CONTROLLING FOR EXTRANEOUS VARIABLES

Imagine that we are examining the effect of an experimental variable RiskTaken? (simply an experimental version of our observational variable RiskTaker?) on ExamGrade. Unknown to us, diligence has a big effect on exam grades. If there happens to be a difference in diligence between our two groups for RiskTaken?, just by chance, this would lead to a difference in exam grades between the two groups but we would be misled into thinking that the difference was because of RiskTaken?. Diligence, this variable that we are not researching and is having an unknown influence on our DV, is an **extraneous variable** and we need to find a way of removing its possible effect on our result. We call the process of removing its effect *controlling for extraneous variables*.

If extraneous variables are likely to be a problem, then recruiting a sample that neutralises their effect is important.

10.2 DECISION 2: HOW TO USE PARTICIPANTS

Once we have our recruitment method, we may have a decision to make about how to use our participants.

10.2.1 OBSERVATIONAL OR EXPERIMENTAL RESEARCH

Our starting hypothesis may lend itself best to an observational study, where we just let events take their course and effectively eavesdrop on what happens to our participants – the people we choose to observe. Here there are no decisions to make about how to allocate our participants. Our RiskTaking and ExamGrades study is an observational study. We have a sample and we are just looking to see whether there is a pattern in the data.

However, we can also conduct an experimental study where we create a Categorical IV and allocate participants to the different categories for that IV. Our example from Section 10.1.4, RiskTaken?, with values yes and no, could fall into this category. The yes group are asked to do something (mildly) risky; the no group are kept away from all risks. We then wait and see what their exam grades look like. In this situation, we need to make a decision about how to allocate our participants to the two Risk groups. The best allocation is random: we allocate each participant to one or another group before we know anything about them. This way, the cause of the variable is known to us.

As well as having implications for uncertainty, as we will see, the way we allocate participants has important consequences for what we can conclude about **causation**.

10.2.2 INTENTION TO TREAT ANALYSIS

There is one very important point to be understood here. The experimental method is a widely recognised route to inferring causation. But it only works if it is done properly. The logic is that it works because the IV value (which group) for each participant is *completely* determined (caused) by the experimenter. If any other factor is allowed to creep in, then the logic of experimental method is lost.

A widespread use of this is for experiments that compare treatment with non-treatment (control) conditions. We randomly allocate participants to one of these two conditions and then we can infer that any difference in outcome must be due to the treatment. That is correct. The issue arises with people who subsequently decline treatment, or don't adhere to the treatment properly. They would seem, after the event, to belong to the non-treatment group and there is the temptation to move them into that group. Leaving them in the treatment group, despite the fact they weren't treated, is likely to reduce the effect size. But the temptation to move them must be avoided to keep the causation logic in place. If we move participants who didn't take the treatment from the treatment group to the control group, then the cause of values for our IV is partly determined by a participant's willingness to take the treatment. Any effect of the treatment might be caused by the treatment itself or, very problematically, by being willing to be treated.

So, we must keep values for the IV according to our original allocation, regardless of what participants actually did. This is called Intention to Treat Analysis.

10.2.3 BETWEEN OR WITHIN DESIGN

With our experimental design, which has a Categorical IV, we can also decide whether to allocate participants to just one group or to all the different groups in turn. We can place each participant into one of the groups so that each group contains a different set of participants. This design is a **between-participants design** (because the comparisons we are going to make are between different sets of participants).

We can allocate every participant to each group in turn so they all do all the different conditions of our experiment. If we do this, each group contains the same set of participants. This is a **within-participants** design (because we can make the comparison within a single set of participants).

For example, if we were interested in the effect of caffeine on memory, we could use either of these options. By splitting the sample in half and giving one half a strong energy drink and the other water, we would utilise a between-participants design. However, if we gave each participant water first and gave them a test, then gave them all a strong energy drink and did another test, we would be utilising a within-participants design.

A within design leads to more precise estimates of effect size and to lower rates of Type II error. There are two reasons why a within design is better:

1. With the same number of participants, a within design has more data from each participant.

2. Extraneous variables will have (almost) the same values in the different groups: we don't know any more about them, but we know, by using the same people in a within design, that their effects are minimised.

When there are more experimental IVs, then the same basic idea applies separately to each one. It is possible to have all IVs set up as a within design, or just some, or none. In the situation where there are several experimental IVs, the within design is sometimes called **repeated measures**. If only some of the IVs are set up as a within design, then we call the design **mixed measures**.

10.2.4 ORDER EFFECTS

Despite the attractiveness of a within-participants design there is one serious problem: **order effects**. Participants have memories and the order that they do different experimental conditions matters. The effects of first being the 'yes' group for RiskTaken? will persist and affect what happens when we subsequently place them in the 'no' group. That is an IV order effect.

There is also a DV order effect: when we make them sit the exam for the second time, they will probably have learned something from their first exam and their score may well be naturally higher anyway. There are many ways in which order effects can happen, such as participants being more relaxed the second time around, or more bored and less engaged with the task they have been given.

Order effects can be dealt with to a degree by **counterbalancing**: by having different participants do the different conditions in different orders. Counterbalancing will remove any bias that might arise from everyone doing the conditions in the same order, but still leaves the contamination in place so that it weakens any effect. For example, half the participants could participate in the RiskTaken? yes group first, while the other half could participate in the RiskTaken? no group, then swap. Really, there is no other sensible way to handle this except counterbalancing and a degree of critical thinking when you consider your results.

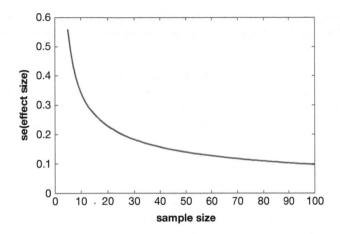

Figure 10.4   An illustration of how the standard error changes as sample size is increased.

Notice that there is a law of diminishing returns: the function flattens off to the right, indicating that there is less benefit gained from increasing the sample size further.

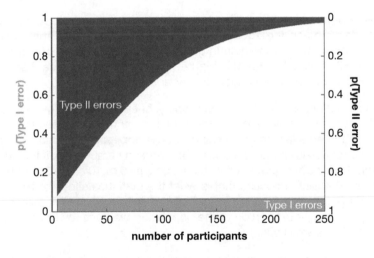

Figure 10.5   The effects of sample size on Type I and Type II errors.

Increasing sample size reduces Type II errors (the dark area) but leaves Type I errors unchanged.

10.3 DECISION 3: HOW MANY PARTICIPANTS?

Once various decisions have been made about how to recruit participants and what to do with them, a final decision must be made: the sample size. Sample size is the number of unrelated participants in the sample. They have to be unrelated: you cannot use the same participant twice in exactly the same condition, but you can use the same participant in multiple different conditions (in a within-participants design).

Despite it being the last of the three decisions, the size of our sample is the most obvious decision that we must make. Using a larger sample size means that we have more information about the population. Having a larger sample size leads to a narrower distribution of sample effect sizes: a smaller standard error. Here is the formula for the standard error for a sample effect size as a reminder:

$$se(r) = sqrt\left(\frac{1 - r^2}{n - 2}\right)$$

where r is the sample effect size and n is the sample size (number of participants).

The important part of this for our discussion now is the bottom part of the fraction: this tells us how standard error varies with sample size. Standard error is reduced as sample size increases, as shown in Figure 10.4.

There is a real benefit in obtaining a large sample size wherever practical. However, the standard error depends on the square root of the sample size and this means a law of gradually diminishing returns: the gain in going from 42 to 62 is greater than the gain in going from 62 to 82. This is illustrated in Figure 10.4, where we can see that the difference each additional participant makes gets smaller and smaller.

In null hypothesis testing, similar observations apply, but with perhaps more impact. A larger sample size also leads to smaller Type II error rates, but unchanged Type I error rates (shown in Figure 10.5). The same law of diminishing returns applies. Note that the probability of making a Type I error (a false positive) does not depend on sample size; if the null hypothesis is true, then you have a 5% chance of it with a sample size of 10 and a 5% chance of it with a sample size of 10 million, because that is what the statistics allow for However, a larger sample allows more chance of getting a significant result for a small population effect size. Because we have a bigger proportion of the population we have lower uncertainty and we are more likely to find a small effect.

So why shouldn't we use extremely large samples? In principle, the more the better. However, there are some important practical considerations. Compare what you are asking the second participant and 2000th participant to do. They both give up their time and effort equally. The second participant massively increases what you know; the 2000th participant probably doesn't change your result even at the third decimal place (go back to Figure 10.4 and look at how small the differences become). If the 2000th knew that, they probably wouldn't want to spend their time helping you with your research.

10.3.1 POWER ANALYSIS

Before we move on, we'll look at the common method used to determine sample size using statistics. It's called **power analysis** and is just a calculation that determines how many participants would be sufficient to expect a significant result on 80% of attempts with a predicted effect size, if it really exists in the population. This is called 80% power. The 80% figure is arbitrary, recommended by most researchers. It's really 'just enough without being too much work'.

To calculate the number of participants that would give us a power of 80%, we have to make a prediction about the population effect size. The calculation is weak because the number of participants is only enough if the effect *really exists* and we have predicted its effect size *accurately*.

Power analyses can be calculated in most popular statistical packages and require a prediction of effect size based on anything from a wild guess to a well-educated, published paper-derived prediction. The basic data required for power analysis are shown in Figure 10.6.

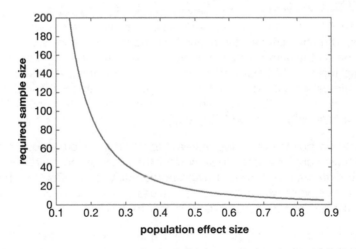

Figure 10.6   The sample size required to have a 50% chance of a significant result as the population effect size varies.

This figure shows the sample size required to have a 50% chance of a significant result as the population effect size varies. Notice how steeply the curve rises for small population effect sizes. And as we have previously mentioned, effect sizes in psychology are usually not very big. We suspect that most research in psychology falls well under this curve: a situation that is described as under-powered.

10.4 PITFALLS IN SAMPLING DESIGN

Now that we've looked at all the decisions that we should consider, let's look at some of the pitfalls that can appear in samples. These are all difficult to diagnose.

We will use a specific example where IV and DV are both Interval variables. Imagine that we have chosen to measure RiskTaking as an Interval variable (recall that usually it's Categorical), keeping our typical (Interval) ExamGrade DV. This choice makes it very easy to see the effects we will explore, but it doesn't mean that the effects we are talking about are limited to this particular combination of variables.

10.4.1 PATCHY COVERAGE OF THE IV

The regression line through a set of data points will always pass through their centre – the place where the value for each variable equals the sample mean for that variable. The slope through that point is determined by the data points: it is calculated to fit as closely as possible all of the data points. The discrepancies between the data points and the regression line are called the **residuals** and the line is chosen to keep the residuals as small as possible.

Look at Figure 10.7, which shows the same data set three times with three different possible regression lines. The thin vertical lines show the residuals between each line and the data points. Focus first on the data points that have IV values that are close to the centre of the graphs. Rotating the possible regression line clockwise or anticlockwise (i.e. the different graphs) makes almost no difference to the size of the residuals for these data points. That means that they make very little contribution to the calculation of the slope of the regression line: they are nearly equally happy with any slope.

Now concentrate on points out to the extreme left or right. Here, those rotations of the regression line have very large consequences for the sizes of the residuals, which means that these more extreme points have a disproportionately large effect on the slope of the regression line. Participants with more extreme values on either side of the mean for their IV will typically be more useful than participants closer to the centre.

More extreme points are more valuable, so the overall width of the distribution of IV values in our sample matters. The wider the spread of IV values, the more accurate the estimate of the effect size. For this reason, it is important for a sample to cover as wide a range of the IV as possible. A wide sample and a narrow sample are show in Figure 10.8; it easy to see how the wider sample constrains the slope of a regression line more than would the narrow sample.

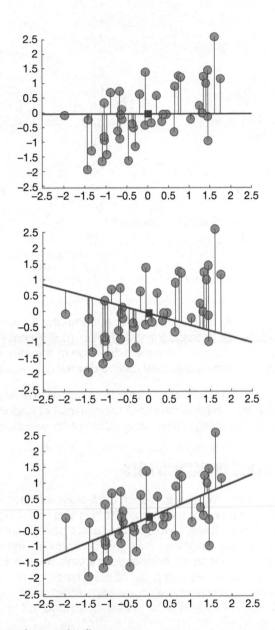

Figure 10.7 Comparison of regression lines.

This figure shows the same set of data with three possible regression lines drawn through it. In each case the lines pass through the centre of the data points, marked by a blue square, but each has a different slope. The size of the residuals for data points that are placed towards the centre of the horizontal axis are relatively unaffected by the regression lines. The size of the residuals for data points that are towards the extreme left or right, on the other hand, are very strongly affected by the direction of the rotation. Because of this, points out here will have a strong effect on the calculation of the regression line.

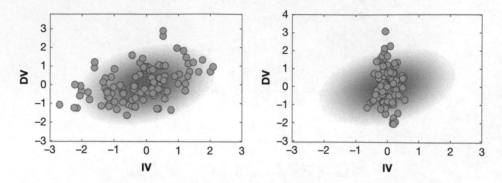

Figure 10.8   Random versus opportunity sample illustration.

This figure shows a simple population where there are two interval variables and an effect size of 0.3. On the left is shown a random sample to demonstrate how most of the population can be covered. On the right is a hypothetical opportunity sample which has a much narrower range of participants. This is quite an extreme example. A considerable amount of the population is missing from the sample in this case and the slope of a regression line is much more uncertain.

Patchy coverage of the IV has consequences for uncertainty. A narrow range of values for the IV will result in a slightly raised standard error (Figure 10.9). In null hypothesis testing, the effects are more marked because of the underestimation of the effect size. The Type I error rate remains at 5%, but the Type II error rate can be dramatically increased.

While proper random sampling is unlikely to suffer from patchy coverage of the IV (and would only do so by chance), it is probably a frequent consequence of opportunity sampling. Given the ubiquity of opportunity sampling in psychology, this set of consequences is quite worrying.

10.4.2 NON-INDEPENDENCE OF PARTICIPANTS

All statistics works on the assumption that each data point we have – each participant – is quite independent of the others in our sample. This is important because it allows us to say how much information we have – two quite separate participants bring quite separate information into our study and together they give us twice as much information as just one of them. But this assumption of independence isn't always true. The classic case of non-independence is where we use a participant twice or we use identical twins. It also happens if we recruit participants who are connected, such as several close family members or close friends on social media (as we illustrated in Figure 10.3).

Connections between participants mean that they probably share similar life experiences and are more closely alike than two random people will be. This in turn means that our sample will have less natural variation in it than we would expect and is therefore less informative about the population. It can be quite difficult to establish whether participants are independent of

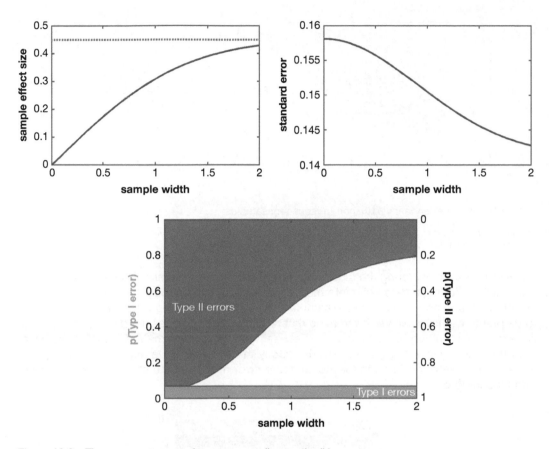

Figure 10.9   The consequences of narrow sampling on the IV.

The upper row of the figure shows the sample effect size (left) and standard error (right). There is a small increase in the size of the standard error at narrow widths; there is a much larger drop in sample effect size. The bottom row shows the consequences for Type I and Type II errors.

each other or not. Figure 10.10 shows two example samples: the left sample is made up of independent participants; the right has quite a high degree of non-independence visible as little clusters of participants.

Before proceeding to understand why this is a problem, we can just remind ourselves that the size of standard error, which is at the heart of uncertainty, depends on the sample size. Its role in that formula is as a measure of how much information we have. If we put too big a sample size into the formula, then we get a standard error that is too small: an underestimate of our uncertainty. This is what happens with non-independence. This is very bad: we are underestimating our uncertainty, meaning that we will be more certain than we should be.

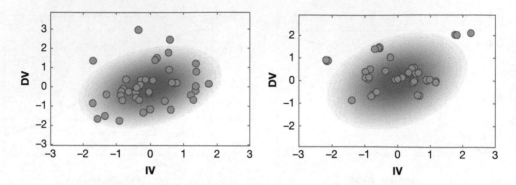

Figure 10.10   Independent versus non-independent samples.

The left-hand scatter plot is a sample of independent participants. The scatter plot on the right, on the other hand, has a high degree of non-independence. This results in the participants forming little clusters.

Let's start with considering the most extreme case where we mistakenly use the same data point twice. Putting a data point into the sample a second time doesn't introduce any *fresh* information and its real value to the sample is zero. However, when we count up how many data points we have, we will be treating that repeated data point as if it did introduce fresh information, resulting in a discrepancy between how much information we think we have and how much we actually have. This is exactly the same as if we had just entered (n+1) instead of (n) into the formula for the standard error: it makes the standard error smaller than it should be.

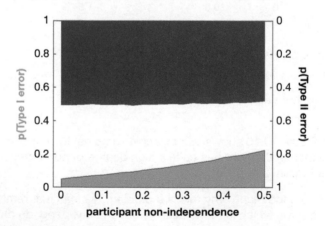

Figure 10.11   The consequences of non-independence in a sample.

As non-independence rises, the probability of a Type I error increases considerably; the probability of a Type II error changes slightly. The increase in Type I errors is particularly serious given the importance attached to getting a significant result.

Using a data point multiple times leads to an underestimate of the real standard error, and an underestimate of the standard error leads in turn to smaller p-value than is really correct. If the null hypothesis is true, then we now have a situation where the probability of a Type I error is greater than 5%. This is one of a very few rare situations where this happens.

Now, of course, we don't usually use the same participant twice. But another example will make this much less far-fetched and easier to recognise. Imagine that we are recruiting participants for our study of risk-taking and exam grades. We want to get lots of participants, so we ask each participant to come along to do the study, and *to bring a friend*. That will certainly double the number of data points that we get. Since friendships work best when the people involved share similar risk-taking and academic performance, the friends brought along to the study are not actually bringing much new information.

When a participant is recruited into the study because they have a connection to someone else who was also recruited, then those two participants are potentially not independent samples and their non-independence is a serious threat to the validity of the study. Whether they are independent, for the purposes of our study, or not depends on the nature of the connection between them. Let's look at two extreme examples to see how the connection matters, using our risk-taking and exam grades study again.

- Example 1: each participant is instructed to bring along another person whose name has the same initials as them. In this case, the connection really has no plausible psychological meaning: we have no reason to suppose that risk-taking or exam grades depend in any way on a person's initials. It would be reasonable to treat these participants as independent.
- Example 2: each participant is instructed to bring along their partner. Here the connection has a very plausible meaning: the pair will match on a whole range of different psychological dimensions, many of which may affect risk-taking and/or exam grades.

Think of the issue in this way: we need to avoid a situation where, somehow, our sampling process means we are likely to recruit as the next participant someone who is connected to a previous participant. This is not to say that the next participant cannot be similar to an already existing participant, just that we mustn't create a situation where it is likely. The sampling process should find someone completely at random for the next participant – so anyone in the population could get chosen.

Non-independence is a serious defect: in practice, we can think of non-independence as being the same as having fewer participants than we think. We may have obtained 42 participants, but because there is some non-independence they are only providing as much independent information as 30 independent participants would. If we overestimate the amount of information in our sample (the number of independent participants), we underestimate the standard error and get a smaller p-value than we really should. This means that we are running a higher probability of making a Type I error than we think. So, a method of sampling that introduces any participant non-independence increases our Type I error rate and is highly undesirable.

10.4.3 RECRUITMENT VIA SOCIAL MEDIA

Recruitment of participants via social media is becoming fairly widespread. We are giving it a section all of its own here because it embodies both of these pitfalls, with who knows what consequences for the validity of the results that are generated. We use it here as a way of tying all of this together into a single big pitfall.

First, let's just make the observation that, for most people, the experience of social media is positive – otherwise we wouldn't persist with it. It is mostly positive because of the way social media works: we are typically interacting with people who do not irritate us. That is because most of our contacts (and their contacts…) are selected by us. It is clear to me (RW) from my social media experience that nearly everyone in the world enjoys a good old statistical problem, enjoys gardening, and posts photos of lovely landscapes; while it is clear to me (EC) that nearly everyone in the world likes cute puppies, holidays in far-away destinations, and taking photographs of their food…

Really, we all live in our own little social media bubbles that keep us in contact with people who match us well and rarely if ever lets us glimpse the people who don't match us. This means that using my contacts as a sample – as I do when I share an invitation to participate in my questionnaire on a social media platform – will result in very patchy coverage of some potentially key variables.

The counter-claim would be that it only takes each of my contacts to share the invitation, each of theirs to do so, and so on, and then very soon we have reached well outside my own particular bubble. That is true, but it doesn't help as much as you might think. Even if the invitation to participate does get shared widely enough to break into a world far beyond (i.e. independent of) my own, there is still a problem. Although the people it eventually reaches are not at all connected to me, each one of them is directly connected to at least one other person in the chain and probably a few more.

Limiting my research to a narrow social media bubble is likely to be a great example of both patchy coverage of key variables and non-independence of participants.

10.5 OUTLIERS

A quick word about outliers. Outliers are data points that appear to be well beyond every other data point in a distribution. Many researchers will remove outliers they detect and there are various different arbitrary rules for determining what might count as an outlier. However, this isn't a simple topic and we would recommend that outliers are potentially too important to remove without good reason.

We can think of three simple ways in which participants appear to be outliers in a data set:

1. They are a measurement error (the number 4.2 was recorded somehow as 42).

2. They are participants who don't belong to this population.

3. They are perfectly correct extreme values, as will happen from time to time.

If it is possible to say without much doubt that a given outlier is a real error and not just a valid extreme value, then it is quite proper to remove them. The decision depends on something other than just their extreme value.

Let's think further. We saw in Figure 10.7 that data points generally have little influence on a sample effect size if their value is close to the centre of the IV distribution. Removing them will make no real difference. This is true regardless of what their value for the DV is.

- Points with typical values for the IV are relatively uninformative, so outlying values for the DV here don't matter.

We also saw that data points that have more extreme values for the IV are very influential and contribute most to the effect size. If we remove them, we lose something important: we reduce the range of the IV, which automatically reduces our effect size (see Figure 10.9).

- Points with outlying values for the IV are the most informative, so the values of the DV here do matter.

The only outliers that might be worth removing are those where the value for the IV is extreme. Since these points generally are the most informative, there is a considerable risk of a loss of information by removing them. Unless we have a good way of distinguishing true outliers (i.e. that don't belong to the population) from points that are rightly in the tails of the distribution, then we should probably respect outliers.

10.6 PRACTICAL MATTERS – OR HOW (NOT) TO CHEAT

10.6.1 GOOD PRACTICE

Decisions 1 and 2 (how to recruit and use the participants) need to be made before you get started, otherwise you will not get very far. Decision 3 (how many to recruit) should also be made before starting, and then adhered to. Good practice is to determine the size of the sample before beginning, using power analysis, and then stick to it.

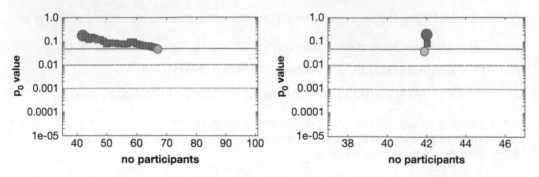

Figure 10.12   Examples of bad practice (cheating).

In this figure, we see some bad practices. In each case the true population effect size is zero, so each example is a Type I error deliberately caused by bad practice. On the left is an illustration of growing a sample, adding additional participants until a significant result is obtained: following an original 42 participants, fresh participants are added one at a time until p<0.05 is reached. On the right is an example of being picky with participants. It only takes the replacement of two in this case to change a non-significant result into a significant one.

10.6.2 BAD PRACTICE

Sample size can be a decision that some researchers don't quite adhere to. There is always a temptation to add a few more participants if the result isn't quite what was desired, but that really must be resisted.

10.6.3 GROWING A SAMPLE

Adding more participants – growing your sample – until you reach a point where p<0.05 is bad practice and is also a bad idea. It is a bad idea for two reasons. First, it is quite ineffectual as a way of converting a non-significant result into a significant one. There is every chance that adding additional participants will make the sample effect size weaker, not stronger: it could just be a waste of time. Second, if this is done systematically, you are setting up a situation where you are deliberately engineering samples with higher sample effect sizes by waiting until you get a suitably high sample effect size. This means that the sample effect size you end up with is artificially high and the p-value is artificially low. An example is shown in Figure 10.12 (left).

Please note that this process, incrementally adding participants up to a maximum of say 100, is radically different from just recruiting 100 participants. Increasing participants involves multiple calculations of *p*, stopping when we get a favourable one; just going for 100 to start with only has one calculation. Multiple tests always increase the chance of a Type I error, because each test has a 5% chance of one in the first place.

10.6.4 BEING PICKY WITH PARTICIPANTS

Another plan might be to recruit 42 participants and do the test; if the result isn't significant, we can look and see whether there is a participant who doesn't quite seem to fit the pattern and replace them with a new participant. Replacing participants until p<0.05 is a very bad idea. It is not difficult to make a dramatic difference to the p-value by removing or replacing participants who don't quite fit. But if you do so, then the sample effect size you end up with and the p-value it leads to will be grossly misleading.

10.6.5 LOOKING FOR THE SUBGROUP THAT FITS

Trying different subgroups (everyone under 25, females, whatever) in your data until you find a subgroup that has a statistically significant effect between your variables is also not recommended. The previous two cases were relatively clear-cut. This is trickier. Taking your data and seeing what the effect size and p-value are for a subgroup of participants will give you accurate effect sizes and valid p-values for those portions of your data. In a sense, doing this doesn't have to be misleading … provided you report all the effects that didn't produce p<0.05 so that anyone following your research can see what has to be explained. If we find that our dandruff cure only works for females under 25 who have IQs greater than 104, then we have to explain why it doesn't work for all other groups. That explanation has to be complete, otherwise we are disregarding most of what the data actually say.

THE BIG PICTURE

The decisions we make about obtaining our sample are profoundly influential. Because the ideal design is nearly always impractical, the art of design is to find good compromises between what is ideal and what is practical.

SAMPLE SIZE

1. Choose an adequate sample size: larger for smaller expected effect sizes.

    a. Sample size affects the standard error: a bigger sample size results in a smaller standard error.

    b. Sample size affects Type II errors.

    c. Sample size does not affect Type I errors.

SAMPLING METHOD

1. Aim for as close to random sampling as you can get and be aware of any compromises you make.

    a. Avoid patchy coverage of the IV: put an emphasis on making sure you have a representative range of values for any IVs.

    b. Avoid non-independence of participants: put an emphasis on making sure that no-one is recruited because of some connection they have with another potential participant.

2. Opportunity sampling might be OK, but it runs the risk of patchy coverage and non-independence. Of these two, non-independence is the most serious. Social media is an attractive sampling method, but really guarantees non-independence of participants.

SAMPLE ALLOCATION

1. A within design for a Categorical variable provides more precise estimates of population effect size and reduces the likelihood of a Type II error.

 YOUR TURN

DEFINE THE FOLLOWING KEY TERMS:

1. Opportunity sampling

2. Stratified sampling

3. Between-participants design

4. Within-participants design

5. Extraneous variables

FILL IN THE GAPS TO COMPLETE THE SENTENCES.

1. .... is the name of the method used to control for order effects.

2. A participant whose data is quite different from the other data points could be called an ......

3.   If two friends participate in a piece of research together, it could create an issue called ......

4.   Patchy coverage of the IV could increase the ....

5.   The calculation used to determine a suitable number of participants is called ......

THE ANSWERS ARE AVAILABLE ONLINE

YOUR SPACE

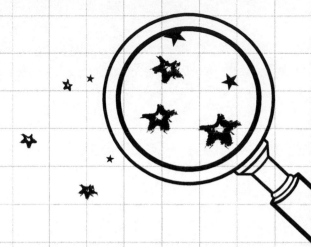

 **REFERENCES AND FURTHER READING**

Cohen, J. (1988) *Statistical Power Analysis for the Behavioural Sciences*. New York: Psychology Press.

The classic text on power analysis.

THERE ARE MORE ACTIVITIES AND A SHORT
SUMMARY VIDEO FOR THIS CHAPTER AVAILABLE AT:
HTTPS://STUDY.SAGEPUB.COM/STATISTICSFORPSYCHOLOGY

INTERMEZZO 3

Replication and Meta-Analysis

Now that we have really covered all the fundamental elements of research, we are going to pause for our final intermezzo. This time, we are going to go on a little tangent that relates to **null hypothesis testing** – covered in Chapters 6 and 7 – and the difficulties it creates for psychology. Here we shall talk about **replication**: the process of repeating a piece of research using a new sample, copying the original conditions as exactly as is possible.

IM3.1 WHY DO WE NEED REPLICATION?

Replication is a cornerstone of science. It is a basic and obvious way of dealing with **uncertainty**: we don't believe a single finding too readily but wait to see if it can be found again. The word 'replication' is used to describe any study that deliberately sets out to repeat a previous one. While it is basic and obvious, it is also not quite what it seems. In this respect, it has issues that are like so many aspects of null hypothesis testing – and the issue arises from that problematical process of attaching a definite conclusion (reject the null hypothesis, or fail to) to an uncertain result. We shall look at this in more detail here.

If both studies produce a failure to reject the null hypothesis, then our confidence that the effect in question does not exist should also be increased, but not by the same degree. For an example, imagine that the first study, unknown to the people doing it, had a **Type II error** rate of 50% (which is not unlikely in psychology, as we have seen when learning about how design choices impact such things), then a failure to reject the null hypothesis twice means that the probability that both studies made a Type II error (a false negative) is $0.5 \times 0.5 = 0.25$ (25% chance). We have already seen that this is how null hypothesis testing works: it is not well suited to establishing the absence of an effect.

In practice, since the probability of making a Type II error is usually much higher than making a Type I error, it is normal to design replication studies that use a larger sample size than the original. The sample size for the replication can be based on the sample effect size found in the original study. If the original study had a sample effect size of 0.3, then a replication study can use that to do a power analysis calculation of the size of sample required to have a very low chance of making a Type II error. It is typical to aim for a Type II error rate of 10 to 20% in the replication study and this will often indicate using a larger sample size than the original study.

IM3.1.1 BRIEF WORD ABOUT COMBINING PROBABILITIES

There are two very simple rules for combining probabilities. Imagine we have two events A and B. The **probability** of A happening is p_A and the probability of B happening is p_B. The two events are independent of each other: one happening has no implications for whether the other will happen.

Rule 1: the probability of both A and B happening is p_A multiplied by p_B: $p_A \times p_B$

Rule 2: the probability of at least one happening is $1 - (1 - p_A)(1 - p_B)$

Rule two needs explaining:

1. Step 1: The probability of A not happening is $(1 - p_A)$ and the probability of B not happening is $(1 - p_B)$. Let's call A not happening, the event *not A*, and similarly for B not happening, *notB*.

2. Step 2: The probability of both *notA* and *notB* happening is then, by Rule 1, $(1 - p_A)$ $(1 - p_B)$. This is the probability of nothing happening.

3. Step 3: The probability of something happening (*A* or *B*) is one minus the probability of nothing happening (*notA* and *notB*). So the probability of at least one event happening is $1 - (1 - p_A)(1 - p_B)$

IM3.1.2 REPLICATION STUDY REPRODUCES THE ORIGINAL RESULT

When an original result and a replication produce the same significant outcome, then there is no problem: we would say that the original result has been replicated. If they both found a **statistically significant** result, then that is quite reassuring because the probability that both studies made a Type I error (found a false positive) is $0.05 \times 0.05 = 0.0025$ (0.25% chance).

IM3.1.3 REPLICATION STUDY FAILS TO REPRODUCE THE ORIGINAL RESULT

When the replication study fails to find a significant result, where the original study did report a significant finding, we have a failure to replicate. Obviously, this is a more difficult outcome to resolve than when the two studies are in agreement. Logically, either the first result made a Type I error or the second study made a Type II error. In general, Type II errors appear to be more likely than Type I errors, although we don't really know, but if the second study had a larger sample size than the first, calculated deliberately to reduce the chance of a Type II error to 10%, then that would appear to lend higher credence to its result being a more accurate reflection of the true existence or non-existence of an effect. At the very least this should reduce our confidence in the existence of the effect.

IM3.2 PUBLICATION BIAS

However, there is a difficulty in the logic here that makes the argument less straightforward than it appears. It concerns a phenomenon that is called **publication bias**. In short, studies with statistically significant results are more likely to be published or reported than those where the outcome was a failure to reject the null hypothesis. In the strictest version of null hypothesis testing, this is right because a failure to reject means that no definite conclusion can be reached – the question behind the research remains unanswered. However, as we know, one result does not ever provide a substantial or certain picture of the real state of affairs, and so failing to publish non-significant findings leads to no end of issues such as overestimation of effects, and misunderstandings about the extent of various psychological ideas.

Consider **Type I errors** for a moment here. What has occurred with a Type I error is that, despite the absence of an effect in the population, the sample effect size is large enough to reach significance. In this situation we can say that the sample effect size has overestimated the population effect size. This overestimation also happens when the population does have an effect. In simple terms, our sampling error has an equal chance of leading to an overestimate or leading to an underestimate. But the overestimates are more likely to lead to significant results than the underestimates. So the overestimates are more likely to be published. Because of this, it is probably safer to suppose that every effect size reported is an overestimate, than it is to suppose that published effect sizes are a mix of over- and underestimates. The problem is that we can't quantify the size of these overestimations.

If publication bias produces overestimates of effect sizes, by only publishing statistically significant findings, then it also means that calculations of replication sample size are going to underestimate the sample size needed to reduce the chance of a Type II error in the replication; recall that using a larger effect size prediction in a power analysis results in a smaller recommended sample. So, replication studies will be making more Type II errors than would be expected at face value.

All of this is irritating, of course, but the real difficulty around all of it is that the key factors in this are unknown and very difficult to estimate. It is a very important issue to be aware of, both when reading about replications and when considering replicating work yourself.

IM3.2.1 REPLICATION IN PRACTICE

A fairly recent study (Open Science Collaboration, 2015) set out to do a systematic replication of a large set of original studies to see how replicable psychology actually is in general. The designers of the replications chose replication sample sizes based on the original sample effect sizes, which would, in the absence of publication bias (or any other bias in reported effect size), produce a Type II error rate in the replications of 8% – not for any mathematical reason, but because 8% is conventionally considered an acceptably low figure. This replication Type II error rate would be the probability of a failure to replicate, if all the reported effects were real. The results were not greatly encouraging: around 60% of studies failed to replicate, which sounds fairly shocking.

If we expected a failure to replicate of around 10–15%, then 60% would indicate something seriously wrong with most of the original studies. That 10–15% expectation doesn't take publication bias into account, a point that the authors of the replication study are clear to emphasise, and it is therefore quite unrealistic. The problem is that it is nearly impossible to know what would be a realistic allowance for publication bias.

Just to explain this clearly, imagine that actually all the population effect sizes in psychology were just 0.1 (using the r-family of normalised effect sizes). With the typical sample sizes that psychology researchers tend to employ, very few studies would come up as statistically significant – perhaps just 10%. But if those 10% of studies then were published, there would be no trace of the other 90% that didn't reach statistical significance. Those 10% of studies would all have sample effect sizes of 0.3 at least, meaning they were very biased. In this imaginary, but not implausible, scenario, the replication failure rate would be expected to be as much as 80%, because there is no awareness of the large proportion of original studies which also produced statistically insignificant results.

IM3.2.2 THE TWO ISSUES

This whole process of replication has two issues. The first issue we have just discussed – publication bias, which is unknown and therefore leads to an unknown expected failure to replicate rate. One can make educated guesses, but these are difficult to justify with real evidence. The missing piece of evidence is that we don't know how often original studies fail to reach significance: this is impossible to really know.

The second issue is deeper. Replication, with the belief that the results of a second study veto the results of a first, as if they are more important or more 'correct' in some way, is a very inefficient way of combining two studies. If we see replication not as a check on the original study but as a second source of evidence about the effect in question, then there are better ways of combining the information from each study. But to do this properly we have to become much more critical of the role of p-values in this process. There is a whole branch of research methodology devoted to finding robust, efficient and safe ways of combining results from different experiments. It is called meta-analysis and has even developed ways of trying to take publication bias into account.

IM3.3 META-ANALYSIS

Meta-analysis is a somewhat different approach to collecting lots of different results looking into the same psychological question. It uses a different approach from a statistical perspective, and also differs in its methodological approach: a meta-analysis can combine results from original and replicated studies, which is what is relevant to our discussion here, but it can also incorporate studies that have used different methodologies. It is not exclusive to replication.

We shall now provide a brief overview of meta-analysis, broken down into three simple steps.

IM3.3.1 STEP 1: AVERAGE EFFECT SIZE

To start with, there is a really easy way of combining the results from several studies: we just calculate an average of their effect sizes (ensuring that the effect sizes are all in the same form, such as r or Cohen's d). This sounds quite crude, but it is quite a sensible choice. A more appropriate way to produce an average effect size – and recall that an average is just a typical value that can summarise a set of values – is by using weighting.

Weighting simply means placing more emphasis on the more trustworthy studies than the untrustworthy studies when putting lots of values together (think of the more trustworthy values being increased, and the less trustworthy ones being decreased, as an oversimplified explanation). To do this, the standard error of each effect size is very useful. We weight effect sizes from different studies by the inverse of their standard error. The inverse of a number is one divided by that number, and can also be written as x^{-1}:

$$inverse(x) = \frac{1}{x}$$

When the number is less than one (and standard errors for effect sizes always are), then the inverse of it is always large, and larger the smaller the number is. So weighting by the inverse of standard errors (recall that a smaller standard error is a good thing) means that the corresponding effect size gets more heavily weighted. Check our online resources for an example of how to calculate a weighted average effect size.

You'll find an example online

Visually, it is useful to provide a graph as well as the average effect size, where the graph shows the effect size from each individual study as a single point to illustrate how variable the effect size has been across the research. This graph is called a forest plot – a term introduced by Cumming (Cumming, 2012). An example is shown in Figure Im3.1.

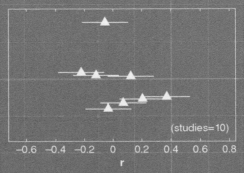

Figure Im3.1   A forest plot of effect sizes.

This forest plot indicates the results from 10 different studies. The triangles indicate the sample effect size.

When doing this process, it is also possible (and desirable) to estimate what the overall standard error for the combined result might be. However, this is a more complicated procedure that we don't need to explore here.

IM3.3.2 STEP 2: COMPENSATE FOR PUBLICATION BIAS

Simply averaging known effect sizes works well only if there are no biases in the selection of studies. This is a very unsafe assumption – publication bias, for example, could be a very large problem. There are several ways of dealing with this and the common methods work on a simple idea.

If we plot a graph showing each study as a single point as in a forest plot, but with the inverse of its standard error used, then we get a plot that is called a funnel plot because the shape of the data on the graph is like a funnel, wide at the base where standard errors are large and narrow at the top where they are small. An example is given in Figure Im3.2. In a funnel plot it is normal to use a measure of effect size called z, which is the Fisher-transformed version of the familiar r. The funnel plot shows z along the x-axis and the inverse of the standard error of z along the y-axis. This means that small standard error (low uncertainty) studies are shown towards the top of the graph, whereas the higher uncertainty ones are lower down.

Recall that the standard error is a measure of the spread of sample effect sizes, so a large standard error (bottom of the graph) means that the sample effect sizes we should expect to see will be very widely spread, whereas a small standard error (top of the graph) means that the spread of sample effect sizes should be much narrower. That produces a funnel shape: narrow at the top, wide at the bottom.

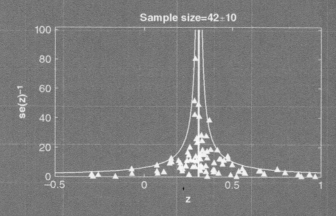

Figure Im3.2   A funnel plot of effect sizes.

A funnel plot with 100 studies plotted and no publication bias involved in their selection.

The average, weighted combined effect size is then the line of symmetry through the middle of the funnel. This is very handy. Publication bias will remove studies that have small effect sizes and large standard errors, and these would all be found in the bottom left corner of the funnel plot. So, if there is publication bias, we know where to look for it in the funnel plot. An example of a funnel plot with publication bias is shown in Figure Im3.3.

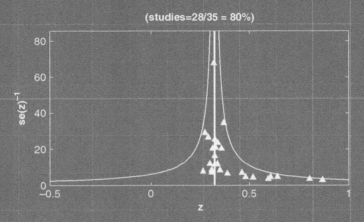

Figure Im3.3   Funnel plot showing publication bias.

In this funnel plot, publication bias is visible as an absence of studies to the lower left.

There are various more or less arbitrary ways of dealing with publication bias that work quite well in the presence of modest amounts of publication bias. They are all methods that try to identify what the missing studies might look like from the pattern already in the funnel plot. They assume that the funnel should be symmetric and then work out where the missing ones should have been. These studies that are thought to be missing are then added in – hallucinated is a better word – to the averaging process.

IM3.3.3 STEP 3: LIKELIHOOD FUNCTIONS INSTEAD OF AVERAGES

In Chapter 5 we explained the likelihood function for a sample effect size, which shows how likely different population effect sizes are. The likelihood function has a very nice property that we didn't mention but we can now use: if we have two different samples, then the joint likelihood function for both samples is simply the product (multiplying together) of the two individual likelihood functions. In this way, we can build a combined maximum likelihood estimate for the population from as many studies as we wish.

However, this process will still require that we attend to publication bias.

IM3.4 SUMMARY AND THE MORAL OF THE STORY

In this brief intermezzo we have explored replication, and how it works traditionally versus how it can be done using a meta-analysis. Traditionally, replication usually exists within the domain of null hypothesis testing and is regarded widely as a necessary check against erroneous conclusions introduced by Type I errors in original studies. Theoretically this is a useful approach, but unfortunately it inherits the deep problems that exist when an uncertain result (statistically significant or failure to reject the null hypothesis) is treated as a definite conclusion.

Realistically, in evaluating the performance of replication there are too many unknowns to reach anything other than a very broad judgement. The probability of a significant result in a replication study can't be calculated without a good estimate of the population effect size. The sample effect size from the original study is used as a guide to determine the sample size of the replication study because that is all that is available. However, if published studies typically contain overestimates of the population effect size, because of publication bias, then the replication rate will not be as high as would be expected from a simple power analysis. A simple power analysis will underestimate the sample size needed, but by an unknown and unknowable amount. Therefore, the traditional method is not highly efficient and not as statistically valuable as it may have been thought to be.

A much better framework is offered by using the newer process of meta-analysis.

 # REFERENCES AND FURTHER READING

Open Science Collaboration (2015) Estimating the reproducibility of psychological science. Science 349, aac4716, DOI: 10.1126/science.aac4716

A careful study of what happens in replication. The results have led to a considerable reassessment of psychology research.

Cumming, G. (2012) Understanding the New Statistics. New York: Routledge.

Covers meta-analysis.

Cooper, H., Hedges, L.V. & Valentine, J.C. (2009) The Handbook of Research Synthesis and Meta-analysis (2nd edition). New York: Russell Sage Foundation.

A comprehensive text on meta-analysis, covers publication bias.

CHAPTER

11

HYPOTHESES WITH MORE THAN ONE INDEPENDENT VARIABLE

IT'S MORE THAN JUST CAKE THAT MAKES WAISTLINES EXPAND

We have now reached the stage where we have explored all of the basic statistical understanding required to plan and carry out research by collecting data and analysing the results. We have seen how to turn ideas into specific, testable hypotheses that involve two variables, make educated decisions about the variables to include, come up with an optimum design and sampling strategy, and then analyse data with descriptive and inferential statistics to examine our sample and relate it to the population we are interested in.

This chapter now takes us on the next step forwards: what happens with more than one **Independent variable** (IV)? In this chapter, we will look at how multiple IVs work together. We will explore the way such systems behave, rather than the practical details of how to analyse data, which we will come to in Chapter 12.

Examples of the use of multiple IVs are shown in Figure 11.1: here we can see our original IV, RiskTaking, alongside other variables that could also explain ExamGrade. Our purpose now is to get you, the reader, to the point where you are looking at data, thinking about diagrams like these, and focusing on what the meaning of the diagrams is: what could the (underlying) statistical analysis tell us about psychological processes?

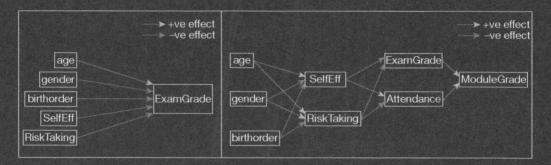

Figure 11.1   Much richer exploration using multiple IVs.

This figure shows a much richer exploration of various influences on ExamGrade, including our original RiskTaking variable. In this chapter, we will focus on the principles and issues when we are assessing the effect of multiple IVs simultaneously on a DV. The situation shown in the left panel is an example where several IVs are considered together. On the right we can see the variables feeding into each other.

In principle, we could just analyse each link between variables in Figure 11.1 separately as a two-variable hypothesis, repeating the process over and over again to explore lots of different influences on, say, exam grades. Typically, however, it is better to explore several IVs at once. So, while we are asking each person about their risk-taking, we could ask their age, measure their self-efficacy, and so on. Any of these – or any other variable you could imagine – might have influences on exam grades. In this chapter we explore the effect of multiple IVs simultaneously influencing a dependent variable (DV). Working with multiple IVs together can lead to a much richer and more interesting understanding of the underlying psychology than we would find by examining IVs separately.

The increase from one IV to many IVs is straightforward. There are three new ideas that need to be understood, each of which concerns ways in which the IVs work together. In this chapter we will work through the first two new ideas, and in Chapter 12 we shall see the third new idea.

11.1 THE BASIC STRUCTURE

The structures in Figure 11.1 are easy enough to understand on a psychological level: they show how influence flows from one variable to another, whether that is in a simple or more complex way. The arrows indicate relationships between variables. For now, though, they are more complicated than we need. We can explore all the new concepts that are relevant to multiple-IV hypotheses with a simplified set up of just two IVs and a single DV, which is shown in Figure 11.2.

Despite being simpler than the structures of Figure 11.1, the use of two IVs creates a more complex structure than we have seen in previous chapters: the single relationship when we only had one IV influencing one DV is replaced now by four relationships (indicated by the variety of arrows in the second part of Figure 11.2) that form a triangle of two IVs influencing one DV. The triangle isn't any kind of a fancy statistical concept that you need to learn about – it's just a very simple way to visualise this scenario that we have designed.

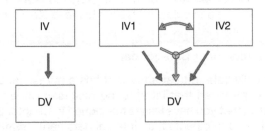

Figure 11.2   Typical diagrams for one-IV and two-IV hypotheses.

On the left, there is the familiar diagram of a two-variable hypothesis: one IV affecting one DV. On the right, we show a new diagram with three variables: two IVs affecting one DV. In this new situation, there are three relationships between the IVs and the DV to consider, each marked by an arrow. The centre arrow has a slightly more complex shape because it involves all three variables.

In this new three-variable scenario, there are three different relationships between the IVs and the DV. By common convention these relationships are called **effects**. We will mention them all here, and then explore each in detail.

- The separate effects that flow directly from each IV to the DV are called **main effects**: these are very much like the effect that exists between one IV and a DV in a simple two-variable hypothesis. These are the simple arrows on the left and right of Figure 11.2. Main effects describe how IVs work separately.

- Then there is a more complex relationship where both IVs in combination affect the DV: this is called an **interaction effect**. This is easiest thought of as a switch: the value of

IV2 changes (switches) the effect of IV1 on the DV. It can equally be described the other way round: the value of IV1 changes the effect of IV2 on the DV. This is shown as the merging arrow in the centre of Figure 11.2. Interactions describe how one IV can alter the relationship between another IV and the DV.

- Finally, there is also the possibility for a relationship between the two IVs themselves – we will call this a **covariation effect**. If there is such a relationship, then it has consequences for how we measure the effect sizes for the main effects. This is shown as the double-headed arrow at the top of Figure 11.2. A covariation is where the IVs overlap in their effects on the DV. Covariation is covered in Chapter 12.

11.1.1 VARIABLE TYPES

In this chapter, we will limit ourselves to exploring the following situations:

1. **The DV is an Interval variable.**

   The principles we will learn here also apply when the DV is **Ordinal** or **Categorical**, but with the additional complication of involving logistic regression. So for now, we are keeping things simple. The particulars that relate to these other variable types are covered in Chapter 12.

2. **The IVs are either Interval or Categorical.**

   It is always statistically safe to treat an IV that has a numerical ordering (i.e. Interval or Ordinal) as Interval, provided that interpreting results is done with care over the true amount of information that you have (as we mentioned in Chapter 3, Ordinal data provides less information about participants than Interval data can). Treating data like this allows the statistical processes to benefit from the inherent ordering of numerical variables.

11.1.2 A NEW DIAGRAM

The material from here to the end of the book is easiest to understand if we introduce a new version of our typical figure to show the different types of effect size. When there is only one relationship, we didn't need a detailed diagram to show the effect size – it is, after all, just one number. However, as we will see, things are a little more interesting now and a different diagram will help.

In Figure 11.3 we show the new diagram, first with just one IV. The amount that is dark blue in the DV shows us how much influence flows in from the IV. Think of this diagram as being part of a set of tanks connected by pipes that the influence flows through. Each tank shows us how much of the influence of other variables it contains. As we move on to two IVs, the diagram will allow us to illustrate how the IVs work together.

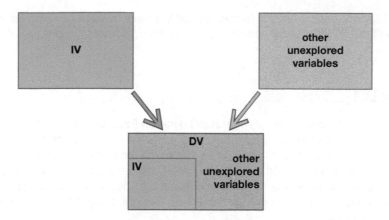

Figure 11.3   Hypothesis diagram including variance explained.

This is a schematic diagram of the effect between an IV and a DV. It shows the familiar diagram with an arrow showing the relationship between the IV and the DV. The box for the DV now has a blue area to indicate how much of the variance of the DV is explained by the IV. The proportion of variance that is explained by the DV is the same as the effect size squared (r^2). In this example, the IV is explaining 30% of the variance of the DV, which is a large effect: if r^2 equals 0.3, then r equals 0.55. The pale grey area is the residual variance of the DV that is unexplained by the IV. In this chapter, we are exploring how that residual area can be examined for the influence of further IVs.

11.2 IDEA 1: MAIN EFFECTS – SEPARATE RELATIONSHIPS FOR EACH IV

Let's think back to Chapter 4 where we looked at relationships between variables. We saw that the value of the DV for each participant can be thought of as the combination of an amount from the effect of the IV plus a second amount, which we called the **residual**, which is made up of all the other unmeasured influences on the DV. The residuals arise from all the other possible variables that are affecting our DV that we haven't considered or don't know about. This starting point is already illustrated in Figure 11.3, which shows how the variance of a DV can be split into the part that is explained by an IV and the remainder: the residual variance.

With our three-variable scenario, we are starting to think about how some of that unknown residual influence may be due to a second IV. When we introduce a second IV, we are building a hypothesis where the DV is affected separately by each of two IVs. These two separate effects of the two IVs are called **main effects**. We can see this situation in two ways:

- Variables and their effects: there are two relationships to consider: IV1→DV and IV2→DV.
- Participants: the value for the DV for any participant is given by the sum of a contribution due to their value for IV1, a contribution due to their value for IV2 and a residual made up of all the remaining unknowns.

There is nothing to stop us adding further IVs (so we have three, four or however many we wish), but we'll stick with just two in this chapter as it is sufficient to explain all of the relevant principles clearly.

11.2.1 EXAMPLE 1

We have already considered the effect of RiskTaking on ExamGrade. Now imagine we have done an experiment. Half of our participants have been asked to undertake 30 minutes of mindfulness meditation the evening before the exam. The remaining half of the participants are asked to go for a brisk walk round the university loch, also taking 30 minutes. Just in passing, notice how making an experiment had led us into a situation where there are considerable ethical implications: we wouldn't be doing this if we thought it might have detrimental effects on any of our participants.

We have created a new Categorical variable which we will call RelaxType – it has two conditions, mindfulness and walking. There is an important detail here: we *randomly allocate* participants to the two experimental groups. With a random allocation, we ensure that this new variable RelaxType can have no relationship with the other IV, RiskTaking: whether you are a risk-taker or not has no bearing on which experimental group for RelaxType you will be assigned to. We can say that the two IVs are *independent of each other*. That means we can use the diagram shown in Figure 11.4.

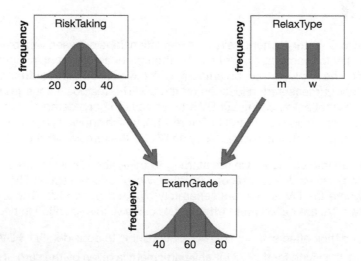

Figure 11.4   The hypothesis for our first example.

This figure shows the hypothesis for our first example. We are expecting that there will be a separate effect of each IV on the DV and that the two IVs are independent. m=mindfulness and w=walking.

11.2.2 VARIABLES AND EFFECTS

Our first new principle is relatively straightforward. Provided the two IVs are independent of each other, then their two relationships with the DV will operate quite separately. If the two IVs are related to each other, then things are a little different, as we will see in Chapter 12.

Let's start with the effect of RiskTaking on ExamGrade on its own. This works in precisely the same way as we have learned in previous chapters. The effect size for this relationship, using the r-statistic as we have done throughout, can be anything from –1 through 0 to +1. The process of finding the effect size of the relationship splits the value of each data point into two parts: the part due to the effect of the IV and the residual which is the part not due to the effect of the IV.

Now we bring in our second IV, RelaxType. We have made the two IVs independent through our design choices, which means that the variability in ExamGrade that is due to RiskTaker? cannot simultaneously be due to RelaxType. If the two variables are not related, they cannot cause related effects in ExamGrade. Any effect of our second IV will be found in the residual left after looking at how much of our DV is explained by the first IV. With the schematic diagram, this is easy to illustrate: Figure 11.5 shows the situation now.

Even with the inclusion of a second IV, there will be a remaining unknown residual, which consists of other variables that we haven't considered. The residual is smaller than when we had only one IV because our second IV will have explained some of the original residual.

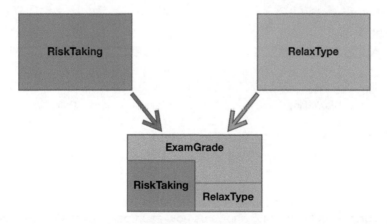

Figure 11.5   Schematic diagram for two independent IVs affecting one DV.

This is a schematic diagram for two independent IVs affecting one DV. Since the IVs are independent, they explain separate proportions of the variance in the DV. In this case, the second IV affects the DV to a slightly smaller degree. The pale grey area is reduced by including the second IV in the analysis because the second IV is explaining separate variance in the DV. The leftover grey space is the residual.

Adding even more IVs at this point just carries that process further: potentially we explain more and more of the residual with each additional independent IV. This schematic graph approach allows us to see how the process works. For any IV in this process, the larger the area of the DV that it fills, the larger the effect size relating that IV to the DV and the more influential that IV is in the DV.

11.2.3 PARTICIPANTS

We now turn to think about individual participants in this process. We have invented some data for this. We have already seen how to visualise the relationships between pairs of variables in graphs. We can do that now for this new situation. First, we can look at the two IVs quite separately and use familiar graphs for that purpose. These are shown in Figure 11.6: on the left is the scatter plot showing the relationship between RiskTaking and ExamGrade; on the right is the equivalent plot of group means for the relationship between RelaxType and ExamGrade. The slope of the regression line and the difference in group means illustrate the respective effect sizes.

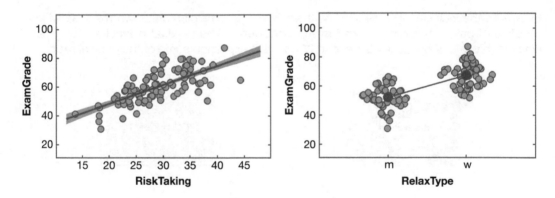

Figure 11.6   Simulated data demonstrating main effects.

This figure shows some simulated data for our first example. The two different panels show the two different main effects arising from the two IVs. Since the two IVs are independent of each other, these are a good representation of the data.

Looking at the graphs in Figure 11.6 shows us how each participant's grade is now related to two different things:

(i)   The effect of their own risk-taking value plus a residual from risk-taking.

(ii)   The effect of their own RelaxType value plus a residual from RelaxType.

The two residuals here are different: one participant may have a tiny residual in the left graph and a large residual in the right graph, or vice versa. We now move to a single graph which shows the two effects simultaneously, and this allows us a way of combining the two variables. That single graph is shown, in two different forms, in Figure 11.7.

The figure is a simple extension of the graphs we already know about, except that we have plotted the participants from two RelaxType groups in different shades (and different depths on the right). The two regression lines have the same slope (warning: we will change this in the next section) and that slope is the main effect of RiskTaking. The two regression lines are separated by a difference in ExamGrade, and that difference is the main effect of RelaxType. So the single graph shows both main effects. The left graph in Figure 11.7 show us how any participant's grade is now seen in a third different way:

(iii) The effect of their own risk-taking value and of their own RelaxType value plus a residual.

This combined way says that each participant's grade is formed by adding up the main effect of each IV and an overall residual. That overall residual is smaller than either of the two previous ones.

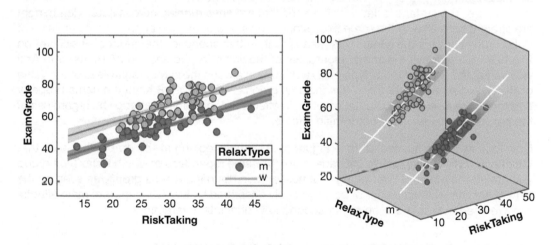

Figure 11.7   Extending one-IV knowledge to two-IV hypotheses.

This figure shows how we can extend our understanding about a single IV to the case where there are two independent IVs. On the left you can see a set of data, plotted to show ExamGrade as a function of RiskTaking score with the two conditions of a second IV, RelaxType, shown by different shades. Beside this, the same data are shown but in a three-dimensional plot where the two groups of RelaxType are distinguished by colour, but also by being separated in depth. The two horizontal axes are the two IVs and the vertical axis is the DV. For this set of data, the three-dimensional graph adds very little to our ability to see the structure in the data, but in other cases it will be very useful.

In this example where the two IVs are independent, this combined approach using the two IVs together leads to nothing different from what we find by treating each IV separately on its own. Our hypothesis that *DV is affected by IV1 and independently by IV2* is just the same as two hypotheses that *DV is affected by IV1* and that *DV is affected by IV2*.

11.2.4 OTHER VARIABLE TYPES

Although our example has illustrated the concept with an Interval and a Categorical IV, there is no limitation on the use of different variable types for three variable hypotheses. The relationships and main effects that are created will depend simply on the type of each IV and the DV – and will follow exactly the same pattern as we saw for a single IV in Chapter 4.

Keeping the DV to an Interval variable, there are three basic types of three variable hypotheses (both IVs are Categorical; one IV is Interval and one is Categorical; both IVs are Interval). The way the data look for each of these is shown in Figure 11.8.

There is one last point to observe here and this point will lead us into the next idea in Section 11.3. If we look at the final graph in Figure 11.8, we can see that the combination of the two IVs is a tilted but flat surface. Technically, a flat surface is called a plane and it is the next step in a simple sequence: you begin with a point, spread points out into a line, then spread lines out into a plane. The surface is flat, which means that any lines running across it from left to right are straight lines all with the *same* fixed slope. The slope of the line at any particular value of RelaxType is always the same. This means that, in this scenario, the effect of RiskTaker on ExamGrade is always the same, regardless of the value for the second IV, RelaxType. And vice versa: the effect of RelaxType on ExamGrade is always the same, regardless of the value of RiskTaker. All the other three-dimensional graphs in Figure 11.8 have the same property and this is the fundamental limitation of main effects. Each main effect applies, regardless of the particular values of any other main effects.

Now look at the (simulated) data in Figure 11.9. Simply looking at the graph shows us that the effect of RiskTaking on ExamGrade is not the same regardless of which RelaxType group you are in: the effect of RiskTaking is almost zero in the mindfulness group, as seen by the almost flat line. This data cannot be adequately described by just two separate main effects, and we need now to move on to our second new principle: interactions.

11.3 IDEA 2: INTERACTIONS – ONE IV SWITCHES THE EFFECT OF ANOTHER

When there are two (or more) IVs, there is the possibility for a completely new type of pattern in the data: the way in which one of the IVs affects the DV could depend on the value of the other IV. We have already seen this effect in the data shown in Figure 11.9. It is called an **interaction**. We are going to start exploring interactions with an example where the two IVs are both Categorical.

Categorical + Categorical → Interval

Participants are divided into four clear categories: those who were in the walking (w) RelaxType group and not a RiskTaker (n), those who were in the meditation RelaxType group (m) and not a RiskTaker (n), and so on. Each dot is one participant.

Categorical + Interval → Interval

If RiskTaker were measured on a scale, the data are illustrated showing the spread of participants along the RiskTaker scale, divided into the two groups of RelaxType. Each dot is one participant.

Interval + Interval → Interval

The hardest to picture as a 3D model: participants are plotted on a RelaxType scale, a RiskTaker scale, and the Exam Grade Scale. Each participant will have a single location (marked as a dot here) within the 3D model of the three variables together.

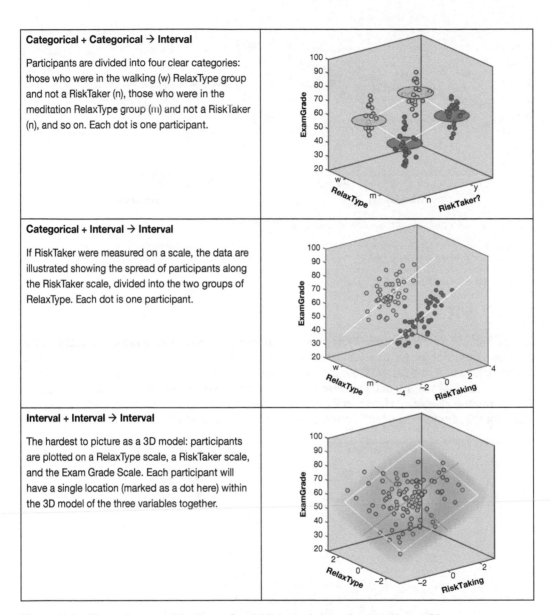

Figure 11.8   The various combinations of variable types in hypotheses with two IVs.

There is a fundamental similarity to these graphs and their appearance is just altered to reflect which, if any, IVs are Categorical. Remember that Ordinal data can look similar to Interval data or Categorical data when plotted, depending on the nature of the data.

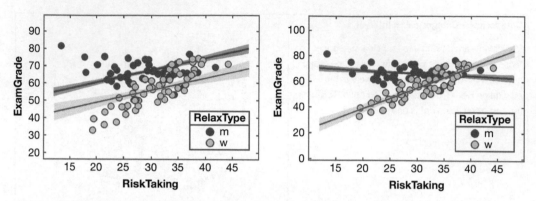

Figure 11.9   Comparison of main effects and data with an interaction.

Here are some hypothetical data where a description of the patterns in the data using just main effects is inadequate. The two graphs show the same data. On the left, the regression lines have the same slope: the analysis uses just main effects. On the right, the regression lines are different: the effect of RiskTaking on ExamGrade is allowed to be different in the two different groups of RelaxType. This is called an interaction.

11.3.1 EXAMPLE 2

For our second example, we will keep very close to the example in the previous section and just make one change: we use the Categorical variable RiskTaker?. Interactions are not limited to situations where the IVs are Categorical, but this is easier to understand to start with. In this second example, we are actively interested in the possible presence of an interaction, and the hypothesis diagram, shown in Figure 11.10, has a new arrow to indicate this: a slightly more complicated arrow which links both the IVs together and then to the DV.

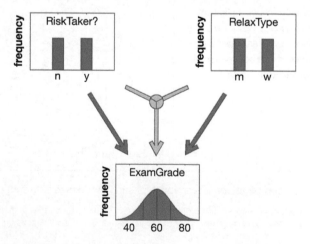

Figure 11.10   A new arrow to illustrate interactions.

The possibility of an interaction is shown in this diagram by the more complicated arrow in the middle, which connects both IVs to the DV. Note that RiskTaker is now a Categorical variable for the purposes of illustrating interactions.

If you look at Table 11.1, you will see a table that illustrates an interaction in this second example. We can see two patterns in this hypothetical situation:

1. *There are no main effects*. There is no *overall* effect of RiskTaker?: the different effects of the other IV (Mindfulness and Walking) cancel each other out across each row. Equally, there is no *overall* effect of RelaxType: the different effects of the other IV (Yes and No) cancel each other out down each column.

2. *There is an interaction*. In the top row of Table 11.1, Walking leads to a higher exam grade than Mindfulness, whereas in the bottom row, the opposite is found. So while each variable separately does not have a main effect, something happens when the different groups of each variable get split apart: they interact. Hence the name interaction effect. Table 11.1 illustrates a relationship that is not the simple combination of main effects – because both main effects are zero. This new type of relationship is characterised by needing to specify the value of IV1 *and* IV2 to describe it.

Table 11.1   A basic interaction.

Whether there is a benefit for exam grades depends on the specific combination of values for the two IVs. The benefit exists for anyone who is either RelaxType=M and RiskTaker?=No or RelaxType=W and RiskTaker?=Yes. The hallmark of this interaction is the need to use the word and to state which combination of IV values gives which outcome for the DV.

		RelaxType	
		Mindfulness	*Walking*
RiskTaker?	*Yes*	ExamGrade lower	ExamGrade higher
	No	ExamGrade higher	ExamGrade lower

This example shows that we can have an interaction when there are no main effects: interactions and main effects are quite separate.

There are several conventional ways of describing an interaction, but none is entirely helpful. Traditionally, it is just called an interaction and, for the more mathematically inclined, is explained as a multiplication. More recently, it has also been described as a moderation. While the effect we are looking at certainly involves two variables interacting with each other, the term 'interaction' doesn't give much of a hint as to what happens and grasping the idea of multiplying values for RiskTaker and RelaxType together takes some effort. To say that one variable moderates the effect of another comes much closer to something we can readily understand, and we will return to this in a few paragraphs.

11.3.2 INTERACTION AS A SWITCH

We are going to introduce interaction as a switch, because that is an easy object to understand and there is no need to make things more complicated than they have to be.

The interaction can also be thought of as a way in which one of the IVs switches the effect of the other IV. In our example in Table 11.1, the effect of RiskTaker? is negative when RelaxType is Mindfulness and is positive when RelaxType is Walking. So, the value of RelaxType *switches* the effect of RiskTaker? on ExamGrade *from negative to positive*. If you look at Figure 11.11, you will be able to see that describing the interaction as a switch can be done both ways: RelaxType switches the effect of RiskTaker? and equally we can say that RiskTaker? switches the effect of RelaxType.

The first example in Figure 11.11 is also a +/– switch. This happens when the two main effects are both zero, or close to it. In the second example, the interaction can switch the IV1 effect on or off. This happens when the two main effects both have the same magnitude of effect size as the interaction.

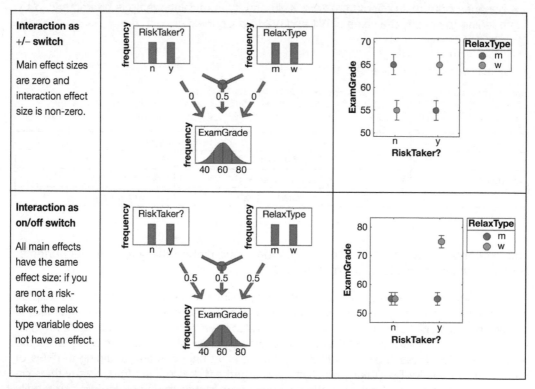

Figure 11.11   A way of visualising interactions as switches.

11.3.3 INTERACTION AS MODERATION

We think of switches as being all-or-none devices. When the IVs are Categorical, that is a useful analogy. A broader concept is the idea of a moderator: the effect of an IV is adjusted by another IV. So instead of on or off, it might be that IV2 reduces the effect of IV1 by a certain amount. The word 'moderation' catches this nicely.

The concept of moderation also makes it easier to see what an interaction that involves Interval variables would be. The second row of Figure 11.12 shows this case. In order to make the interaction easy to see, we have switched here to the three-dimensional graph. The interaction means that the lines running left to right across the RiskTaking dimension now have slopes that change depending on where they are placed from front to back (i.e. what the value of RelaxAmount is). Although the surface now looks curved, in fact all of the lines that run parallel to either axis (i.e. lines where one or another IV has a fixed value) are still straight lines.

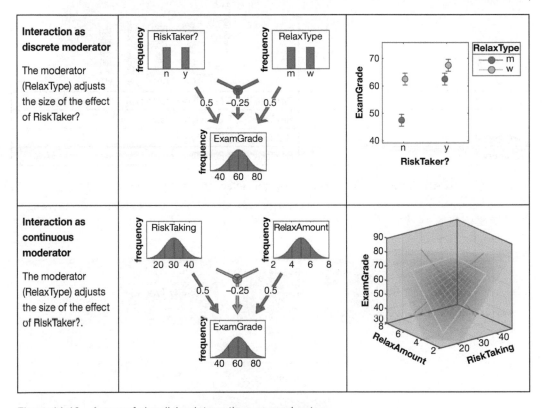

Figure 11.12   A way of visualising interactions as moderators.

This is just another way to visualise interactions.

11.3.4 INTERACTION AS A SEPARATE VARIABLE

Although the interaction involves the two IVs, its effect is independent of the two main effects. This means that an interaction behaves exactly as if it were just another IV.

This is the easiest to see when the two variables are both Categorical: this new 'Interaction' variable is also Categorical, with four categories. The number of categories is the product of the number of categories for the two IVs (2×2). This is shown in Figure 11.13.

It is important to understand that the interaction really does just work as another variable. We can add it into the schematic diagram as a separate entity that explains variance in the DV independently (i.e. not overlapping with the main effects). This is shown in Figure 11.14.

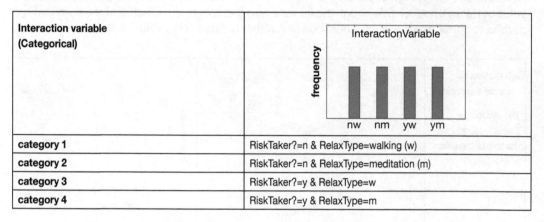

Interaction variable (Categorical)	
	InteractionVariable (frequency — nw nm yw ym)
category 1	RiskTaker?=n & RelaxType=walking (w)
category 2	RiskTaker?=n & RelaxType=meditation (m)
category 3	RiskTaker?=y & RelaxType=w
category 4	RiskTaker?=y & RelaxType=m

Figure 11.13   Interaction as another variable having an effect on the DV.

This table shows interaction as another variable having an effect on the DV. There are four possible combinations that may lead to different outcomes of the DV in this example.

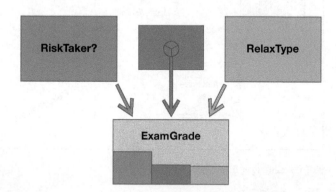

Figure 11.14   Schematic diagram showing how the interaction is a separate effect from the two main effects.

This schematic diagram shows how the interaction (the darker colour in the middle) is a separate effect from the two main effects – and explains a different proportion of the variance of the DV from either of the main effects.

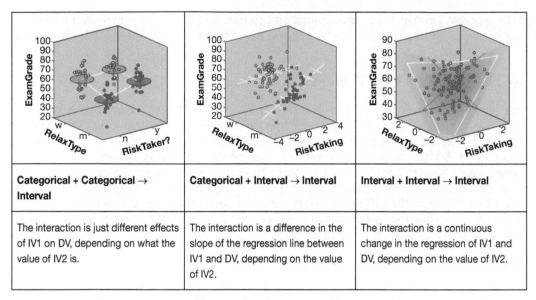

Categorical + Categorical → Interval	Categorical + Interval → Interval	Interval + Interval → Interval
The interaction is just different effects of IV1 on DV, depending on what the value of IV2 is.	The interaction is a difference in the slope of the regression line between IV1 and DV, depending on the value of IV2.	The interaction is a continuous change in the regression of IV1 and DV, depending on the value of IV2.

Figure 11.15 Example data sets with interactions between different variable types.

11.3.5 INTERACTIONS BETWEEN OTHER VARIABLE TYPES

As with the main effects, there are no limitations on what variable types can be involved in an interaction. Take a look at Figure 11.15 for more information.

11.4 PUTTING IT ALL TOGETHER

We have left behind the simple world of a single effect linking two variables. Now we have seen how multiple IVs can affect a DV in a richer pattern of ways. The pattern so far is made up of two basic types of effect linking IVs to the DV: main effects and interactions. With these different types of effect, we can build hypotheses that are sophisticated and that can make quite complex predictions.

Nothing we have covered so far should be discarded. The variables we are talking about here are the same concept as we had back in Chapter 3. When we talk about all the effects involved and their effect sizes, we are talking about relationships between variables that are not different from the relationships we looked at in Chapter 4; and they are subject to sampling error and the resultant uncertainty just as we explored in Chapter 5. We can apply null hypothesis testing to these effects, following exactly the logic of Chapter 6. We will no longer need the different specific tests of Chapter 7 – in Chapter 13 we will see how they are all incorporated into just two fundamental procedures. And we can design research that has multiple variables to minimise uncertainty using all the same ideas that were in Chapters 8–10.

11.4.1 LIMITATIONS ON EFFECT SIZES

The effect size relating a single IV to a DV can range from 0 up to 1 using our preferred normalised type of effect size. This is still true when there is more than one IV, but with an important qualification: the combination of all the different effects relating IVs to the DV cannot exceed one. So, for example, if the effect size of one single IV was actually 1, then all the others would have to be 0. Recall that *the square of the effect size is the proportion of DV variance explained by the effect of the IV*. Taken all together, the various effects of our IVs cannot explain more than 100% of the DV variance. So, if we have one IV with an effect size of 0.5, then the effect size of an independent second IV cannot be greater than 0.87. This is explained with examples in Table 11.2.

Table 11.2   How independent effect sizes are combined.

This table only applies to the situation where the two IVs are independent. The first two columns have the individual effect sizes. The third column shows the proportion of variance in the DV that each IV is explaining. These figures are the square of the individual effect sizes. The fourth column adds the proportion of variance explained by each IV to find a total proportion of variance explained. The final column shows that we can convert that back to a combined effect size by taking the square root.

IV1 effect size	IV2 effect size	DV variance explained	Total DV variance explained	Combined effect size
0.5	0.87	$0.5^2 = 0.25$ $0.87^2 = 0.75$	$0.25 + 0.75 = 1.00$	$\mathrm{sqrt}(1) = 1$
0.3	0.3	$0.3^2 = 0.09$ $0.3^2 = 0.09$	$0.09 + 0.09 = 0.18$	$\mathrm{sqrt}(0.18) = 0.42$
0.4	0.14	$0.4^2 = 0.16$ $0.14^2 = 0.02$	$0.16 + 0.02 = 0.18$	$\mathrm{sqrt}(0.18) = 0.42$

THE BIG PICTURE

Moving on to consider the situation when we use more than one IV at a time marks the start of the last big step forward in our thinking.

MULTIPLE IVS

1.   It is possible to use multiple IVs simultaneously to explain the variance in a DV. Looking at more than one IV is a way of learning more about the residuals left over when only one IV is examined.

MAIN EFFECTS

1.   Each IV may have its own separate main effect on the DV. If the IVs are independent, then these main effects explain different variance in the DV.

INTERACTIONS

1.   Two IVs may interact (an Interaction Effect) where the strength of the relationship between one IV and the DV depends on the value of the second IV.

     a.   Think of this like a switch mechanism.

     b.   It can also be thought of as moderation.

     c.   Interaction operates the same as a third independent variable.

     d.   Any types of variables can interact: it is not restricted to just Categorical variables.

IMPORTANT CONSTRAINTS

1.   All the principles that we have explored so far, such as uncertainty and errors, still apply to scenarios with two or more IVs.

2.   All the effect sizes found working together must add up to a maximum of 1, as explained in Table 11.2.

YOUR TURN

CROSS OUT THE WRONG WORD IN EACH SENTENCE:

1. The effect of each IV independently on the DV is called a Main Effect/ Interaction Effect.

2. An easy way to think about interactions is to think of them like an addition/ a switch.

3. When added together, IVs can explain up to 100%/50% of the variance of a DV.

Fill in the table with the missing values. You may find it useful to look back at Section 11.4.

IV1 effect size	IV2 effect size	DV variance explained	Total DV variance explained	Effect size
0.15	0.6	$0.15^2 =$ $0.6^2 =$	$(0.15^2 + 0.6^2) =$	$\text{sqrt}(0.15^2 + 0.6^2) =$
0.3	0.1			
-0.25	0.4			

THE ANSWERS ARE AVAILABLE ONLINE

YOUR SPACE

 # REFERENCES AND FURTHER READING

Flora, D.B. (2018) *Statistical Methods for the Social Science & Behavioural Sciences*. London: Sage.

A good general text that uses some mathematics with helpful explanations.

Hayes, A.F. (2013) *Mediation, Moderation and Conditional Process Analysis*. New York: Guilford Press.

The section on moderation is relevant to this chapter.

THERE ARE MORE ACTIVITIES AND A SHORT
SUMMARY VIDEO FOR THIS CHAPTER AVAILABLE AT:
HTTPS://STUDY.SAGEPUB.COM/STATISTICSFORPSYCHOLOGY

CHAPTER 12

COVARIATIONS: RELATIONSHIPS BETWEEN TWO INDEPENDENT VARIABLES

↳ TURNS OUT IT'S NOT CAKE'S FAULT AFTER ALL: BLAME ANOTHER VARIABLE

BUILDING   USING

In the previous chapter we began our exploration of what happens when we use several different Independent variables (IVs) at the same time. In that chapter we saw that the influences on a Dependent variable (DV) are of two basic types: **main effects**, which link individual IVs to the DV; and **interactions**, which are where one IV can switch or moderate the effect of another IV on the DV.

Now we turn to something that is going to be more dramatic in its consequences. It is often a possibility that the two IVs are themselves related. When this happens, the relationship between the IVs is called **covariation** (Figure 12.1). They are said to covary ('co-' means 'together', so they vary together), and this has important effects for both the statistics and the understanding of what the statistics are telling us.

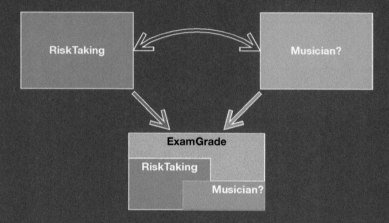

Figure 12.1   Illustration of covariation.

This diagram shows the effect of covariation. Covariation is marked by the double-headed arrow between the two IVs. The arrow is double-headed to indicate that the relationship can work in both ways. It causes an overlap of the DV variance explained by the two IVs: their shared effect.

We are going to start with using our usual research idea. So let's suppose that we have already established that there is a relationship between RiskTaking and ExamGrade. Now, our next question is whether being a musician or not has an effect on exam grade. We add into our analysis a second IV, Musician?.

From here onwards, the effect sizes we draw on arrows in these types of diagram will be called **direct effect sizes** to distinguish them from two other types of effect size that we will meet soon: total and unique. Direct effect sizes show how much influence flows from one variable to another through that arrow. They work in the same way we have seen throughout this book.

12.1 STEP 1: TOTAL EFFECT SIZES

If we take our IVs quite separately using each one on its own and ignoring any covariation it may have with other IVs, the effect size we obtain is called the **total effect size**. It is the sum total of all the information that flows from the IV to the DV. This approach is illustrated in Figure 12.2. In two-variable hypotheses like these, the total effect sizes are the same as the direct effect sizes on the arrows because there are only single arrows.

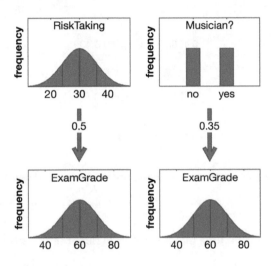

Figure 12.2   Illustration of total effect sizes.

Total effect sizes are the effect sizes we measure when we look at just one IV and one DV. These two here show the total effect sizes for our example. There are strong effects of both IVs on the DV.

12.1.1 RELATION TO DIRECT EFFECT SIZES

We have found a strong, positive effect of Musician? on ExamGrade. But perhaps musicians are simply very good at managing their nerves and using anxiety to maximise performance: maybe, for the purposes of our study, being a musician is no different from being a scuba diver. By thinking like this, we are splitting the concept of our variable Musician? into two parts: a risk-taking part and everything else, which we will call MusicNotRisk. The total effect size between Musician? and ExamGrade that we measured could be mostly due to the risk-taking part of being a musician and hardly at all due to MusicNotRisk. Our positive effect of Musician? may really only be because it is related strongly to risk-taking habits.

To see this graphically, look now at Figure 12.3. Focus on Musician? and how it can influence ExamGrade. There are two routes for that influence: a direct one and an indirect one via

RiskTaking. The total influence of Musician? on ExamGrade is the combination of the influences carried by each route. We have supplied some direct effect sizes that produce the phenomenon we are describing. The direct effects from each IV to the DV are now rather different, although the total effect sizes will be the same. We must explore why this is.

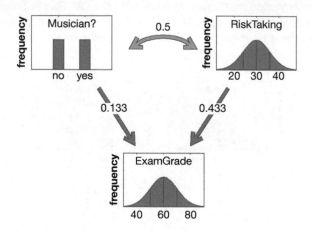

Figure 12.3   Illustration of direct effect sizes.

This diagram introduces a double-headed arrow between the two IVs to indicate the presence of covariation. The diagram shows the direct effect sizes between the three variables in this example.

Two rules allow us to calculate total effect sizes from direct effect sizes.

1. *Combining a sequence of steps*: the effect size for any single whole route is calculated by multiplying together the direct effect sizes for the individual steps. In doing this we must be careful with effect signs.

2. *Combining parallel routes from the same IV to the same DV:* the effect sizes of the routes are added together.

We can apply these two rules to the example in Figure 12.3, using Rule 1 to calculate the indirect route and then Rule 2 to combine the direct and indirect route. The calculations are shown in Table 12.1. The two total effect sizes are the same as those in Figure 12.2, so we know that the new diagram in Figure 12.3 is consistent with that old one.

Table 12.1   Calculations of total effect sizes from direct effect sizes.

IV	Direct route	Indirect route	Total effect size
Musician?	0.133	0.5×0.433=0.217	0.133+0.217=**0.35**
RiskTaking	0.433	0.5×0.133=0.067	0.433+0.067=**0.5**

12.2 STEP 2: UNIQUE EFFECT SIZES

Now we will go one more step and look at **unique effect sizes**. Unique effect sizes measure the effect of an IV that doesn't overlap with any other IVs. It is what is left when any overlapping effects are simply removed. In our example, the unique effect of Musician? is what is left after the overlap with RiskTaking is subtracted from it, as shown in Figure 12.4.

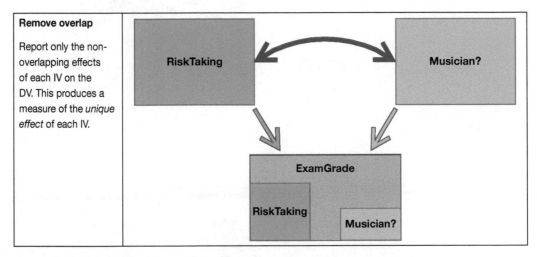

Figure 12.4   Unique effects come from removing overlap in variance explained.

This schematic diagram shows how the unique effects of each IV can be found by removing any overlap between them. In this situation, we are underestimating the amount of variance in the DV that our variables are accounting for because we are ignoring a portion of it.

12.2.1 RELATION TO DIRECT EFFECT SIZES

The variable Musician? in our example can be thought of as having two parts: the risk-taking part and everything else. These two parts are variables: one of them, RiskTaking, we already have, but the other (MusicNotRisk) is new. We can illustrate this with an extension to the diagram, as shown in Figure 12.5.

The variable we have labelled as (MusicNotRisk) represents all of the causes of Musician? except for those which overlap with RiskTaking. We have drawn the name of this variable in brackets and italics to show that it is not a variable we have measured: it is a latent variable. The direct effect size between it and Musician? is calculated to explain all of the remaining variance in Musician? after RiskTaking is taken into account. Its value is given by:

$$\text{sqrt}(1 - 0.5^2) = 0.87$$

where the 0.5 is the direct effect size linking RiskTaking to Musician?

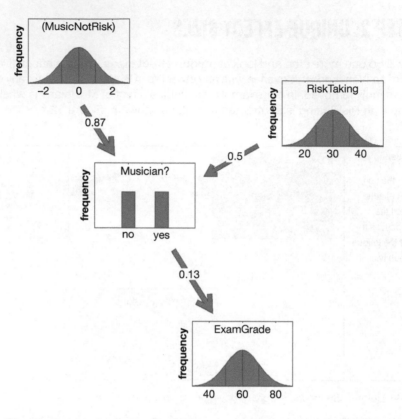

Figure 12.5   Hypothesis including a latent variable.

This is an elaboration of Figure 12.3, where we have added in a latent variable (MusicNotRisk) that corresponds to everything that contributes to the IV Musician? except risk-taking. The two variables (MusicNotRisk) and RiskTaking now explain all the variance of Musician?. For simplicity we have left out the link from RiskTaking directly to ExamGrade.

To find the unique effect of Musician? on ExamGrade, we must remove the effect that it shares with RiskTaking. In Figure 12.5, this is very easy to see: the unique effect of Musician? is the effect of (MusicNotRisk) on ExamGrade via Musician?. The unique effect of Musician? on ExamGrade is equivalent to the total effect of (MusicNotRisk) on ExamGrade. There is only one route between these two variables: an indirect route. Using Rule 1, we calculate the effect size for this indirect route by multiplying the direct effect sizes together: $0.87 \times 0.133 = 0.12$. So the unique effect size for Musician? is 0.12, which is the effect of being a musician after the risk-taking component of it is removed.

We can do the same calculation for RiskTaking: find the unique effect size of this variable. This unique effect size for RiskTaking is the effect of risk-taking after the being a musician component of it is removed.

12.3 THE TWO MEANINGS OF COVARIATION

When there is no covariation between the IVs, then the three sorts of effect size – direct, total and unique – are all the same. We have just seen that when there is covariation between the IVs, then the they are not the same. This matters for how we interpret any results that we get: what they mean. Up until now, interpreting a relationship between two variables, an effect, has been simple. But unlike most of the material so far, we now have to deal with the meaning of the different effect sizes.

There are two types of meaning we can understand. First, we will look at the statistical meaning: how the different relationships and routes work together in these diagrams. That will be the easier part of this. Then we will look and see what the psychological meaning of this all is. It might seem a little more tricky to grasp, but we'll get there.

12.3.1 STATISTICAL MEANING

The statistical meaning of the situation that arises with covariation is actually straightforward. There are three ways we can describe the situation: (i) using direct effect sizes (as in Figure 12.3, or converting these to (ii) total effect sizes or (iii) unique effect sizes. The values for these are shown in Table 12.2. Looking at this table, we can see easily that it is no longer possible to simply talk about the effect size of an IV on a DV. There are three different ways of describing it and we need to think about which we should use.

Table 12.2   Calculations of unique effect sizes from direct effect sizes.

IV	Direct effect size	Total effect size	Unique effect size
Musician?	0.133	0.133+0.217=0.35	0.87×0.133=0.115
RiskTaking	0.433	0.433+0.067=0.5	0.87×0.433=0.375

Here are various considerations to take into account:

- Total effect sizes in all the examples here have turned out to be potentially misleading. If taken together, they give an overestimate of how much variance in the DV we have explained.

- The direct effect sizes have the benefit that they are complete: they say everything that we know about the effects of these variables. They provide a correct estimate of how much variance in the DV we have explained. Compared to the other two, however, they are actually quite hard to interpret.

- Unique effect sizes are not complete: they leave out any overlap because of covariation between IVs. They are easier to interpret than the other effect sizes.

Ultimately, this is a choice to be made depending on the purpose of the research. It is important to bear in mind that neither total effect sizes nor unique effect sizes on their own provide a full picture.

12.3.2 PSYCHOLOGICAL MEANING

Once we have identified the covariation and its statistical consequences, then we have to think about what it means. If we use the unique effect size of an IV to characterise the relationship, then we have removed part of the IV (that overlaps with the other IV) and are using only what remains. We should work out how to describe that remaining part. Once we take risk-taking out of being a musician what is left?

The starting point is to realise that (looking at Figure 12.5) the unique effect size is really the relationship between the variable (MusicNotRisk) and ExamGrade. So, although we talk of it being the unique effect of Musician?, that is really just a shorthand way of avoiding having to spell out the latent variable.

When we analyse both IVs at the same time, the process finds their separate contributions to the exam grade. Specifically, the presence of the RiskTaking variable means that the **meaning** of the unique effect of the Musician? variable is changed to something that doesn't involve risk-taking. We call this *controlling* for the second variable: our analysis of Musician? has controlled for (i.e. removed) the effects it shares with RiskTaking. The effect we see, after controlling for RiskTaking, is the effect of a specific subset of the components of being a musician: the ones that aren't related to the willingness to take risks. Perhaps playing music requires great skill at recognising scales and arpeggios and these are what remains – in which case we could have discovered that these characteristics are not helpful in an exam. That makes sense.

The point here is that the meaning of each IV can be changed when our analysis includes their covariation to reveal their unique contributions to the DV. That leaves us with the important task of working out what the variables now mean. There is no statistical answer to that: the answers are all psychological. This is a clear example of how statistics can be thought of as a tool that allows us to see inside the data to a rich underlying psychology. You may feel that you want to be skilled at statistics, but really the key skill to aim for is the ability to think like a psychologist about what statistics shows you.

12.4 ANOTHER EXAMPLE OF COVARIATION

This principle of covariation is so important that we are going to look at another example. We have chosen a puzzling finding. Imagine we have measured the effect of the amount of time a student plans to spend preparing for exams on their exam grade. We would do this with the intention of using some real data to persuade students to plan out their preparation for exams by being able to demonstrate vividly the actual benefits.

We are looking at two new IVs, from which we hope to give students some sensible advice. The variable we are most interested in is the number of hours that participants plan to spend preparing for their exam; we will call it PlannedTime. Our main hypothesis is therefore that PlannedTime affects ExamGrade. We feel sure you will agree that this is a very sensible hypothesis but, like everything that is sensible, it is rather dull and obvious. To make it more interesting we have also measured participants' attitudes towards exams.

12.4.1 THE DATA: IVS SEPARATELY FOR TOTAL EFFECT SIZES

We show some simulated data for the effect of PlannedTime in Figure 12.6. The result looks clear-cut: planned preparation time has a strong influence on exam grades and the **total effect** size is 0.29. Using this, we begin to formulate the advice we will offer students. The result tells us that every hour of planned preparation time, on average, increases a student's exam grade by 5.5 points. That seems like a very useful piece of evidence to use to persuade students of the value of preparation.

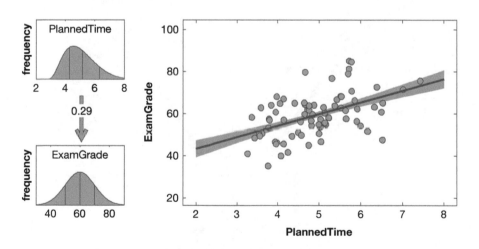

Figure 12.6   Hypothesis diagram and related scatter plot.

Our hypothesis is that the amount of time participants plan to spend preparing for their exam has a strong positive effect on their exam grade. We have placed a scatter plot of our data beside the hypothesis: it is clear that there is a strong positive relationship between the two variables.

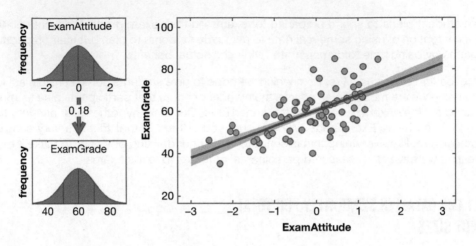

Figure 12.7   Second example including hypothesis diagram and related scatter plot.

This is our second example, after we have also measured ExamAttitude. There is, as expected, a positive relationship between attitude to exams and performance on exams.

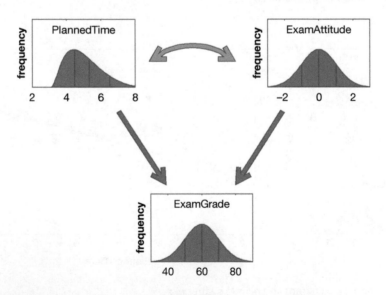

Figure 12.8   Hypothesis where two IVs are both included.

This figure shows the hypothesis when the two IVs are both included. We have every reason to expect that there will be covariation between the two IVs, so we have included an arrow for that.

Before committing to the simple advice, we return to the data and analyse our second IV, their attitude to exams. This hypothesis is shown in Figure 12.7 along with the simulated data for the effect. The total effect size for the effect of ExamAttitude on ExamGrade, obtained by just analysing those two variables on their own, is 0.18: a positive but rather modest effect.

12.4.2 THE DATA: IVS TOGETHER

Now we take the two IVs and put them both into a single hypothesis, which is shown in Figure 12.8.

When we examine the data with the two IVs together to get their direct effect sizes, the first thing we discover is that there is still, not surprisingly, a strong positive relationship between exam attitude and exam grade: participants with a positive attitude to exams do better than those with a negative attitude. The **direct effect** size for this relationship is 0.61.

Table 12.3   The different effect sizes for this example.

IV	Total effect size	Direct effect size	Unique effect size
PlannedTime	+0.29	−0.22	−0.123
ExamAttitude	+0.18	+0.61	+0.34

However, there is also a big unwelcome surprise. We now find that by including ExamAttitude in the analysis, the direct effect size for PlannedTime is −0.22, which is quite strongly negative. By adding more information into our analysis, the effect of PlannedTime we initially saw has changed radically. This would seem to mean that there is a reduction in exam grade of −2.4 for each hour planned for revising. To be clear, there are no mistakes in this: that is exactly what the data say. So what advice should we now be telling students? We clearly can't say that they should avoid preparing for exams because it reduces their exam grade.

We need to work through the two meanings of this data: the statistical and then the psychological.

12.4.3 STATISTICAL MEANING

The statistical meaning of this is straightforward. The total effect of PlannedTime on ExamGrade is the sum of the various routes (a direct route and one indirect route here). The direct route has a negative effect size of −0.22; the indirect route has a positive effect size of $0.83 \times 0.61 = 0.51$. The sum of these two is $-0.22 + 0.51 = 0.29$.

So, overall there is a positive total effect size of 0.29. The statistics have shown us that this total effect size is made up of two parts: (i) the direct route has a medium negative effect size (−0.22) and (ii) the indirect route has a strong positive effect size (+0.51).

12.4.4 PSYCHOLOGICAL MEANING

The psychological meaning of this is less straightforward. It hinges on what we think the variable PlannedTime means after we have removed the part of it that relates to ExamAttitude. One possibility is that if you remove attitude to exams from the amount of time people plan to spend preparing for exams, what you have left is a measure of how much they are being over- or under-ambitious in their plans. If the thought of exams fills you with horror, then planning to spend 8 hours per day, 5 days per week for 4 weeks is quite possibly a bad idea. Making such a plan would mean for me that either (i) I am going to spend most of that time in a panic convincing myself that I cannot do it or (ii) I am going to fail to keep it up and end up feeling guilty, with a strong aversion to revision.

Disclaimer: None of this is real advice by the way: the data are simulated just to make the point.

The negative unique effect of planned preparation time on exam grades, after attitude to exams has been taken into account, is a measure of how far our plan is realistic for us. If we are planning more revision time than we will achieve, then that will be bad for us, as the data show.

The advice? The advice would seem to be that students should prepare while that is productive, but if the preparation becomes a negative experience, then stop.

This is still not real advice by the way... although there may be some wisdom in it.

12.4.5 THE LESSONS OF THIS EXAMPLE

There is an activity for this online

The first lesson is that the statistics side of things is very simple: multiply effect sizes along a sequence of steps; add effect sizes where different parallel routes starting at the same original variable join up again. Bookmark these pages to come back to them or find additional examples in our online resources to get some more practice.

The second lesson is that the psychology side of this is perhaps quite complicated. Essentially, we have seen how the direct and unique effect size that joins an IV and a DV is changed every time we add in a new additional IV. There is nothing wrong in that, it is just that the meaning of the effect is itself also changed – and that is where the hard work will often lie: working out the new meaning of our variables.

However, there is a little bit of comfort here. To make the whole thing clear, we had to use very large effect sizes along the indirect route in our example. If they had been 0.25 each, which is certainly more likely generally, then the indirect effect size would be $0.25 \times 0.25 = 0.06$, which is so small as to be negligible.

It is sometimes possible to make two IVs to be completely independent of each other, such as our first example in Chapter 11, where we could randomly assign participants to groups of the second IV, which means that they have a relationship with a zero effect size. In this situation, the direct, total and unique effect sizes from an IV to the DV all have the same value.

12.5 PUTTING IT ALL TOGETHER

Covariation is common in psychology, probably more common than is realised. When we have understood how it happens, then there is nothing much more in statistics for us to learn.

The analysis of covariation has many different names. Mathematicians call this process conditioning because the analysis will look for any effects of Musician? after the condition of RiskTaking is fixed. Sometimes, psychologists call a partial version of it controlling for the second IV. By this they mean that it allows them to look at the purer effect of being a musician, after the risk-taking aspect of that has been controlled for – that is, removed. Another partial version of it can also, in some circumstances, be called mediation analysis, where the analysis would focus on whether the effect of being a musician on exam grades is mediated by (carried by) the effect of risk-taking. We will examine mediation briefly in Chapter 14.

We have seen how the existence of covariation creates a much richer picture of the psychology of a situation than we could see by looking only at total effects – by looking at each IV separately. That richer picture has a relatively straightforward statistical meaning, but it can require considerable thought to understand the psychological meaning.

12.5.1 EFFECTS AND EFFECT SIZES

We are now quite used to two key concepts of descriptive statistics: the idea that there are relationships between variables and that those relationships have a strength that we call the effect size.

In the topics we are now covering, the term **effect** is commonly used to describe a relationship: does RiskTaking have an effect on ExamGrade? Now we have multiple IVs, there are three different types of effect:

(i)   Main effects

(ii)   Interactions

(iii)   Covariations.

The strength of an effect can be presented in three different ways:

(i)   Natural effect sizes

(ii) Standardised effect sizes

(iii) Normalised effect sizes.

In this more complex situation of more than one IV, there are three different types of effect size:

(i)   Total effect size

(ii) Direct effect size

(iii) Unique effect size.

THE BIG PICTURE

Covariation is when there are relationships between IVs. It can have consequences for the effect sizes that we measure. When we use multiple IVs, there is a high chance that there will be some covariation.

VARIABLES AND ROUTES

1. We can think of the links that connect variables as being like pipes along which information flows. The variables are like tanks that hold that information.

2. The presence of covariation leads to there being multiple routes between IVs and the DV.

   a. Direct routes: any link that connects two variables without an intervening variable.

   b. Indirect routes: a sequence of direct links.

WAYS OF DESCRIBING EFFECT SIZES

1. Covariation means that there are three different ways of describing the sizes of effects.

   a. Total effect size: the effect size you would see if you just used a single IV. It is the sum of all the different routes from an IV to a DV.

   b. Unique effect size: the effect size seen when all overlap between IVs is removed.

   c. Direct effect size: the effect size that determines the flow of information through a direct link.

2. When there is a single IV, or the multiple IVs are all independent of each other. The total, unique and direct effect sizes are all the same.

3. When multiple IVs covary, the effect sizes are all different and may even have different signs.

MEANING

1. There are two rules for combining effect sizes:

   a. Sequence of links: multiply the direct effect sizes together.

   b. Set of parallel routes between the same two variables: add effect sizes.

2. The presence of covariation often requires us to change our understanding of the psychological meaning of IVs. The unique effect size is that part of the effect of an IV that it doesn't share with any other IVs.

 # YOUR TURN

DEFINE THE FOLLOWING KEY TERMS IN THE SPACE PROVIDED:

1. Covariation

2. Total effect size

3. Unique effect size

FILL IN THE GAPS TO COMPLETE THE SENTENCES.

1. In a route that is a sequence of steps, the direct effect sizes are .... together to give the effect size for the route.

2. When there are multiple routes between an IV and a DV, the route effect sizes are .... together to give the total effect size.

THE ANSWERS ARE AVAILABLE ONLINE

YOUR SPACE

 **REFERENCES**

Ellis, P.D. (2010) *The Essential Guide to Effect Sizes: Statistical Power, Meta-Analysis, and the Interpretation of Research Results*. Cambridge: Cambridge University Press.

Quite technical but very useful summaries.

Flora, D.B. (2018) *Statistical Methods for the Social Science & Behavioural Sciences*. London: Sage.

A good general text that uses some mathematics with helpful explanations.

IIIIIIIIIIII➤ THERE ARE MORE ACTIVITIES AND A SHORT
SUMMARY VIDEO FOR THIS CHAPTER AVAILABLE AT:
HTTPS://STUDY.SAGEPUB.COM/STATISTICSFORPSYCHOLOGY

CHAPTER

13

ANALYSING DATA WITH TWO OR MORE INDEPENDENT VARIABLES

GENERAL LINEAR MODEL VERSUS ANOVA: WHO WILL WIN?

BUILDING   USING

In the previous two chapters we have examined the three fundamental ways in which independent variables (IVs) can work together: **main effects**, **interactions** and then **covariations**. In this chapter we will now explore how to analyse data that has come from hypotheses with multiple IVs.

There are two fundamental ways of analysing data that has multiple IVs. These methods of analysis are going to be somewhat familiar to you as we have already seen scaled-down versions of them in Chapter 7: **regression** and analysis of variance (**ANOVA**).

In the past there were many more approaches that were all treated as distinct but are now seen as falling into these two fundamental categories. We will close this chapter with a brief look at those so that you will understand them if you encounter them.

13.1 DIFFERENT WAYS TO DESCRIBE EFFECT SIZES

If two or more IVs are completely independent, then each explains a separate amount of **variance** in the Dependent variable (DV). If they are not independent and there is covariation between the IVs, then the variance of the DV that is explained by them has two parts:

- There is variance in the DV that is only explained by one IV.
- There is variance in the DV that is simultaneously explained by two or more overlapping IVs.

In Table 13.1 we list the three basic effect sizes that can be used when there is overlap between two IVs. In the previous chapter we saw how these different ways of describing an effect work. In thischapter we will see how these can be estimated from data.

Table 13.1   The possible ways of dealing with the overlap between IVs when there is covariation.

Ignore overlap: total effect sizes	Report each **total effect** size separately.
Remove overlap: unique effect sizes	Report only the **unique effects** of each IV on the DV. This produces a measure of the unique effect of each IV.
Partition overlap: direct effect sizes	The overlap can be split between the IVs. This results in what we have been calling the **direct effect** of each variable.

13.2 GENERAL LINEAR MODEL

The first for analysing data with more than one IV is called a **General Linear Model**. Actually, it works perfectly well for data when there is only one IV and will produce the same results (in a slightly different way). However, it hasn't really caught on in psychology yet for single IV testing: the older tests that we looked at in Chapter 7 persist in analysis, probably because they are more familiar.

The process builds a model – a General Linear Model – of what the data tells us using principles we have already covered, so although it is a new name, most of the details will be familiar. We are going to use some formulae in this section because they are good ways of explaining what General Linear Models are. We will explain each formula as we go along – and none of them involves more than adding and multiplying. Even if you don't like maths, this is going to be simple. Remember that we have included a table of common formulae meanings in the 'How to Use This Book' section.

13.2.1 FORMULAE

Look at the following formula. The right side of it (to the right of the =) is a recipe for calculating the left side where each letter stands for a number:

$$y_i = a + e_i$$

y = DV value, a = constant number, e = variable number; the subscript, i denotes any specific participant

This formula says, in mathematical notation, that the value of a variable y for participant i (the bit that says 'y_i') is made by:

(i)   taking a constant value (a)

(ii)   adding a variable extra amount (e_i) which has a specific value for each participant i.

The right-hand side of the formula is said to have two terms, separated by the + sign. These terms correspond to the steps in the calculation. Notice also that the right-hand side of the formula has two types of number: one that doesn't depend on the particular participant (a) and one that does depend on the individual (e_i). The first term in the formula does the same thing for everyone, which is why a is called a **constant**; the second term has a different consequence for each participant.

Now we can let y_i stand for the value of the DV for participant i. Let's also set the constant a to the mean value of the DV. This would mean that e_i is the difference between the participant's value and the mean – the residual. So this formula would say that we can calculate the individual value of the DV for participant i as the sum of the mean of the DV plus the individual residual for that participant (e_i).

In Chapter 4 we learned about regression lines. We can write the regression line down as a similar formula:

$$y_i = a + bx_i + e_i$$

b = slope of regression line, x = value of IV

In formulae, it is conventional to miss out the times character for multiplication. So, bx means b times x.

This formula is very similar to the previous one, it just has one more term. It says that y_i, the value for the DV for participant i, is made by:

(i)   taking the constant a

(ii)   adding the constant b times x_i, the value of the IV for participant i

(iii) then adding e_i, the residual for this participant.

There are still some numbers in this formula that apply to all participants (a and b) and numbers that do not (y, x and e). The numbers of the formula that apply to everyone (a and b) are now going to be called **coefficients**. This formula is slightly more complex than the previous one. It calculates the DV value for a participant with two coefficients (a and b) instead of one.

13.2.2 MODELS

The formula we have been looking at tells us how to calculate the specific value of the DV for a given individual. Now we are going to drop the term e_i, so that what we have left is a formula that tells us what the general pattern in the population is:

$$y_i = a + bx_i$$

This is now a **model**: it is a statement about the overall effect in the population. It is possible to think of the model as being a formula that allows us to make a prediction of what value of DV (y) we should expect given a value for the IV (x). In this case, it is a statement that says 'the predicted value of y for any participant or other member of the population i is a plus b times x_i'. This is a model in the sense that it captures what we think of as the important information (the coefficients) and disregards the specific details (the residuals); because of this, it now works for the whole population.

In this model, the coefficient, a, has a special name: it is called the **intercept**. Its value is the same as the value of y when x is zero, because when x is zero the second term in the model is also zero. Usually the intercept is not of any interest.

With more than one IV, we can just continue adding coefficients to the model. So, with two IVs, we can have a model that contains the effects of both IVs:

$$y = a + b_1x_1 + b_2x_2$$

x_1 = IV1 value for that participant, x_2 = IV2 value for that participant b_1 = coefficient for IV1, b_2 = coefficient for IV2

This time, just to avoid having a formula that is difficult to read, we have left out the subscripts (the i bit) to show which participant we are describing. That means that we have to understand that some of the quantities are coefficients (a and the various b terms) and some are values for an individual with a missing subscript (y, the various x terms).

The procedure for estimating the (finding the best-fitting) regression line when we had just one IV involved finding values for the coefficients (a and b) that resulted in the smallest possible sum of squared deviations. Since the deviations are residuals, we can describe the process as finding values for the coefficients (a and b) that produce the minimum (smallest) sum of squared residuals.

The model with two IVs is just a simple extension of the model with one IV. So, although mathematically it is a bit more complex, we can again estimate the values for the coefficients by finding a combination of values for them that minimises the sum of squared residuals. As a result of doing this, we might find that our model becomes this:

$$\text{ExamGrade} = 60 + 5 \times \text{RiskTaking} + 2 \times \text{Musician?}$$

This formula tells us that the exam grade for any person is predicted by the model to be a combination of a constant 60, plus five times their RiskTaking score plus two times their Musician? score. This is useful:

(i) It shows us that a person's exam grade goes up by 5 (on average) for every increase in their RiskTaking score of 1.

(ii) It shows us how much benefit (on average) a person gets for being a musician (2 extra grade points).

13.2.3 COEFFICIENTS AND VARIABLE TYPES

Look at this model again:

$$y=a+b_1x_1+b_2x_2$$

x_1= IV1 value for that participant, x_2= IV2 value for that participant b_1 = coefficient for IV1, b_2 = coefficient for IV2

In simple regression involving only Interval variables, it is easy to see how the individual values for the IVs can be used as x in the model and multiplied by the coefficients, b. With Categorical IVs, the values are not numerical and it doesn't really help us to talk of multiplying the category labels by coefficients (e.g. two times 'Yes').

The model we saw at the end of the last section implicitly assumes that if you are a musician, then that variable has a value of 1 and if you aren't then it has a value of 0. That works nicely: if you are a musician then you get two extra grade points (two times 1 is 2), and if you aren't, then you get 0 extra grade points (two times 0 is 0). It would have been more complete to write the formula like this:

ExamGrade = 60 + 5 × RiskTaking + 0 × (Musician? = No) + 2 × (Musician? = Yes)

which then makes explicit what we are doing. This way, we can also deal with a different version of the variable Musician? which has three categories (No, Amateur, Professional). Then the formula might look like:

ExamGrade = 60 + 5 × RiskTaking + 0 × (Musician?=No)
+ 1.5 × (Musician? = Amateur)
+ 2.5 × (Musician? = Professional)

This formula has split the variable Musician? into its three different categories and estimated a separate coefficient for each possible value. The categories are all mutually exclusive, so each participant gets one and only one of the list of three possible coefficients. So the above formula means that if you fit into the professional category, you would have a value of 0 for 'Musician?=no' because you don't fit that category, and a value of 0 for 'Musician?= amateur' because you don't fit that category, then a value of '1' times 2.5 for 'Musician?= professional'. So, written out again, we have:

$$ExamGrade = 60 + 5×RiskTaking + 0×(0)$$
$$+ 1.5×(0)$$
$$+ 2.5×(1)$$

$$ExamGrade = 60 + 5×RiskTaking + (0×0) + (1.5×0) + (2.5×1)$$

We can always set the coefficient for one of the categories (by default, it's always the first) to zero. Then we can simplify the formula by dropping the term that is zero because it is unnecessary to write a part of a formula that means 'if this is true, then add zero'. The remaining two coefficients then show us the difference between those two categories and the missing category. So, an amateur musician scores, on average, 1.5 grade points higher than a non-musician and a professional scores 2.5 points higher than a non-musician. So, we can write:

$$ExamGrade = 60 + 5 × RiskTaking + 1.5 × (Musician? = Amateur) + 2.5 ×$$
$$(Musician? = Professional)$$

This business of splitting a Categorical variable with g categories and creating $(g-1)$ coefficients to show the differences between the first category and the other categories is called creating **dummy variables**. Once we have done this, then all the values are numerical: for the dummy variable they are always 0 or 1. What we have here are now two dummy variables: one for being an amateur or not, and one for being a professional or not.

13.2.4 USEFULNESS OF THE GENERAL LINEAR MODEL

The General Linear Model makes two very important contributions.

The first contribution is that the coefficients that we estimate are measures of the direct effect size of the variables concerned. The coefficients themselves give us direct effect sizes in **natural effect size** units, as they are expressed in units of the variables: the 5 in the formula above is 5 grade points (DV units) for an increase of 1 in the RiskTaking score (IV1 units).

It is possible to convert these direct effect sizes from natural units to normalised units. A simple formula does this:

$$r_1 = b_1 × \frac{sd(IV1)}{sd(DV)} \quad r_2 = b_2 × \frac{sd(IV2)}{sd(DV)}$$

Where r_1 is the normalised effect size for the first IV, r_2 is the normalised effect size for the second IV.

The second contribution of a General Linear Model is that it represents everything we know about the DV from our sample. Any possible overlap between IVs, like we looked at in Section 12.1, are included (but not duplicated) in the coefficients for those DVs. The whole model can have its own effect size, which then tells us how much of the variance of the DV is explained by the model as a whole. We will call this the **model effect size**.

To calculate the model effect size, the right-hand side of the model formula can be thought of as a recipe of how to combine the various IVs into a new single combined IV. For each participant we can apply this formula and get a new value for them. If we had a participant with a RiskTaking score of 0.5 and who was an Amateur musician, then the formula would give us this value as the model prediction for them:

$$60 + 5 \times 0.5 + 1.5 = 64.$$

Their actual value for ExamGrade might be 71, and the difference is their residual. We can get a predicted value for each participant in this way and in so doing we have created a new variable, which is the value predicted by the model for each participant. We can write down the formula like this where $model_i$ is the value of this new variable for each participant:

$$y_i = model_i + e_i$$

where e_i is the residual

This new formula is a simple regression line (it uses a new Interval variable, $model$, predicting an Interval variable, y) and we can calculate a normalised effect size for the relationship between the new variable model and the original DV.

Adding up the total effect sizes of each IV includes any overlap between them multiple times and will overestimate the amount of variance in the DV they jointly explain. Adding up the unique effect sizes of each IV omits any overlap between them and will underestimate the amount of variance in the DV they jointly explain. The model effect size for a General Linear Model properly estimates the amount of variance in the DV explained. In that way it is a substantially better description of what our data tell us than the sum of either the total or unique effect sizes.

13.2.5 UNCERTAINTY AND GENERAL LINEAR MODELS

There is one more thing that we need to explore before moving on: **uncertainty**. In Chapter 5 we saw that uncertainty arises when we estimate a population effect size from a sample. That is equally true here for General Linear Models. Each estimated (sample) coefficient has an associated uncertainty about the value of the coefficient in the population. It is normal to express these uncertainties as **standard errors**, just as we discussed in Chapter 5. As we saw in Chapter 6, a common way of examining the uncertainty is to use **null hypothesis testing**. There we saw that, to do this, we convert an effect size and its associated standard error into a t-value and then convert the t-value with its degrees of freedom into a p-value. We can do all of this for the coefficients of a General Linear Model in exactly the same way.

Table 13.2 shows *simulated* results for the General Linear Model we were considering above in a format that is similar to the output of most commonly used statistical software. Each row in the table shows us an analysis of one of the coefficients In the model, so the variable Musician? has two rows – one for each dummy variable.

- Estimated value: the estimated value for the coefficient.
- SE: the standard error for that estimated coefficient.
- t: the **t-statistic**. You can check that the t-value is just the estimated value of the coefficient divide by its standard error.
- df: the **degrees of freedom**. This is the sample size (n) minus the number of coefficients estimated for the whole model (including the intercept).

Table 13.2 is a straightforward replacement for the APA statement that we saw in Chapter 7 (e.g. t(40)=2.67, p=0.011). The table has the same information, plus a bit more, for each coefficient. This table would be reported in its entirety to show the results of this analysis. It would also be expected that the conclusions reached about the different coefficients (which of them are significant, for example) would be reported.

Table 13.2   The full analysis of a General Linear Model.

This table is an example of the full analysis of a General Linear Model. It shows for each variable (note that there are two dummy variables for the Categorical variable Musician?) the estimated value of each coefficient, the standard error of that estimate, the t-value and degrees of freedom for the coefficient, and then the p-value for the null hypothesis that the population value for that coefficient is zero. Df = 38 because we have three coefficients and the intercept, and n=42. The degrees of freedom are n minus the number of estimated coefficients, so 42 − 4 = 38.

Coefficient	Estimated value	SE	t	df	p-value
Intercept	60	10			
RiskTaking	5	2	2.5	38	0.017
Musician=Amateur	1.5	1.05	1.43	38	0.16
Musician=Profess	2.5	0.94	2.67	38	0.011

The analysis behind the General Linear Model has given us the two different types of measure of uncertainty: standard errors as a means of understanding how wide the likelihood function is and also **p-values** for null hypothesis testing. These p-values are tests of the null hypotheses that each coefficient in turn is drawn at random from a population with zero coefficients. A p-value that is significant for any given coefficient would indicate that we can reject the corresponding null hypothesis, which is that the population value of that coefficient is zero. Notice that the Categorical variable, which gives rise to two coefficients in this case because there are three categories, has two null hypothesis tests.

The model effect size for the whole model will have an associated standard error and can be compared with the null hypothesis that the sample whole model is drawn from a population where the whole model has a zero effect size.

13.3 ANOVA

ANOVA is an acronym of analysis of variance, and we first encountered it back in Chapter 7 with the one-way ANOVA. What we learned there is that an ANOVA is used to compare the effect of different groups of a Categorical IV on an Interval DV. It achieves that by calculating and comparing:

(i)   the variance in the DV that is explained by the IV

(ii) the variance in the DV that is unexplained.

Where ANOVA differs from General Linear Model is in its treatment of overlap: General Linear Model looks for a combination of IVs that will include all the variance in DV that is explained, whereas ANOVA examines the variance in the DV that is uniquely explained by each IV. Any overlap is disregarded. ANOVA works on unique effect sizes.

There is nothing special about Categorical IVs and the ANOVA procedure is one that we can use with Interval as well as Categorical IVs to identify the unique effects of each variable in the model.

It is easiest to think of the process like this. An ANOVA starts with the amount of variance in the DV explained by the whole model. Then it takes one IV and removes it from the analysis and fits the new model without this variable to the data. The only thing that is removed by doing this is the unique effect of that IV, as any covariation or overlap it has with other IVs is still in the model – that is, covered by them. So the difference between the new model and the full model can tell us the unique effect of the IV we removed:

Variance uniquely explained by IV1 = Variance explained by full model –
Variance explained by model without IV1

If the model with one IV removed shows a large reduction in variance explained compared to the full model, then the IV that has been removed must have a strong unique effect size.

The proportion of variance in the DV that a model explains is the square of the r-family version of the model effect size and is usually written as R^2. We can find the value of R^2 for the full General Linear Model and then the value for a model without a specific IV. The difference in R^2 between the two models is an R^2 measure of the unique effect of the IV in question.

R^2(unique effect of IV1) = R^2(full model) – R^2 (model without IV1)

By doing this for each variable in turn (and when we say 'by doing this', we mean 'when a chosen piece of software runs these calculations'), we can produce a table of effect sizes: one for each IV.

13.3.1 UNIQUE EFFECT SIZES, η^2 AND PARTIAL η^2

Often an ANOVA analysis is reported with an effect size called η^2 (pronounced eta squared). This quantity is just the square of the unique effect size, as we have described it (i.e. using normalised effect sizes). It is also sometimes called a semi-partial effect.

A related quantity that ANOVA software can provide is partial η^2. This quantity is the square of the standardised effect size version of the unique effect size. The formula is:

$$R^2(\text{unique effect of IV1}) \,/\, (1 - R^2(\text{model without IV1}))$$

13.3.2 UNIQUE EFFECT SIZES AND VARIABLE TYPES

An ANOVA finds the variance in the DV uniquely explained by each IV. It does that for one IV by comparing the variance explained by a full model and by a model with that IV removed. This process does not depend on what the variable types are. A consequence of this is that, although the full General Linear Model potentially has more coefficients than variables (recall that every dummy variable created will have its own coefficient), the ANOVA has the same number of results as the number of variables.

13.3.3 USEFULNESS OF THE ANOVA

The ANOVA makes two important additional contributions to the analysis of data with multiple IVs.

The first contribution is that the effect sizes that an ANOVA produces are the unique effect sizes for each variable. Recall from earlier that these are a measure of any effect a variable might have that does not overlap with any of the other variables.

In a situation where we are aware of a confounding variable, then it makes sense to try to remove that variable. Sometimes we can do this by design: choosing our sample carefully to avoid it. If we thought that there might be an effect of Musician? on ExamGrades but wanted to remove any possibility of that being due to a tendency among our musicians to take risks, then we might try to set up two groups, musicians and not, but ensure that the two groups had very similar distributions of risk-taking, so that it couldn't influence the results. This can be very difficult to achieve sometimes, and usually there is no need to because if we measure risk-taking as a second variable, then we can allow the statistical analysis to remove its influence. An ANOVA allows us to look for the unique effect of Musician? alongside RiskTaking.

The second contribution is that a unique effect size assessed by an ANOVA often provides the most persuasive answer to a question about the existence of an effect. In this circumstance, the most persuasive answer arises when we ask a question not about the total effect of a variable (which, as we have seen, could be contaminated with influences of other variables), but instead when we ask a question about the unique effect of a variable: is there anything in our second variable that is explaining otherwise unexplained variance in the DV?

13.3.4 UNCERTAINTY AND ANOVA: NULL HYPOTHESIS TESTING

Normally, the end result of ANOVA is a null hypothesis test which compares the unique effect of each variable with the null hypothesis that the population unique effect of that variable is zero. This is achieved by an F-test (the same F-statistic that we saw in Chapter 7).

In practice, although this is the logic of what is done, it is usually reported slightly differently. R^2 is the same thing, as the proportion of variance explained. To be more precise, we can write a simple formula:

$$R^2 = \frac{variance\,(due\;to\;variable)}{variance\,(DV)}$$

R^2 is the variance in the DV that is due to the variable divided by the total variance of the DV.

The standard practice in ANOVA is to use a slightly different quantity:

$$F = \frac{variance\,(due\;by\;variable)\,/\,df\,(variable)}{variance\,(unexplained)\,/\,df\,(unexplained)}$$

Instead of comparing the variance in the DV that is explained by the model to the total variance of the DV, this formula produces an F-statistic by comparing the variance due to the model with the unexplained variance. This F-statistic is the same as the one we encountered in Chapter 7 where we were also looking at it as a route to null hypothesis testing. In the same way as then, it leads easily to a p-value.

There is a common approach to reporting an ANOVA. An example is shown in Table 13.3. The table lists the different IVs with a row for each plus a row marked error – this corresponds to the quantity e in the formulae for General Linear Models above and is the residual for the model: the difference between what the model predicts for each participant and their actual value. It is also therefore unexplained variance.

For each variable, the results table gives:

- SumSq: the sum of squared deviations that are due to the corresponding variable (and the error number is just what is left over).

- df: the degrees of freedom associated with that variable. It is actually the number of coefficients in the General Linear Model associated with that variable. For an Interval variable, this is just 1; for a Categorical variable it is the number of different categories minus 1 (which is the number of coefficients needed for the dummy variable). The total count of degrees of freedom must equal the number of observations, and so the Error row has a value for df that is n (the sample size) minus all the other df values.
- MeanSq: SumSq divided by df (just provided for convenience).
- F: the F-statistic, calculated as the SumSq divided by the df for each variable divided by the SumSq for Error divided by its df.
- p: the result of a null hypothesis test using the F-statistic for that variable.

Table 13.3 would be reported in its entirety to show the results of this analysis. It would also be expected that the conclusions reached about the different coefficients (which of them are significant, for example) would be reported.

Table 13.3   A typical ANOVA output.

Here is a typical ANOVA output reported as a table of values. SumSq = sum of squares; df = degrees of freedom; MeanSq = sum of squares divided by degrees of freedom; F = F-statistic (test-statistic for ANOVA as seen in Chapter 7); p = p-value. If you wish, you can check that the numbers in this table are consistent with each other – that the MeanSq numbers are the SumSq numbers divided by df, and that the F values are MeanSq divided by MeanSq(Error).

Variable	SumSq	df	MeanSq	F	p
RiskTaking	3.47	1	3.47	3.16	0.084
Musician?	1.05	2	0.526	0.478	0.624
Error	41.8	38	1.1		

13.4 GENERALISED LINEAR MODEL

You may have just read this section header and gone 'well hang on a minute, we've already done General Linear Models'. And you would be correct. But this section is actually about the similarly named but slightly different General*ised* Linear Models.

Back in Chapter 4 we explained how linear regression only works for a continuous DV, and that we need to use logistic regression for a Categorical DV. Logistic regression is based on similar logic to linear regression, but since the DV has category values not numerical values, logistic regression predicts the relative probability of a particular category occurring, depending on the value of the IV. The same logic applies here. A General Linear Model works for a continuous (Interval) DV, but if the DV is Categorical, then we have to use its close cousin the **Generalised Linear Model**. Although the details are more complex, at a conceptual level we can think of it as being essentially the same process. If our DV was ExamPass? with values Yes and No, then the Generalised Linear Model would be something that meant this:

logit(ExamPass? = Yes) = 0.8 + 0.1 × RiskTaking + 0.024 × (Musician? = Yes)

There are many different ways of providing that left-hand part of the formula and we will leave the details of this for your further reading. As with all other types of analysis, a Generalised Linear Model can be calculated using most common statistical software packages.

13.5 THE HISTORICAL STATISTICAL TESTS

Although General Linear Models and the application of ANOVA to them is now widespread in psychology, this is a relatively recent development. Historically, the analysis of data with multiple IVs has used a small bag of special-purpose tools, each of which is a particular variant on the General Linear Model idea. We don't wish to devote much time to these as they are now really best treated as a remnant of the past. However, you will still encounter them in research papers and may work with researchers who stick to the traditional methods, and so it is worth knowing a little about them. Our descriptions here are therefore kept brief.

13.5.1 INTERVAL DV VARIABLE TYPE

Historically, there are three types of analysis that have been used when the DV is an Interval variable, depending on the combination of IV types involved. The name of the analysis in each case is provided in Table 13.4.

Table 13.4 Historical tests for hypotheses with multiple IVs and Interval DV.

This table shows the historical tests for hypotheses with an Interval DV and two (or more) IVs. Although there are four cells in this table, two of the cells are effectively the same because they each involve a combination of Categorical and Interval variable.

		Categorical	Interval
IV2	Categorical	Factorial ANOVA	ANCOVA
	Interval	ANCOVA	Multiple regression

FACTORIAL ANOVA: ALL IVS ARE CATEGORICAL

When all of the IVs are Categorical, the analysis that was used was called either a **Factorial ANOVA** or, more specifically, a two-way ANOVA, three-way ANOVA, etc., where the numbers refer to how many Categorical IVs there are.

In practice, the outputs of a Factorial ANOVA are the same as would be obtained by applying an ANOVA to a General Linear Model. Therefore, they are measures of the unique effects of each variable and remove any overlap.

MULTIPLE REGRESSION: ALL IVS ARE INTERVAL

When all of the IVs are Interval, the analysis that was used was called a **multiple regression**. The analysis behind a multiple regression is identical to that in a General Linear Model (and multiple regression is sometimes called linear modelling). Since it only uses Interval variables, there is only one coefficient for each variable (there are no dummy variables). The coefficient, analogous to the slope term in regression with one IV, is a direct effect size measured in natural effect size units.

In order to obtain the unique effect size in multiple regression, a variant was developed where the variables are taken in turn. We would do a multiple regression analysis with the variables we are least interested in to begin with. Then we add in some more variables that we are interested in. If the overall model is substantially improved, then we know that our second set of variables is important. This is a method that removes overlap for the variables we are most interested in by implication.

ANCOVA: MIXTURE OF CATEGORICAL AND INTERVAL IVS

The last variant is where the IVs are a mixture of Categorical and Interval variables. The special purpose analysis for this situation was called an ANCOVA (analysis of covariance). Its working and outputs are essentially the same as a General Linear Model followed by an ANOVA.

13.5.2 CATEGORICAL DV VARIABLE TYPE

Historically, there are two types of analysis that have been used for a Categorical DV, depending on the combination of IV types involved. The name of the analysis in each case is provided in Table 13.5.

Table 13.5   Historical tests for hypotheses with multiple IVs and Categorical DV.

The historical tests for hypotheses with a Categorical DV and two (or more) IVs. Although there are four cells in this table, two of the cells are left blank as they never had a special purpose analysis devised for them.

		IV1	
		Categorical	Interval
IV2	Categorical	Chi-square test of independence	
	Interval		Logistic regression

We will not dwell on this as the two analyses in this section are simply extensions of the equivalent two variable analyses that have the same names.

13.6 USING THESE ANALYSES

The two basic processes described in this chapter lead themselves to a very clear work flow.

1. A General Linear Model produces estimates of the model coefficients. From these we can calculate the direct effect sizes.

2. ANOVA estimates the unique effect sizes for each of the variables.

Using both of these sets of results, we can build a comprehensive picture of the relationships between the IVs and the DV.

As we emphasised in Chapter 12, the most important part of the procedure (and often the most difficult) is not the statistical analysis provided by these two processes, but is instead working out what the meaning of the variables in the results is. And we wish to finish this chapter with another paragraph to draw attention to this.

It is a mistake to take a set of data with several IVs and just apply an ANOVA analysis to it. This is easily done – all modern software makes this readily available. The problem with this approach is that it overlooks the possibility of covariation between the IVs. If there is covariation between the IVs, then the psychological meaning of the unique (i.e. ANOVA) effect size for each IV may have been altered.

We have considered how to analyse the individual coefficients and/or variables in a General Linear Model. We've said rather little in this chapter about what to do with the whole model. In the next chapter we will look at this and specifically consider how to compare different models, such as you might get by adding in or removing variables.

THE BIG PICTURE

TWO DIFFERENT ANALYSES

1. There are two basic forms of analysis:
    a. General Linear Model
    b. ANOVA.

2. The two approaches estimate effect sizes:
    a. Direct effect sizes can be calculated using General Linear Model.
    b. ANOVA can be used to calculate unique effect sizes.

3. Table 13.6 captures the most important differences between the two approaches to multiple-IV analysis.

Table 13.6   A side-by-side comparison of the two main types of data analysis.

General Linear Model	Analysis of Variance (ANOVA)
Find a combination of the IVs that predicts the DV as closely as possible.	Find out how much of the variance in the DV each IV uniquely predicts.
Where IVs overlap, share it between them.	Where IVs overlap, discard.
Split Categorical variables into dummy variables.	Keep Categorical variables whole.
Give result as coefficients and SEs. Calculate t-statistic.	Give results as SSQ. Calculate F-statistic.

WORKFLOW

1. The two processes can be used on the same set of data to provide a comprehensive insight into the variables. Alternatively, the one that better suits the purposes of research should be chosen.

2. Bear in mind that where unique effect sizes differ considerably from total effect sizes, the psychological meaning of the variables must be considered.

 # YOUR TURN

FILL IN THE ANSWERS TO COMPLETE THESE SENTENCES.

1. A continuous (Interval) DV requires the use of a _____ model.

2. A Categorical DV requires the use of a _____ model.

3. If you are interested in whether or not a variable is having a unique effect on a DV, then use _____ .

BELOW ARE THE RESULTS OF A GENERAL LINEAR MODEL ANALYSIS LOOKING
AT THREE VARIABLES THAT MIGHT INFLUENCE A STUDENT'S OVERALL GRADE.
THERE WERE 51 PARTICIPANTS. FILL IN THE GAPS IN THE TABLE AND IN THE MODEL
FORMULA TO COMPLETE THE RESULTS.

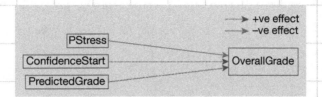

Figure 13.1   Some sample results from a General Linear Model.

OVERALL GRADE = 52 - 0.521*_____ + __*CONFIDENCESTART +
0.401*PREDICTEDGRADE +

Table 13.7   Some sample results from a General Linear Model.

Coefficient	Estimated value	SE	t	df	p-value
Intercept	52.5	13.41	n/a		n/a
PStress		0.380	-1.37		0.174
ConfidenceStart	0.010	0.067	0.15		0.882
PredictedGrade		0.147	2.72		0.008

ANSWER THIS QUESTION:

ARE ANY OF THE VARIABLES A SIGNIFICANT PREDICTOR OF OVERALLGRADE?

_____

THERE ARE MORE ACTIVITIES AND ANSWERS ONLINE

YOUR SPACE

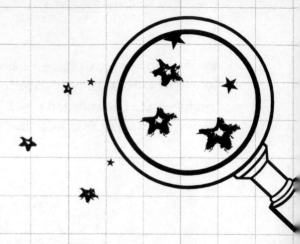

 # REFERENCES AND FURTHER READING

Dobson, A.J. & Barnett, A.G. (2008) *An Introduction to Generalized Linear Models* (3rd edition). Boca Raton, FL: CRC Press.

Advanced classic text.

Flora, D.B. (2018) *Statistical Methods for the Social Science & Behavioural Sciences*. London: Sage.

A good general text that uses some mathematics with helpful explanations.

Fox, J. (2016) *Applied Regression Analysis and Generalized Linear Models*. London: Sage.

Advanced but comprehensive.

THERE ARE MORE ACTIVITIES AND A SHORT SUMMARY VIDEO FOR THIS CHAPTER AVAILABLE AT:
HTTPS://STUDY.SAGEPUB.COM/STATISTICSFORPSYCHOLOGY

CHAPTER

14

WHICH MODEL IS BEST?

MY GENERAL LINEAR MODEL IS BETTER THAN YOURS

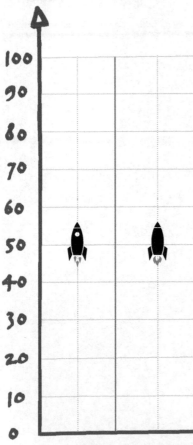

BUILDING   USING

This chapter introduces one last concept that will let us take a brief tour of some more advanced topics. With the understanding of statistics that we have been building up, this last step is surprisingly easy to take.

For each topic that we have included here, we will explain the purpose and concept behind it and provide you with enough information to go away and discover the 'how-to' of doing it for yourself. We felt it important to include this content because, even though the topics here deserve a book of their own, the way they work underlines a significant change in how statistics can work for psychology.

All the topics we will be considering have at their heart a simple but new type of question: which model is best?

14.1 CHOOSING BETWEEN MODELS

A **model**, as we saw in the previous chapter, is a mathematical way of saying what we think the population is like, given our **data**. The mean exam grade from a sample is a model: if that is all we know, then it is the best guess we can make about the exam grade that anyone in the population might get in the future. If our data have told us that there is an effect of being a risk-taker on exam grades, then we can build that effect into our model to produce a more detailed model that should make a more accurate prediction for anyone in the population.

When we have more than just a few IVs, then we have the potential to use them in many different ways to make many different models. There are important decisions to be made about which IVs to include and which to leave out, and each decision leads to a different model. The last concept we need is a way of understanding how to choose between these different models.

Just like General Linear Models are a broader, bigger picture version of regression, our last concept is a broader, bigger picture version of several earlier concepts.

14.1.1 NULL HYPOTHESIS TESTING AS MODEL COMPARISON

We have seen in Chapter 6 how a simple, frequently used way of deciding whether there is an effect is to use **null hypothesis testing**. The null hypothesis is that there is no effect of the Independent variable (IV) on the Dependent variable (DV) and we hope to reject this null hypothesis. Another way of thinking about the logic of the null hypothesis test goes like this. We have two models: (i) the null hypothesis model and (ii) the model which is the null hypothesis plus the effect of the IV. The null hypothesis test is then rather like a way of deciding which of these two models is the better one (with a very particular way of making the decision).

The way that null hypothesis testing chooses between the two models (null hypothesis and alternative hypothesis) is to use a heavy bias towards the status quo: no effect. It asks that the proportion of **variance** in the DV that is explained by the model for the alternative hypothesis should be enough to make the null hypothesis much less likely than the alternative.

14.1.2 MAXIMUM LIKELIHOOD AS MODEL COMPARISON

Recall the **likelihood function** from Chapter 5: a plot of the likelihood of different possible population effect sizes. The peak of the graph indicates the most likely population effect size. The area under the likelihood function has to sum up to 1. This means that a narrow likelihood function, where the uncertainty in the result is small, will have a higher maximum (peak) than a wide one which represents higher uncertainty. Two examples are shown in Figure 14.1.

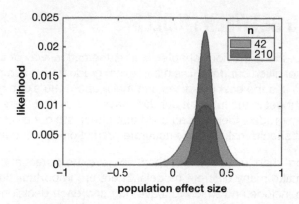

Figure 14.1   Likelihood functions for two different sample sizes.

This graph shows two likelihood functions. They differ in sample size. The smaller sample size (n=42) leads to a much wider function than the larger sample size (n=210). Since the area under each function must sum up to 1, the height of the narrower function is higher.

If we now think of all the different possible population effect sizes as being different models, then we have been using a rule that says prefer the model with the highest likelihood given our data. When we moved on to General Linear Models, the same principle applied. We choose the combination of values for the **coefficients** that creates the maximum likelihood.

14.1.3 BROADER BASIS FOR MODEL COMPARISON

When we were only interested in the rather oversimplified situation of just comparing the null hypothesis with the alternative hypothesis, the significance test was problematical but acceptable. Now we have reached a point where we might want to compare several quite different models, and null hypothesis testing isn't really that helpful any longer.

If we think of the different population effect sizes in a likelihood function as different models, then we have been choosing the model with the maximum likelihood. Since all the models in this situation are the same except for the values of their coefficients, they are equally complex.

We now broaden this process out to comparing likelihoods for models of different complexities. Given a set of data, we can calculate the likelihood of any model we might be interested in and of any complexity we wish. We can therefore use a broader version of the rule: prefer the model with the highest likelihood while taking complexity into account. The fundamental basis for comparing between models is a balance between two factors:

(i)   Likelihood: how well do the models explain the variance of the DV?

(ii)   Complexity: how many coefficients does the model have?

Adding IVs to a model will always make some improvement in the variance explained. A model with 10 IVs will explain more variance in a set of data than a model with only two IVs would, regardless of whether the extra IVs are valid in reality. If we just use likelihood, we will end up always preferring models with more IVs. Complexity provides a counterbalance: a way to prefer models with fewer IVs. A broader process of model comparison requires a single number that will balance these two factors in a sensible way. This is what we discuss next.

14.1.4 MODEL COMPARISON BY AKAIKE INFORMATION CRITERION (AIC)

There are quite a few ways to balance model likelihood and complexity. We will describe one that is representative of the others. It is called the Akaike Information Criterion (**AIC**).

The AIC is a number that can be calculated for some data and any model of those data. Several models are created, and their AIC values are compared to see which model is best.

This is explained in further detail online

The AIC is a combination of complexity and likelihood set up so that a smaller value is better. The formula for it is quite straightforward:

$$AIC = 2(k-\log(L))$$

where k is the number of coefficients and L is the likelihood of the model, given the data.

A low value for AIC means some combination of low k (few coefficients) and high likelihood (low uncertainty). There's a little bit more detail about the AIC in our online resources.

There are other statistics that are also used to answer the new question (some are close cousins, as you can see from their labels: AICc, BIC, CAIC), but they all work in similar ways, with each representing a slightly different balance between variance explained and number of coefficients.

14.2 A NEW CONCEPT: STATISTICS FOR BUILDING AND COMPARING MODELS

We are now seeing the role of statistics in psychological research as being about choosing between different models. The statistical process we use to assist that choice has at its heart the likelihood function and the number of coefficients that the model has. Between them, these two parts represent both the need to acknowledge the uncertainty in the data and a preference for simpler models.

The procedure we are now exploring consists of simple stages: design some possible models, estimate their coefficients from the data, and then choose the best model using a criterion like AIC.

AIC = 787

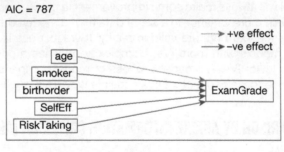

$R^2 = 0.04$, or 4%

AIC = 777

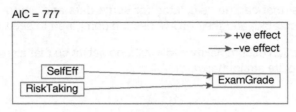

$R^2 = 0.02$, or 2%

Figure 14.2   Two different General Linear Models, with the AIC value for each.

This figure shows two different General Linear Models, with the AIC value for each. The upper one has five IVs, including three demographic variables (age, gender and birth order) that are quite uninteresting and are not included in the bottom one. Although the top one has a higher value for R^2 than the lower one, the AIC values tell us that the lower model is the better fit to the data. Those extra demographic variables are not worth including in the model.

In the previous chapter we saw how the question of interest when conducting an **ANOVA** is whether a particular variable changes R^2, the amount of variance explained by the model, sufficiently compared to the unexplained variance for the **p-value** to allow us to reject the null hypothesis. Here we go one step further: does a variable change the amount of variance enough to justify the cost of adding that variable into the model? AIC does this by penalising models that have unnecessary variables.

An example of two models fitted to the same data is shown in Figure 14.2. The top one has more variables and has the larger R^2. Larger R^2 is generally a good thing, but the bottom model in the figure, despite having a poorer R^2, has a better AIC value. The statistics are telling us to prefer the lower model because it is simpler.

In this new approach to General Linear Models, we are seeking the best model we can find to explain our data. We've got some more information about fitting complex models in our online resources.

This is explained in further detail online

14.3 THINKING ABOUT CAUSATION IN MODELS

There is an important final consideration before moving on. The statistics part of this becomes conceptually simple: make models; use software to find their respective AIC; choose the lowest AIC. This describes a simple sort of a machine really: think hard and make some models and sit back and let the statistics choose between them.

In theory, one could take a set of data with lots of different variables and work out what all the possible models might be. Then, apparently, the analysis of that data comes down to choosing the model with the lowest AIC. Suddenly, one might think, machines can even do this. That is certainly a view that some hold, but it is wrong because it overlooks one thing that statistics cannot yet do adequately. Look at the two models in Figure 14.3, one of which is logically implausible. There is no statistical procedure that can identify any difference between these two models. Only thinking and psychological insight can do that.

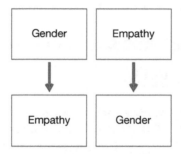

Figure 14.3   Thinking psychologically about asymmetry.

Which of these models is the best? Statistics cannot tell us, but there is a definite answer. Hint: the definite answer most probably isn't the diagram on the right-hand side.

The fundamental issue here concerns **causation**. The model on the left of the figure is plausible as an account of causation; the one on the right is not.

When we choose between models, we have to be aware that there are psychological issues of causation that will rule out models. Sometimes the issue of causation is very clear-cut, as in this example. Often it isn't so. It becomes a topic we have to think about.

All the statistical analysis we have explored is very much blind to causation. There are some recent techniques that can sometimes identify causation from specific types of pattern in data. These are called Structural Causal Models (SCM).

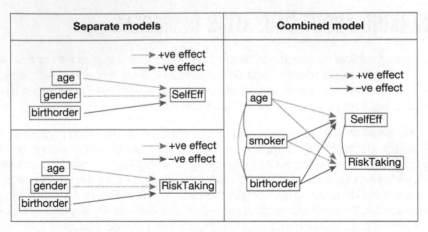

Figure 14.4   A multivariate model.

This diagram shows a multivariate model. We are using three IVs to simultaneously predict two different DVs. The process of multivariate analysis allows for the exploration of models like this one, which may have co-variation between the IVs and between the DVs.

14.4 MULTIVARIATE MODELS

So far, we have only examined models that have a single DV. Although there is no real statistical reason for this, we think that the type of situation where it is possible to justify having two or more DVs from the psychology is quite rare. If you aren't certain whether you are interested in a person's anxiety score or their depression score and are tempted to use both as DVs, hoping that something interesting will come out of it all, then our advice is simple: go away and think. Statistics is never a good replacement for thinking and using psychological insights. It is not a good idea to take the lazy – and statistically misleading – option of simply putting all your data together to make analysis faster.

Regardless, let's look at multiple DVs here. Just as with more than one IV, it is possible to approach the situation of more than one DV by taking them individually and making a set of General or Generalised Linear Models. In our example in Figure 14.4, this approach would mean that there would be two models, one for each of the two DVs. In some ways, this is analogous to treating the various IVs in a simple General Linear Model separately. Just as in that case, the best reason for treating all the DVs as part of a single model is because that allows you to explore the ways in which any covariation (relationship) between the DVs may have an effect on how the model works.

Finally, the process of fitting a model that has multiple DVs is a variant on the process of fitting a model with a single DV. It is done by finding a set of coefficients for all direct effects in the model (i.e. to both DVs at the same time) that best fit the data. In this type of model, the key issue is the psychological justification. We saw in Chapter 12 that covariation between IVs means we may have to think carefully about what the IVs mean, psychologically. That applies here as well: just what do the DVs mean in the presence of covariation between them?

To begin to repeat ourselves: the statistics here is easy, the psychology often isn't.

14.5 MEDIATION

Mediation is the name given to a model where, instead of an IV directly affecting a DV, it instead affects another variable (called a mediator), which then in turn affects the DV. This is illustrated in Figure 14.5. It is really a version of covariation where you analyse the different routes, direct and indirect, to see whether your data are consistent with a particular hypothesis for how the variables relate to each other.

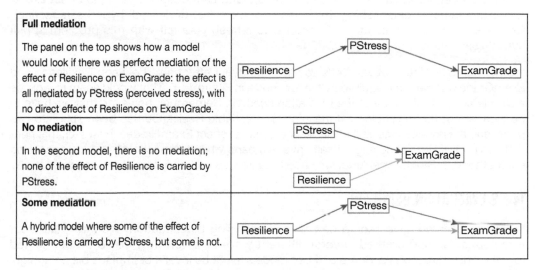

Figure 14.5   A typical mediation scenario.

This diagram illustrates a typical mediation scenario. Three possible models are shown. We can use what we know about effect sizes and indirect routes to work out how the different models would work. We can use AIC calculations to choose between the models.

A lot of the work on mediation analysis has focused on how to get p-values from complex models like this so that null hypothesis testing can be done. We think, as always, that the desire to do null hypothesis testing is misplaced. But here it is positively unhelpful. To reach a satisfactory outcome and conclude that the effect of Resilience on ExamGrade is mediated by

PStress, we need to establish that one of the direct effects is zero (the one between Resilience and ExamGrade). That is very difficult without leaving the framework of null hypothesis testing.

14.5.1 EVALUATION USING DIRECT EFFECT SIZES

In Chapter 12 we covered two rules about how **total effect sizes**, **unique effect sizes** and **direct effect sizes** relate to each other in a diagram like Figure 14.5. With this, we can ask some potentially interesting questions. All of the three models shown in Figure 14.5 are variants on the basic triangle that we used in Chapter 12. In the top model, the direct effect from Resilience to ExamGrade is zero and the other two are non-zero. In the middle model, the direct effect between Resilience and PStress is zero. In the bottom model, none of the direct effects is zero. In principle, we can establish which model is best by seeing which direct effect sizes, if any, are zero.

A caveat here is that it is critically important for mediation analysis to be able to demonstrate which direct effect sizes are zero. Establishing that an effect size is zero (no effect exists) is not the same as establishing that it isn't non-zero (i.e. under null hypothesis testing). Go back to our conversation in Chapter 6 to refresh yourself with this problem in null hypothesis testing.

We need another little caveat. Let's say that the direct effect size between Resilience and ExamGrade was zero, as required by the top model in Figure 14.5. That would seem to indicate a simple account of the data: the mediation account. Remember, however, that we have to be clear about the psychological meaning. The variable Resilience has been split into two parts, and the non-PStress part of Resilience does not affect ExamGrades. However, that non-PStress part of Resilience might itself have two parts whose opposite effects are cancelling each other out. Strictly speaking, we should be very careful about what we conclude.

14.5.2 EVALUATION USING AIC

In this chapter we have seen a new way of analysing this situation. We have taken our three variables and created several different ways in which they could be connected together: different models. Some of those models might be invalid or implausible on straight psychological grounds and we could drop them for that reason. If there were several left, then we would now know how to ask a simple question: which of these models best fits the data we have?

The procedure is simple: compare AIC. In this case, it is actually even simpler as the number of coefficients is the same in all three models, so with the AIC we are simply comparing their respective likelihoods and choosing the most likely model. In doing this we would be wise to be aware of the uncertainty that is built into the AIC itself. Obviously, small differences in the AIC are less meaningful than large ones.

14.6 PATH MODELS

The next step is one of those small steps that places a new perspective on everything. All of the previous examples can be collected under the broader umbrella term of a **path model**, a fairly new idea in psychological research. The only new feature we need to add in to our thinking is to allow there to be several steps in the model, rather than just one step from IV(s) to DV as you've seen in previous figures in this chapter.

An example of a path model is shown in Figure 14.6. In this model, we are thinking that the basic demographic variables on the extreme left might be the causes of a person's risk-taking (RiskTaking) and self-efficacy (SelfEff), which are the DVs of the first stage of the model. Then these DVs become IVs for the second stage of the model where they become the causes of a further set of DVs. The new DVs are attendance at tutorials, hours spent using statistics software, and diligence in collecting data for the module (did we say that all through the book the ExamGrade variable that we have been examining was from a statistics exam?). Then these three variables, DVs in the second stage, in turn become IVs for the third stage where they are the causes of variation in exam grades and coursework grades.

This step of going to a path model is a big leap from simple two or three variable hypotheses to an undoubtedly richer and far more informative psychological model. It feels rather good to have reached a point where such a model is understandable as a statistical proposition as well as a psychological one.

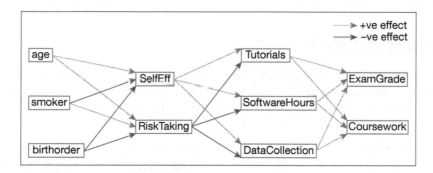

Figure 14.6   A more general path model.

This diagram shows a more general path model. In this model, most variables are now IVs to some variables and DVs to other variables.

For the new situation where variables can be IVs and DVs at the same time, we switch to a slightly broader terminology. Any variables (like the three on the left in Figure 14.6) that are only IVs and never DVs are called **exogenous variables** in this type of model. Their causes are outside the scope of the model, which has nothing to say what their cause might be. The other variables which are DVs at some place in the model are called **endogenous variables** because we hope that some of their causes are inside the model.

A moment's reflection on what we have said about the arrows in the basic triangle for two IVs will show us the importance of the rules for how to compute the effect size of a route and how to combine the effect sizes from different routes from the same source to the same destination. Looking at Figure 14.6, and wondering about the total effect of risk-taking on exam grades, we can see that there are now various routes (one via each of the variables in the next stage). So we would work out the effect size for each route and then add those together. If we look at the situation for being a smoker or not and exam grade, there are even more routes this time and we would need to combine them all.

14.6.1 A PATH MODEL AS A SET OF GENERAL LINEAR MODELS

One way of thinking about a path model is to notice that each endogenous variable is the DV for a little local General Linear Model. For example, right in the middle of Figure 14.6 there is a simple linear model with SoftwareHours as the DV, and SelfEff and RiskTaking as IVs. Seen like this, we can then simply think of estimating the coefficients for this local model and each of the other local models.

In fact, this is unwise. It is analogous to treating a General Linear Model with two IVs as two separate hypotheses and analyses (so you get only the total effects, not the informative direct or unique effects). In extreme circumstances you may be quite badly misled.

14.6.2 A PATH MODEL AS A SINGLE MODEL

Instead, it is possible to estimate the coefficients for the model in a single whole step. We won't provide details, but we have already touched on the principle. The process of estimating the whole model is a case of finding a complete set of coefficients for every stage in the model that best fit the data.

This is important because, implicitly, most path models have lots of zero links. A path model is likely to have lots of pairs of variables that are not linked together. This means that the direct effect between those two variables is zero. That needs to be built into the model. Here we hit, yet again, a point where the importance of zero direct effect sizes can hardly be underestimated.

14.6.3 EVALUATION OF PATH MODELS

When we evaluate a model like this, we can, if we really insist, look at each link in it and ask the p-value question, hoping perhaps that the bits of the model we like best will be statistically significant. As we said above, this is not really the best way to think about these models. The better question instead is this: among the (large) number of psychologically plausible combinations of these variables into different models, which one is best and by how much? Then we just compare AIC values.

Notice that the judgement about the models involves both statistical considerations and also, and most importantly, psychological considerations. Imagine, just for a moment, the mirror image model for Figure 14.6, where a person's age and birth order are determined in part by their risk-taking behaviour. Such a model is implausible, and even if the data fit it really well, we would not consider it further. Usually in path models there is a high number of possible models, but many of them can be ruled out on psychological grounds.

14.7 SEM ANALYSIS

There is another new and intriguing further step that we can now take, using the latest developments in statistics: we can place latent variables (variables that weren't measured) into a model. This sounds impossible: how can we use data that we don't really have? There are new methods, such as structural equation models (SEM), which can use covariation and the unexplained relationships between the variables that we do have to infer the presence of latent variables. We aren't going to go into them here: we mention them only to remind you that statistics and the way it can interact with psychological thinking is always evolving. Who knows what will be possible as you do research of your own?

14.8 A SUMMARY: BIGGER AND BIGGER PICTURES

This chapter introduced a new type of statistical question: which model is best and by how much? We have seen how it encompasses older questions, like the null hypothesis test question, but that it is a bigger, broader perspective that can be used to achieve more interesting results.

For that new question, we have introduced a way of answering it with one last statistic: AIC. AIC is a broader concept than null hypothesis testing or likelihood.

With the new question and the means to answer it, something rather interesting has happened. The machinery for comparing two different models – calculating AIC or whatever – is conceptually very simple. It is easy to agree that a new model that is better should replace an old model that is worse. Since the process involves a penalty for the complexity of the model, the process is slightly predisposed towards simple models, which is also easy enough to agree to.

We want to persuade you to adopt an attitude. Here are the principles that got us to this point:

(i)   Variables: the way we split the world into pieces we can study.

(ii) Relationships between variables: the way we recognise how variability works.

(iii) Likelihood: uncertainty about the population given just a sample.

(iv) Covariation: all variables may be related to each other.

(v)   Statistical models: a way of stating precisely what we know about a population.

If you understand these principles, then you can now understand the statistical part of data analysis. There is no mystery about statistics. Think right back to the start. Statistics has two purposes: to describe what our sample has to say about the population it came from; and to quantify how much uncertainty we should have about that description. The attitude we think you could adopt is this: because there is no mystery about statistics, you are freed-up to think about the psychology of the data analysis. And since you collected that data, you are the expert about what it means: your data, your analysis, your interpretation.

THE BIG PICTURE

Once we understand how main effects, interactions and covariation work, we can easily take the next step to more complex arrangements of variables. The result of analysis of a set of data is a statistical model: a representation of the salient patterns of relationship between variables in the data.

MODELS AND MODEL COMPARISON

1. The new concept we need is the idea of comparing different models to establish which is the best.

2. There are two considerations that work in opposite directions:

   a. How well the model describes the data.

   b. How simple the model is.

3. We have used a quantity known as AIC to compare models.

4. We must also always think about psychological constraints on models.

THREE EXTENSIONS TO GENERAL LINEAR MODELS

1. Multivariate models:

   a. Have multiple DVs.

   b. Are of interest when there may be covariation between the DVs.

2. Mediation models are:

   a. A version of indirect and direct routes.

   b. Of interest when the direct route has zero effect size.

   c. Difficult to establish using null hypothesis testing.

3. Path models:

   a. Are a general form of model.

   b. Could be estimated as lots of local General Linear Models.

   c. Are better to estimate in a single complete model.

YOUR SPACE

REFERENCES AND FURTHER READING

Flora, D.B. (2018) *Statistical Methods for the Social Science & Behavioural Sciences*. London: Sage.

A good general text that uses some mathematics with helpful explanations.

Hayes, A.F. (2013) *Mediation, Moderation and Conditional Process Analysis*. New York: Guilford Press.

The section on mediation is relevant to this chapter.

Kline, R.B. (2016) *Principles and Practice of Structural Equation Modeling*. New York: Guilford Press.

A good first step in Structural Equation Modelling.

Pearl, J. (2009) *Causality: Models, Reasoning and Inference* (2nd edition). Cambridge: Cambridge University Press.

An advanced account of Structural Causal Models.

Pearl, J. & Mackenzie, D. (2018) *The Book of Why: The New Science of Cause and Effect*. London: Allen Lane.

A popular account of new approaches to causality.

Tabachnik, B.G. & Fidell, L.S. (2014) *Using Multivariate Statistics* (6th edition). Harlow: Pearson.

Multivariate analysis: the classic text. Advanced.

THERE ARE MORE ACTIVITIES AND A SHORT
SUMMARY VIDEO FOR THIS CHAPTER AVAILABLE AT:
HTTPS://STUDY.SAGEPUB.COM/STATISTICSFORPSYCHOLOGY

FINISHING WITH ONE BIGGER PICTURE

Now that we have taken you on a journey through all the principles and methods that are important in the research process, it is time to consider the very last step: presenting and persuading. In Chapter 2 we introduced our research cycle image. Here we provide it again in Figure PS.1, with some modifications:

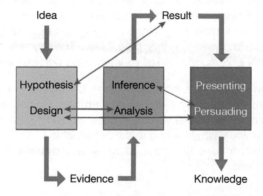

Figure PS.1   The research cycle: a set of interconnected decisions and actions.

These arrows here are just some of the possible connections: every element is connected in some way with all of the others.

In all of the preceding chapters, we have explored the first two phases of the research cycle (hypotheses, designs, analysis and inferences) in great depth. But we have ever so slightly neglected phase 3, despite its importance: presenting results to persuade readers. It would be unethical to do research and not share it: even if you haven't found an effect, or a statistically significant outcome, that knowledge itself may benefit someone else. And what use is knowledge if it is not shared?

Really, we have provided you with most of the information you need to know to do this well: we have shown you clear and varied graphs, given you the shorthand abbreviations and formulae symbols that help effectively summarise results, and included the various APA requirements for presenting the results of two-variable null hypothesis statistical tests. This very short chapter is merely a way to tie all these loose threads together.

PRESENTING RESULTS

When it comes to presenting results, there is only one piece of advice that is meaningful: results should be clear, simple and linked in a narrative. We often have students come to us and ask for a set of clear instructions: What information should they include in their work? What order does it need to come in? It can be very tempting to just provide a short list for students to tick off, but that has not been our approach so far and we're not going to start now. Instead, we shall ask this: What do you want to share with your audience? What story are you trying to tell? What does your audience need to know? It is up to you how many descriptive statistics you include; how you present them; and how many graphs are needed for your audience to easily grasp what you have found.

It is also up to you what story you tell with your inferential statistics: What tests have you carried out? What models have you proposed? What insight have you gained? We have two small pieces of advice here. The first is that if you have carried out exploratory research, you don't need to report p-values. Instead, report your confidence intervals to demonstrate the level of uncertainty in your results. Save p-values for hypothesis testing; and remember that statistical significance is not a gold medal. There are far more interesting things that you can express than simply whether or not $p<0.05$. The second piece of advice is this: be ruthless. The process of testing and reporting every single detail probably isn't a good use of your time and will likely irritate your audience.

If now you are still reading this but thinking 'yes, but *how* do I write all of this up?', then we shall provide one more piece of advice for you: read journal articles. Do not read them as a textbook but instead read them with the critical skills of someone who has just finished this book: What do they tell you? What do you wish they had told you? What is clear, and what isn't? Draw on what you learn in order to produce the most informative and well-considered work that the publishing world will ever see.

PERSUADING AN AUDIENCE

Of course, presenting your results in a way that an audience can understand is not really the end. The last important task is to take those results, and your knowledge of statistics, and use both to persuade your audience that you have something meaningful. Imagine that your audience is made up of amiable sceptics: they are willing to be persuaded, but you must demonstrate your case.

Persuasion is really where all of the interconnected principles of this book come together.

It may seem that statistics is the most important jigsaw piece, but start by answering these questions instead: Can you justify your decisions psychologically? Have you measured what you set out to measure? What have you learned from your data, even if it did not support your hypotheses? Then you can put your statistical cap on. Have you optimised your sample size to reduce Type II errors? Can you justify your measurement choices, and explain the small impact they have statistically?

The most important thing that you need to know as you reach the end of this book is that this is not a rule book: there are no rules, even if it has appeared that way at times. Instead, the best psychological research comes from finding the place where you are doing the best research possible, from a psychological and statistical perspective. There will always be compromises and restrictions (perhaps not if you win a million-pound grant, but we shall assume that as you read this, you have not for now), and good research is about making good decisions. Once you realise that data analysis is not an island, or a mountain to be climbed, but instead weaves its way through the decisions you make from the beginning, it becomes far easier to realise that you are very capable of doing it all.

A COMMENT

We just showed you our revised edition of the research cycle: not a smooth continuous flow, but a network of connections. Really, we could go one small step further, and present it like this instead (see Figure PS.2). This figure shows how the goal of presentable and persuasive research overshadows everything we do. Everything we do in the bottom level of the figure, interconnected as it is, becomes the raw material for the next level. And that is our route to new knowledge.

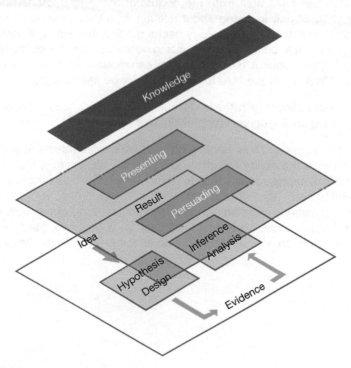

Figure PS.2   The research cycle as a set of layers.

Really, the whole research cycle is about discovering knowledge, and sharing it.

OUR FINAL OBSERVATIONS

We want to finish this book with a thought for you, our faithful reader. What do we hope lies ahead for you in this specific business of using numbers and labels to advance psychological knowledge? Psychological research cannot exist without the methods it uses – as you have seen from the web of big and bigger pictures that we have accumulated in this book – but there are three enormously difficult obstacles it has to overcome.

First, there is the difficulty of relying on small samples to inform us about whole populations. Statistics was invented to illuminate the importance of this unavoidable difficulty and we hope you feel at home by now with the uncertainty it brings.

Second, there is the difficulty of knowing how to measure thoughts, feelings, attitudes and all the other richness of mental life. The meaning of things we measure is changed by what other measurements we place them alongside. If you have learned here that statistics requires flexibility in how we approach our psychological understanding of our data, then we are pleased.

Third, psychology has been built from the dogma of trying to demonstrate the existence of effects. The value of only knowing about relationships that have non-zero effect sizes is questionable on logical terms. Psychology needs models and ways of comparing different models. That turned out to be the most surprising consequence of allowing more than one IV at a time. And a key component in choosing between models is knowing which relationships have zero effect sizes. If you are able to see that, then we are delighted.

We know that feeling secure with these difficulties in our science and how statistics deals with them makes psychological research exciting, as it should be, rather than intimidating.

Our final reminder as we end this book is that, as we explained at the start, the really big picture to be seen is the ability to turn your research back into a focus on psychology instead of a string of numbers and tests. Once you have understood the web of relationships between variability and statistics and decisions and outcomes, you can start asking far more interesting questions and finding much more interesting outcomes. It is much more important – and much more interesting – to think as a psychologist than to think like a statistician. What story are you able to tell with all the skills that you have gained?

REFERENCES

Nuijten, M.B., Hartgerink, C.H.J., van Assen M.A.L.M. et al. (2016) The prevalence of statistical reporting errors in psychology (1985–2013). *Behavioural Research Methods 48*: 1205.

Open Science Collaboration (2015) Estimating the reproducibility of psychological science. *Science 349*, aac4716, DOI: 10.1126/science.aac4716

Rosenthal, R. & Rubin, D.B. (1982) A simple general purpose display of magnitude and experimental effect. *Journal of Educational Psychology 74*: 166–169.

RECOMMENDED FURTHER READING

Barford, N.C. (1985) *Experimental Measurements: Precision, Error and Truth* (2nd edition). Chichester: Wiley.

Cohen, J. (1988) *Statistical Power Analysis for the Behavioural Sciences*. New York: Psychology Press.

Cooper, H., Hedges, L.V. & Valentine, J.C. (2009) *The Handbook of Research Synthesis and Meta-Analysis* (2nd edition). New York: Russell Sage Foundation.

Cumming, G. (2012) *Understanding the New Statistics*. New York: Routledge.

Dobson, A.J. & Barnett, A.G. (2008) *An Introduction to Generalized Linear Models* (3rd edition). Boca Raton, FL: CRC Press.

Efron, B. & Hastie, T. (2016) *Computer Age Statistical Inference*. Cambridge: Cambridge University Press.

Ellis, P.D. (2010) *The Essential Guide to Effect Sizes: Statistical Power, Meta-Analysis, and the Interpretation of Research Results*. Cambridge: Cambridge University Press.

Flora, D.B. (2018) *Statistical Methods for the Social Science & Behavioural Sciences*. London: Sage.

Fox, J. (2016) *Applied Regression Analysis and Generalized Linear Models*. London: Sage.

Hand, D.J. (2008) *Statistics: A Very Short Introduction*. Oxford: Oxford University Press.

REFERENCES

Harlow, L.L., Mulaik, S.A. & Stegier, J.H. (eds) (2016) *What If There Were No Significance Testing?* New Tork: Routledge.

Hayes, A.F. (2013) *Mediation, Moderation and Conditional Process Analysis*. New York: Guilford Press.

Kline, R.B. (2016) *Principles and Practice of Structural Equation Modeling*. New York: Guilford Press.

Lambert, B. (2018) *A Student's Guide to Bayesian Statistics*. London: Sage.

Pawitan, Y. (2013) *In All Likelihood*. Oxford: Oxford University Press.

Pearl, J. (2009) *Causality: Models, Reasoning and Inference* (2nd edition). Cambridge: Cambridge University Press.

Pearl, J. & Mackenzie, D. (2018) *The Book of Why: The New Science of Cause and Effect*. London: Allen Lane.

Popper, Karl R. (1959, 2005 revised edition) *The Logic of Scientific Discovery*. New York: Routledge.

Rosenthal, R., Rosnow, R.L. & Rubin, D.B. (2000). *Contrasts and Effect Sizes in Behavioral Research: A Correlational Approach*. Cambridge: Cambridge University Press.

Rosnow, R.L. & Rosenthal, R. (1997) *People Studying People: Artefacts and Ethics in Behavioural Research*. New York: Freeman and Co.

Tabachnik, B.G. & Fidell, L.S. (2014) *Using Multivariate Statistics* (6th edition). Harlow: Pearson.

INDEX